HELPING NETWORKS

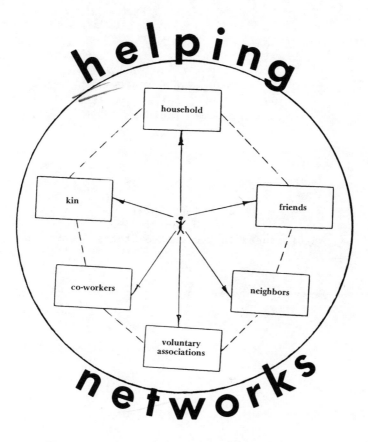

helping networks

How People Cope with Problems in the Urban Community

Donald I. Warren

University of Notre Dame Press
Notre Dame, Indiana 46556

CONTENTS

Preface   vii

Acknowledgments   ix

Introduction   xi

   I. Focus of the Helping Network Study   1

  II. A Theory of the Help-Seeking Process   7

 III. Using Helping Networks: The Overall Patterns   25

  IV. The Neighborhood Context of Helping Networks   55

   V. Community Patterns and Problem-Coping   99

  VI. The Helping Networks of Different Social
       Groups   121

 VII. Helping Networks and the Use of Formal
       Services   133

VIII. Varieties of Urban Social Ties: A New
       Framework for Understanding Community   159

  IX. Findings and Implications of the Helping
       Network Study: An Overview   181

   X. Programmatic Uses of Helping/Social Network
       Analysis   199

Notes   215

References   231

PREFACE

The present volume is a result of a special contract from the Center for the Study of Metropolitan Problems of the National Institute of Mental Health. Based on the original research study funded by this same agency--entitled "Helping Networks in the Urban Community" (USPHS-3 RO1-24982)--the goal is to provide both a description of the basic findings of the core study and to allow a wider audience of researchers to pursue further investigation of the same "data base." References to the Appendix allude to a companion volume which contains extensive tabular results of the original study, elaboration of the methodology and survey design, as well as information on the key variables utilized in the original analysis. A list of all components of the available data tape is also included in the second volume, which is available on request from the University of Notre Dame Press. Both this book and its accompanying research-oriented volume have been published by special arrangement with the University of Notre Dame Press.

ACKNOWLEDGMENTS

Many individuals have contributed to the content and research background of this book. I am especially indebted to the Metro Center of the National Institute of Mental Health and its Director--Elliot Liebow--who has been so consistently supportive of the work contained in these pages. From the original discussion of a research proposal to the design of the field study, he and his staff have been extremely helpful.

The Institute of Labor and Industrial Relations through its Research Director, Dr. Louis A. Ferman, provided the "home base" for the helping network study. Dr. David Clifford was a co-author of the original research proposal and contributed substantively to the design of the project. Dr. Rachelle Warren directed the ethnographical field work of the study (and analyzed portions of the data dealing with women and stress). Dr. Forrest Graves, Jr., worked on the phase of the core study dealing with mental health implications of perceived differences in neighborhood patterns. James Dries coordinated survey data management and contributed substantively in analyzing the effects of the study's panel design.

Also, much appreciation is owed to the field survey director, Mina Cuker, and her staff of devoted and highly competent interviewers, whose mastery of a complex task greatly aided the successful completion of the helping network study.

I wish to express my gratitude to James Langford, Director of the University of Notre Dame Press, for his help and encouragement in the publication of this volume.

The diligent work of Carol Crawford in typing and helping to edit major portions of this manuscript is much appreciated, as is the assiduous typing of the final draft by Cheryl Reed and Sandy DeWulf.

Finally, the author must accept responsibility for the flaws--conceptual and practical--in this book. Readers are invited to assess the value of this analysis in the light of

its theoretical and programatic concerns.   Judgment of the
success of this effort must inevitably be theirs.

Donald I. Warren
Ann Arbor, Michigan
April, 1981

INTRODUCTION

As a nation we have become very much aware in the past several years of the threat to the physical environment of our communities. Although there are setbacks, efforts at the local and national levels frequently result in action. But we have paid too little attention to the equally serious problem of the eroding social fabric of our communities and its detrimental impact on individual well-being.

There is a new direction of community research bearing on the way our society is bound together. "Social networks" or "helping networks" refer to the various individuals to whom each of us turns for coping with daily and more serious problems of living. They are not groups. They often do not know each other. They are combinations of people we turn to: a spouse, a neighbor, friends, relatives, and co-workers. Together they form the "natural helping networks" of an individual.

The neglect and loss of natural helping networks is a major source of social alienation, isolation, and burgeoning public-agency work load.

There are many causes for this trend. Increased social mobility, geographic mobility, family dissolution, the generation gap, loss of trust in neighbors, overspecialization in professional training, and community segregation by race, social class, age, and social attitudes.

Additionally, research has shown that those people involved in ongoing relationships through work, family, or friends are those most likely to be sustained in the community after discharge from a mental hospital. Those sources of help provide the vital margin of recovery.

There are several reasons for carefully examining the natural helping systems of communities and individuals. The time for better understanding is well spent if it leads to new insights about urban life. But perhaps even more valuable than basic knowledge per se is the potential that such new information provides about what we take for granted in human communities. Such understanding can be harnessed by volunteer citizen groups, public service agencies, mental health professionals, and all individuals who want to gain a greater degree of control over their lives.

There is a basic need to consider the capacity--both of neighborhoods and local communities--to encourage forms of mutual aid and helping. This need not be competitive with, or totally independent of, the formal problem-solving agencies. Each can work in conjunction with the other not only to provide a sound quality of life and to focus attention on the delivery of services to those in crisis, but also in a preventive way.

Because what we report here is based on a single study, the findings must be subjected to further verification. The dynamics of what we call "problem-anchored helping networks" are seemingly so mundane and "built into everyday life" that up to now they have been taken for granted or been invisible to government agencies, urban planners, service agency administrators, and social researchers alike. We need to know more about how healthy these natural systems are, how they work, and what can be done to strengthen them. It is toward each of the audiences we have mentioned and with these broad social considerations in view that we offer this analysis.

CHAPTER I

FOCUS OF THE HELPING NETWORK STUDY

This book is about systems of help, not simply those with which bureaucracy and professionalism are assocated, but also a vast set of almost invisible threads of human contact used in times of crisis and need for everyday problems. Of course, such problems sometimes can multiply and become crises. Typically, the need for help is finite and does not recur. Yet, beyond sudden emergencies, people in our complex urban society often need to gradually master a situation of life change and desired life improvement. Such an incremental, cumulative coping process may be composed of discrete bits of advice, information, emotional support, referral, and direct actions of helping that can only be recognized when we trace the help over extended periods of time.

Our research has identified several systems of helping for different types of problem situations. These are not typically systems in the literal sense of the word. Yet we can approach the subject of helping and problem coping insightfully by treating the process in this structurally concrete way.

Given a society of mobile people in search of a better life, the vitality of natural helping networks can no longer be based exclusively on local ties. Helping networks reach out via long-distance telephone and rapid travel. Understanding these crisscrossing patterns and how they function to provide individual well-being is a vital task of governmental service agencies or programs funded to give professional help.

The neighborhood helping network project was undertaken to study the ways in which different populations in a

1

community deal with their problems independently of professional service agencies and, at the same time, how formal
service agencies are utilized by different groups of people.

The purpose of this book is to present a conceptual and
empirical base for understanding the predominant modes by
which individuals use the helping resources--formal, semi-
formal, and informal--to respond to the daily and more sudden
losses and problems with which they must cope. It is based
on a major study of the mental health stresses of given
problems and of the kinds of resources people use to cope
with them.

A variety of social environments are represented in the
findings we shall review, yet there is a common theme which
directs the analysis: namely, the normality of problem
coping. Instead of focusing on pathologies of urban life, we
seek an understanding of day-to-day use of personal help and
social contact.

Perhaps in the widest sense the research reported here
describes the crucial social-change processes of our society.
This occurs for individuals in terms of very small incremental responses. Taken as a whole, life styles and values
are altered significantly. The motivation and the resources
for coping with life are to be significantly found in the
"mediating institutions" of communities. Neighborhoods,
local organizations, and a diversity of individuals tie the
loose elements of urban society into a social fabric that
functions. Isolation from such an integrating process can be
detrimental to mental and physical health. Communities themselves may be debilitated in a similar fashion.

This volume is organized in a developmental fashion to
reflect the several focal points of the basic research from
which it is derived. Specifically, we begin with a discussion of some core questions about how people cope with a
range of different kinds of problems and what individual and
organizational human resources they use to deal with those
issues.

In this first chapter we shall briefly describe the
field methodology and the focal research topics. Chapter II
presents a review of research regarding helping behavior and
suggests a theoretical strategy for understanding how different kinds of help are linked to unique types of problems. In
Chapter III we focus on several major operational research
questions in the core helping network study and present the
key findings.

Chapter IV is centered on the role of different neighborhood settings--both "real" and "perceived." It reviews
findings from survey data and gives detailed descriptions of
the life of people in a wide variety of local residential
areas. Chapter V supplements the major attention of the

study on neighborhoods to consider the wider unit of the municipal community. In Chapter VI the focus is shifted to the social background characteristics of people and how these relate to the type and variety of helping resources used in problem coping.

Chapter VII zeroes in on the role of professional agencies and their relationship to helping--their actual use and perceptions about their effectiveness. We next review the entire range of findings presented and set the stage for discussing some new perspectives on the nature of urban community in modern society. Finally, we consider some of the broad social policy issues, as well as specific mental health and human service outreach issues, that grow out of the findings and conceptual focus of the helping network project.

STUDY DESIGN AND SAMPLING

The helping network study had three major research goals. The first of these was to describe the importance of the local community and neighborhood in their ability to provide help and problem-solving resources. The second goal of the study was to obtain a more complete picture of the types of choices people make when they experience a problem and are seeking help. Such an inquiry also requires that we investigate what kinds of things are in fact sought in the "helping transaction." Is it emotional support, specific information, a new way of thinking about a persistent problem? A methodology was developed for measuring such variability in what constitutes help. Thirdly, the study was aimed at an implicit evaluation of the degree to which people used and trusted various types of helping resources--formal agencies as well as the next-door neighbor.

All of the information obtained in the helping network study was gathered during 1974 and 1975. A staff of professional interviewers and a number of trained neighborhood observers provided the personnel to complete the research.

To carry out the substantive task of the study several different data gathering techniques were employed. A central source of information was the systematic survey interviews that were conducted. An initial "baseline" sample included over 2,500 persons. They were chosen in two ways. First a one percent random sample of eight communities surrounding Detroit was undertaken. At the same time, a completely separate representative sample of 32 non-Detroit and 27 Detroit neighborhoods was drawn. This was based on a "walking distance" definition of neighborhood using the local elementary school district as a sampling unit. Approximately

40 adult heads of household or their spouses were interviewed
in this way. A number of the neighborhoods had been included
in an earlier 1969 study comparing black and white areas. In
both the municipal community sample of 770 persons and the
neighborhood samples the vast majority of persons were of
moderate income rather than affluent. The Detroit SMSA was
typified in this way. The 59 neighborhoods yielded
approximately 1,700 completed interviews with adults in these
areas. Each interview lasted an average of 80 minutes.

     The baseline survey instrument focused on six basic
areas. (1) A series of individual concerns related to job,
personal attitudes, crime, and change in family and
life-cycle roles such as retirement, additional schooling,
etc. Where a person had experienced a problem recently, we
charted the pathway by which they sought help. We asked them
not only what people (ranging from primary group members to
professionals) they talked to, but also what happened in the
interaction with the "helper." (2) Use of professional
helping agencies. (3) Occurrence in the past year of
critical life events such as major illness, death of a family
member, loss of job, etc. (4) A check list of psychosomatic
symptoms and other questions on health. (5) Helping roles
played by different family members. (6) Neighborhood social
interaction, perceived resources, and use of actual
resources.

     One of the unique parts of the helping network study is
the design of a follow-up survey paralleling the original
1974 interview. A total of 1,531 persons were contacted
successfully one year later. This group forms a special
facet of the overall project--"a panel sample." Because of
this feature of the study, we can explore how helping
networks--kinds of helpers and their behaviors--develop from
the onset of a problem through the continual coping with that
concern over an extended time period.

     The second type of data collection pertains to the use
of systematic ethnographic observation in each of the
neighborhoods to supplement the survey interviews and to
generate independent sources of measurement for major
variables. The methodology employed in the ethnographic work
consists of a form of open-ended interview and observation
effort using a set of guiding concepts and dimensions of
local community from previous research. A training manual
for this methodology has been developed as a by-product of
the field work conducted in the project. Graduate students
in social work, anthropology, psychology, sociology, and
urban planning programs at the University of Michigan,
Eastern Michigan University, and Oakland University provided
members of the various observation teams. In this manner a

total of twenty-five neighborhood studies were completed.
These case studies focus on the following topics:
1) social reality or validity of neighborhood boundaries;
2) social structure in terms of a sixfold neighborhood
typology; 3) distinctive informal institutions or institutional patterns of problem-coping within the neighborhood;
4) neighborhood "cultural norms" and values regarding problem
definition, coping styles, and help-seeking; and 5) behavior
patterns and settings of key types of individuals (e.g.,
"opinion leaders," neighborhood activities, "gatekeepers") in
terms of the process of coping with mental health problems in
the neighborhood.

Between March 1974 and August 1975 over 4,100 interviews were completed in the two waves of survey information
used in the helping network study. Each interview yielded
over 1,000 items of information. Seventeen black, 38 white
and four racially mixed neighborhoods were included in the
core study.

The utilization of a neighborhood typology was
developed following a conceptualization utilized in earlier
research by D. I. Warren Black Neighborhoods and Rachelle B.
and D. I. Warren, The Neighborhood Organizer's Handbook.
This technique is based on the aggregation of information for
each neighborhood cluster sample.

The use of survey interviews coupled with ethnographic
observation provides a knowledge base that has both breadth
and depth in terms of number of respondents interviewed and
the quality of their responses. The ethnographic work has
the added function of systematically assessing the neighborhood and community as a behaviorial setting for helping.

Since the helping network study began, a total of five
doctoral dissertations, one master's thesis and a number of
research papers have been generated from the data gathered.

From the initial stage of work an important byproduct
of the original helping network research project was
envisioned to be direct utilization by local human-service
agencies. In fact, collaborative arrangements were established with several universities in adjacent areas where
seminars and feedback discussions were held. In turn, a
specific research team was linked to a local community mental
health organization, the Six Area Coalition. This umbrella
agency drew upon initial research findings and field methods
in evaluating and planning part of its community outreach
effort.

Because the helping network project generated information about a cross section of people in many communities,
its findings offer a valuable comparison to studies which
rely on problem-coping data drawn from individuals who are
clients of various human service agencies. The possibility

of treating the "normal" population versus a "clinical" sample can offer useful insight about pathways to formal agencies and selective utilization of their services by particular segments of a general public. Thus, the issue of underserved groups and those who may tend to monopolize professional services is addressed by the core research.

One practical application of the helping network study is that knowledge about how people define and cope with common life decisions and challenges can suggest new roles for professionals and nonprofessionals.

Throughout the study we were concerned the effectiveness of the outreach of formal agencies. With a greater understanding of how people seek help the research findings lead to a potential for redirecting many service interventions to make them more effective.

If the desired outcome of helping institutions is to facilitate problem-coping, then we must take stock of what those problems are and how they are being dealt with at present by a wide range of populations. Only then can we plan for the future. Knowledge about how people actually deal with personal, family, and collective problems and crises, especially outside the purview of professional agencies, is vital to any effort to develop better human-service delivery systems.

The essential research questions that guided the helping network study can be effectively summarized as follows:

1) What are the helping resources individuals utilize for a range of frequently experienced problems, and how are these distributed between informal and formal systems of helping?

2) How are the patterns of help-seeking of the individual related to the individual's social context—class, race, age, local neighborhood, and community social organization?

3) What are the effects of using particular kinds of helping resources (or not using them) on the individual's well being?

Throughout the subsequent portions of this volume each separate area of analysis can be linked back to these key issues. Upon this base the applied and service-related implications of the helping network study can be developed.

CHAPTER II

A THEORY OF THE HELP-SEEKING PROCESS

For many decades we, as a society, failed to understand
the ecosystem of our surrounding environment. Similarly, we
are just beginning to investigate and identify the components
that make up the social fabric of human communities. This
fabric is woven from the complex interdependencies that are
the formal and informal helping systems of our society.

Increasingly our highly trained and dedicated professional helping institutions have begun to recognize that
they alone cannot provide the resources and social supports
which are so vital to the well-being of the communities in
which we live. There is an invisible partnership of which
they are unaware: it is a web woven by a combination of
neighbors, friends, co-workers, relatives, voluntary
agencies, and formal human service organizations.

We use natural helping networks to get help for daily
life problems such as simple depression (feeling blue),
wanting to get a better job, wanting to get more education,
dealing with retirement, crime in the neighborhood, family
planning, and youth problems.

HELPING NETWORKS AND HUMAN SERVICE SYSTEMS

Knowledge of how people actually deal with personal,
family, and collective problems and crises, especially
outside the purview of professional agencies, has been the
concern of much research aimed at the development of better
social services. To a large extent, these studies have been
concerned with the effects that professionalizing and insti-
tutionalizing problems has on community-based helping
systems. For example, in an early study (Jahoda, 1958), the

7

importance of social norms and values indigenous to the
community was realized in defining symptoms of mental illness. The informal social network appears to serve as a
natural support system that functions to counteract the
effect of stressful life events. Among women who experienced
multiple life changes prior to and during their first
pregnancy, only those with minimal social supports developed
serious medical complications (Nuckolls, et al., 1972). In a
later study, Liem and Liem (1976) discovered that the proportion of network members providing emotional support and the
frequency of contact with network members were inversely
related to psychological distress among college students.

Collins (1973:46) described "natural neighbors," who
comprise a natural system of service delivery, as a
". . . network of relationships in which individuals seeking
a specific service find it, without professional intervention." A number of studies were reviewed by Collins and
Pancoast (1974) which indicated that the frequency of contact
with friends, relatives, and neighbors is an important factor
in providing support and help within natural networks.
Collins and Pancoast stress that:

> Informal, spontaneous helping activities occur so
> often all around us that they usually pass
> without notice. Except for spectacular rescues,
> instances of helping behavior are much less
> likely to be reported than are instances when
> bystanders failed to act on behalf of someone in
> distress (1974:24).

In an effort to identify indigenous helping activities
among various age groups, Patterson (1971, 1974, 1977)
studied a population in a rural Kansas county ranging in age
from sixteen to eighty-three. Her major research findings
indicated that the type of helper (natural helper versus professional) was an important factor in the helping process in
terms of: 1) type of problem encountered; 2) type of helping
approaches or techniques utilized; and 3) the type of
relationship between the helper and the helpee (1977:164).
An important difference between natural helpers and professional helpers is that the natural helpers provided both
support and helping "because they cared rather than out of
expectations of future rewards" (1977:165).

Networks operate by 1) giving emotional support, 2)
providing specific information, 3) filling in when a close
relationship is severed by death, illness, divorce, or
separation, 4) helping identify arenas of good professional
help, and 5) serving in place of professionals when they are
not trusted or not available.

Basic to our theory is the idea that bypassing existing helping structures within the community may systematically lower the adaptive capacity of many human populations and weaken those indigenous resources which in times of crisis may be the only ones available and operative.

Helping network analysis does not simply look at the direct contact that an individual makes with a helper. An individual is part of a system of networks that can provide resources or pathways to help. The individual may not know directly about useful help, but he or she may be in a context in which other people know about a resource and can provide that information. It is an issue of community social integration—patterns in which people relate to each other and to the community as a whole, and ways in which resources are coordinated and used for the common good—and this can be contrasted with the disintegration of resources and links.

HELPING NETWORKS AND WELL-BEING

Numerous studies have shown that many more people are physically or mentally impaired than seek professional help and thus are recorded in official incidence figures. The Midtown Manhattan study of Srole and his colleagues (1962), the Stirling County studies of Leighton (1959), the national survey of mental health by Gurin, Veroff, and Feld (1960), and the studies of mental illness prevalence by Phillips (1966) have shown that as many as 50% of those who have psychological impairment and are even "mentally ill" may never seek and receive any kind of help. Even more dramatic figures have been found for the incidence of physical disease and impairment. Further, Gurin in his national survey found that, for both worries and unhappiness, people turned to "informal" sources of help (Gurin, et al., 1960, p. 366).

Other studies have shown that, through a variety of processes (value conflicts, lack of convenient facilities, refusal to give service and termination of contracts), many people—low income, aged, minorities are underserved by formal agencies. These same groups have a disproportionate incidence of problems (Hollingstead and Redlich, 1958; Gardner and Babigan, 1966; Schaefer and Myers, 1954; Gurin, et al., 1960). Such studies suggest that people are both voluntarily turning to and are being forced to rely on non-professional sources of help in order to survive, cope with, and resolve their personal problems.

A vital (and inadequately researched) question is immediately raised by such statistics: Who are people turning to for help, how are they coping with life stress and problems? This question becomes even more important if one

considers that the studies cited (as well as many others)
have most often focused upon what they have labeled
"pathology," "impairment," or "crisis;" and yet there exists
a vastly greater volume of life events which cannot clearly
be so labeled but may be problems requiring the mobilization
of coping resources. Such problems might include marital
adjustment, career change and planning, friction on the job,
child rearing, crime in one's neighborhood, or just feeling
"blue." The successful resolution of, or coping with, these
kinds of situations is intrinsically important to the healthy
functioning and development of an individual in society. It
is also clear that unresolved conflicts of this kind eventually become disturbing or dysfunctional, and eventually may
develop into crises.

COPING AND SOCIAL SUPPORT SYSTEMS

     The concept of a social support system has received
much attention recently from social scientists concerned with
understanding how persons seek help and cope with a variety
of life crises and stresses. In decribing the linkage
between health and social support systems, Broskowski (1974)
uses phrases such as "social support systems that the
individual has to buffer himself" from a "turbulent
environment." Caplan (1972) refers to the "support and
task-oriented assistance provided by the social network
within which the individual grapples with the crisis event."
Such terms connote an active engagement with a problem by a
person and their "supporters." Such images parallel closely
Webster's (International Dictionary, Unabridged, 1962)
definition of coping:

          Cope: a) to maintain a contest of combat usually on
                    even terms or with success;
                b) to face or encounter and to find necessary
                    expedients to overcome problems and diffi-
                    culties.

     David Mechanic also offers a definition of coping which
maintains this active thrust while providing a clear bridge
to the earlier discussion of social supports:

          Coping, as I use the term, refers to the instru-
          mental behavior and problem-solving capacities of
          persons in meeting life demands and goals. It
          involves the application of skills, techniques,
          and knowledge that a person has acquired. *The
          extent to which a person experiences discomfort*

*in the first place is often the product of the
inadequacy of such skill repetoiries* (Mechanic,
1968:302--emphasis ours).

Coping is the process which describes the mobilization
and utilization of the supports, skills, and assistance
available in a person's "social network" for dealing with and
solving problems. The supports, skills, and assistance act
not just in direct coping (i.e., problem-solving or stress
alleviation), but also in preventing their rise by buffering
and protecting the individual from environmental stress and
uncertainty.[1]

HELPING RELATIONSHIPS AND COPING

On one level the connection between a person's capacity
to cope and the quantity and quality of help available from
others seems obvious and intuitive. Those instances of
dramatic action such as a neighbor driving an injured child
to a hospital or people taking up a collection to assist the
widow of a co-worker are clear examples. Such actions as
these are essential for coping with the major and minor
crises of life.

> Less apparent, but perhaps more important in the
> long run, are the everyday, incidental acts of
> assistance which help hold together the day's
> events into a smooth sequence. All but the most
> lonely and isolated persons take for granted the
> loan of a dime or pencil, or a casual offer of
> "give you a hand with that." Without help-giving
> acts like these life might not be a disaster, but
> it would be a continual nuisance. (Todd,
> 1971:1).

On another level, helping and the relationships of
interpersonal interaction of which they are a critical part
define not only coping but the processes by which people are
kept healthy (buffered from stress).
    The barriers to seeking help from anyone, a psychia-
trist, a family counselor, a neighbor, or even a spouse,
emanate from a number of sources. The person must decide
something is wrong and go to others despite societal value
orientations stressing self-reliance which militate against
the use of such outside help in fulfilling emotional and
material needs. Help-seekers face the probability that
friends and family will question their role fitness.
Receiving help may entail having to admit failure in some

aspect of one's life. If one doesn't feel that he/she can
trust a friend, then help must be sought from a stranger
which may involve even greater suspension of one's identity
in order to bridge barriers of age, sex, religion, and class
between the person and the helper. This may also entail sub-
ordinating oneself to the helper in a client- or patient-
professional relationship. A person may never find someone
who can provide help because such helpers lie outside one's
lay referral network. Additionally, seeking help for a
problem can mean time lost and economic cost beyond these
somewhat intangible personal costs.

The theme of rejection of the help-seeker by family and
friends is especially important. This rejection, however,
may not be at all related to the objective facts of a
person's problem or even the manifestation of deviant
behavior. The research strategy involved a survey which presented people with descriptions of the behavior of a number
of individuals. The vignettes included people who were
perfectly normal and others who behaved in a manner which
ranged from mildly to seriously disturbed. Included in the
description was a statement of from whom these individuals
were receiving help. The respondents were asked to make
evaluative statements about the condition of these people.
Phillips found that individuals described to the respondents
as exhibiting identical (even normal) behavior were rejected
increasingly as they were described as utilizing no help, a
clergyman, a physician, a psychiatrist, and finally, a mental
hospital. Rejection was based on help-seeking biases and not
objective conditions.

These barriers to usage, whether they be normative,
social structural, facilitative, or personal, are felt
differently by various elements of the population. Some
peole are more ready to rely on professionals than others,
while some have closer ties to informal helpers such as
relatives, friends, neighbors, and co-workers. In a national
survey it was found that one-seventh of the people had sought
help for problems while one-fourth had problems for which
professional help would have been useful. (Gurin et al.,
1960)

There also seems to be a strong dynamic operating which
leads many people into seeking professional help more often
than can be explained by differences in stressful experiences
or actual sickness. Those who have a higher frequency of
visits to a professional may have no more sickness than
others, but merely a preference for dealing with their
problems in that way.

Investigations of the provisions of help and help-
seeking behavior have concluded that many persons in need of
help never receive it because they do not contact prospective

helpers (Srole, 1962; Phillips, 1963). These findings have
been elaborated in continuing research on the problems and
barriers of seeking help for social, physical, and psychiatric problems. To a large extent, these studies have
focused on various psychological barriers to help-seeking
such as a perceived threat to self-esteem (Tessler and
Schwartz, 1972), fear of rejection (Phillips, 1963), possible
stigmatization (Goffman, 1963), and social-emotional isolation (Weiss, 1974), as well as the influence of socio-
cultural factors such as class, ethnicity, status, and community. Moreover, information regarding the existence and
availability of both informal and formal helping resources
may be viewed as barriers to seeking and receiving help.

Seeking and receiving help from others in American
culture is constrained by dominant cultural values
emphasizing a propensity for self-reliance and avoidance of
dependency upon others except among the very young and very
old in society. Therefore, the necessity of having to seek
help may result in risk to one's ability to perform essential
tasks or may entail having to admit failure in some aspect of
one's life. These situations have been related to a number
of psychological and social consequences resulting from
help-seeking behaviors.

In the work of Robert Weiss (1974) the "provision of
social relations" becomes a major focus of the social support
and helping process. The severing of a social tie or the
failure to establish a helping network may be seen as a major
source of risk to mental health as well as to general well-
being. In light of this basic assumption about the role of
helping, the absence of helpers might be considered a barrier
that the individual has in coping with a range of problems in
daily life. A major function of informal social networks is
to provide social support which acts to integrate people
sociably into meaningful primary group relationships as well
as provide helping behaviors when group members experience
problems. Weiss (1974:20) points out that failure to
establish such relationships may result in "social and
emotional isolation." He defines social integration as the
network of relationships in which participants share common
concerns. Once one is socially integrated into such a
network, it functions as follows:

> Membership in a network of common concern
> relationships permits the development of pooled
> information and ideas and a shared interpretation
> of experiences. It provides, in addition, a
> *source of companionship and opportunities for
> exchange of services,* especially in the area of
> common interests. The network offers a base for

> social events and happenings, for social
> engagement and social activity. In the absence
> of such relationships life becomes dull, perhaps
> painfully so (1974:23--emphasis added).

While these researchers emphasize the psycho-social
barriers to seeking and receiving help for problems, others
attribute differential patterns of help-seeking to various
cultural and socio-demographic factors. Addressing both the
psychological and social aspects of help-seeking, Gurin and
his colleagues noted salient features in groups that sought
help:

> This group that "went for help" was dominated by
> women, younger persons, and the better educated.
> These types, as we have observed, are inclined to
> be introspective, self-critical, and more
> concerned about themselves (1960:xx).

To summarize, it appears that seeking help for problems
involves a multiplicity of psychological and socio-cultural
factors which can be construed as barriers to effective
helping resources for various segments of the population.
Thus, many people with problems never reach professional
helping resources and never receive help. At best, these
people must look for assistance within the context of
informal social support networks.
    The critical question is: To whom do these people turn
for help and what kind of help is both available and
provided?

SOCIAL SUPPORT VERSUS HELPING

    Studies concerned with the nature and utilization of
social networks tend to agree that networks operate by
providing socio-emotional support for members; filling in
where a close relationship is severed by death illness,
divorce, or other life crises; helping to identify or
recommend where to get professional help; and serving in
place of professionals when they are not available or not
trusted. The mere existence of social networks may function
to banish the isolation which can itself be a source of other
personal and social problems.
    It is clear from the social network literature that
social support networks can serve a variety of individual
psychological functions for maintaining social integration
within the network and helping mechanisms for coping with
problems. What is less clear is the conceptual and

operational definition of these social support networks. An immediate question that arises is: What is the difference between social support and helping? We suggest that social support is not necessarily the same as helping behavior and further, social support is not synonymous with social interaction and network contacts. Yet the concepts of social support and helping have been used interchangeably and the differences that may exist between them have been largely neglected in the literature.

High rates of social interaction do not guarantee that help will be available from other people. Assessing the relationship between "perceived" support for everyday versus emergency problems, Wellman and his colleagues (1971:27) found an association between frequency of contact and support for everyday problems, but a much weaker association for emergency help:

> Our data shows a strong positive association
> between frequency of contact and the provision of
> support. The association is somewhat weaker in
> the case of emergency support, revealing the
> existence of a number of intimates who are con-
> tacted relatively infrequently but who can be
> called upon for help in times of need (1971:27).

The link between social support and helping has been manifested in the recent emergence of self-help groups and organizations. Self-help or mutual-aid groups have developed, in part, as a reaction to various limitations of professional organizations. Such limitations included an "unwillingness of professionals to deal with certain problems, a limited reach with regard to various populations, an overly intellectual orientation, and monopolistic credentialism" (Gartner and Riessman, 1976:785).

The styles of helping within self-help groups vary according to the balance between social supportive functions and problem-specific helping. Abrahams (1976:257) has noted that

> . . . variations in styles of helping range from
> a style approximating the profesional/client type
> of relationship to a style approximating
> friendship, as social distance diminishes
> between helper and recipient of help and as the
> area of mutual sharing of emotional inputs
> increases.

Addressing the role of social support in mutual aid organizations as a preventive means of coping with stress, Gore

(1978:157) has observed that "the concept of support has been incorporated into new models for community mental health and health care delivery " Support is regarded as the core of mutual-help organizations which have proliferated in response to the increased incidence and awareness of stressful life situations.

THE PROBLEM-TRACKING APPROACH

Various methods for tracking problems in terms of analyzing the processes by which people seek help has been referred to as "client careers" (Goffman, 1961). These processes represent different behavior patterns anchored in some combination of preference for help sources. The notion of career has also been defined as a series of stages or phases through which a person passes toward some end point or goal which involves defining problems, sorting them out, and seeking help for problems at various stages of problem development. Moreover this definition of career implies a series of events and corresponding help-seeking behavior patterns shared by several people concurrently. As Roth (1963:93) points out, ". . . when many people go through the same series of events, we speak of this as a career and the sequence and timing of events as their current time tables."
Tracking problems based on the availability and nature of people's support and referral networks has been referred to as "pathways of help-seeking."[2] This approach suggests that after initial self-perception and definition (diagnosis) of a problem, people will often consult with significant others or lay people for concurrence or referral. Essentially, the careers or pathways of help-seeking involve a preference for help sources, availability of various kinds of professional or non-professional resources, the nature of the person's lay support and referral networks, and various personal and social characteristics of the individual.
The specific career or help-seeking behavior people will adopt is dependent, we suggest, upon a number of psychological and socio-cultural factors. These factors have been categorized into four major groups and discussed in terms of their influence on illness and help-seeking behavior. They are 1) the social status of the individual, including such demographic characteristics as age, sex, marital status, socioeconomic status, type of disability, and socio-cultural setting; 2) the individual's view of health including self-conception, cultural values regarding health, views toward medical practice and practitioners, inclination to adopt the sick role, and information about medical problems; 3) the existence, nature, and utilization of lay

support and referral networks; and 4) the nature and types of
life crises, corresponding stress associated with these
crises, and the means by which the individual adapts to or
copes with these life stresses (Safilios-Rothschild,
1970:62).

The way an individual seeks out help to handle problems
or crises is dependent in part upon how the problem is sub-
jectively perceived. Apart from any pathological condition,
the course that the individual will follow is influenced by
the social behavior brought on by a specific pathology. This
behavior has been referred to as "illness behavior" and
defined as "the way in which symptoms are perceived, evaluated, and acted upon by a person who recognizes some pain,
discomfort, or other signs of organic malfunction" (Mechanic
and Volkert, 1961:52). Thus, how one acts upon these perceptions and evaluations determines to a large extent the
specific career or pathway one will choose to handle the
problem.

HELP-SEEKING: A NETWORK PROCESS

What leads one person to choose a particular agency,
professional, or helping resource and another person to
reject these and make completely different choices? These
questions are difficult ones to answer and yet have not been
looked at extensively or very systematically by agencies or
social researchers.

From that vague, indeterminant point at which a problem
begins to the receipt of effective help is often a long road.
Unlike many physical diseases, the symptomatic manifestation
of psychological or social problems represents the culmi-
nation of a long period of accumulated symptoms, events, or
behaviors and not the initial onset of a problem.

Differences in patterns will be due to some combination
of the variables discussed above, including preferences for
help sources, availability of various kinds of professional
and non-professional help, personal and local values, the
character of a person's lay support and referral network, and
various other personal and social characteristics of the
individual. Particular populations will, in turn, be characterized by the predominance of certain routing or decision
pathways.

It is useful to consider four levels of help sources or
service delivery systems that individuals may utilize. These
include:

The Lay (Informal) Service System: This phenomena includes
        the friendship and kinship network in which an

individual is involved and which can be mobilized for
help in problem definition, referral, and direct
service. It also embodies selected community members
who have developed a reputation for help giving.
Quasi-Formal and Self-Help Systems: This includes voluntary
organizations, help-giving activities of churches and
community groups whose primary function is not to
operate as a service agency, and various local
community services which do not have the credentials or
wide community acceptance of formal service agencies.
Such operations often service a limited local community
and, although they may employ or be connected with one
or two professionals, the bulk of their work is carried
on by non-professional staff.
Professional Service Agencies: These organizations operate
primarily as social services. They have credentials
and are generally recognized. Their staffs are for the
most part professional and they service a wide
community.
Inter-Organizational Relationships: The combination and coordination of two or more agencies, either formal or
quasi-institutional, creates a special set of activities, structures and administrative problems which
shape the design and implementation of service
delivery. In some cases, these coordinated activities
are established as separate administrative units and
essentially form an agency of agencies. In other
cases, the coordination is short-term to meet immediate
problems and the relationship is dissolved when the
issue which led to its establishment is resolved.

To date, we find in the literature many studies dealing
retrospectively with help-seeking behavior. That is, after
someone has sought help, networks are plotted by which these
same individuals chose a course of action resulting in
differential patterns of help-seeking.
Several studies suggest these conclusions:

1. Who gets help depends upon normative, cultural, and
    structural barriers; only a minority of those in
    need ever reach the professional help-givers in our
    society.
2. The very decision to seek professional help is
    dependent upon problem perception which is
    conditioned by the environment of social networks
    itself.
3. While the help-seeker faces rejection in certain
    social environments, the literature on the effects
    of social class on help-seeking seems inconclusive

because situational variable are often of great
significance.
4. Informal social relationships provide support and
aid when people fail to seek professional help.
5. Professional helping is highly dependent upon an
elaborate referral process whereby individuals must
pass through a referral network before they may
reach professional help. Also, those from
"socially disintegrated" sub-communities are less
likely to have informal support and referral
networks.

The argument that help seeking is importantly altered
and shaped by the social milieu as well as by an individual's
social background and personality is critical to the research
strategy of our own study. In addition, differences in the
helping networks that are available or utilized, in turn,
affect the capacity of the individual to handle problems with
greater or lesser amounts of stress as reported by respondents. The data are approached using a mix of descriptive
and exploratory analyses coupled with more comprehensive
multivariate methods.

A CONCEPTUAL TYPOLOGY OF INDIVIDUAL PROBLEMS

In their "balance theory" of the roles of primary
groups and bureaucratic organization, Eugene Litwak and Henry
Meyer distinguish between two kinds of tasks, "uniform" and
"nonuniform."[3] Nonuniform tasks are those events which are
unique or idiosyncratic and nonrecurring. These kinds of
problems may require complex knowledge and multiple responses
in quick succession. These kinds of tasks or problems are
also generally simple and do not require expert knowledge.
By their nature (according to Litwak and Meyer's theory)
these kinds of problems are most suited to be dealt with by
primary groups. Uniform tasks, on the other hand, are most
suited to solution by bureaucracies. These tasks usually
involve recurring events that can be broken into components,
are solvable by specific rules, and, most critically require
expert knowledge and a complex division of labor.
Building upon the notions of Litwak and Meyer, Warren
and Clifford (1974) developed the concept of "invoked
expertise." This term refers to the level of technology or
specialized knowledge seen necessary and then invoked by a
person to cope with a problem. Using the three core elements
of this concept, problems can be dimensionalized and distinguished along a continuum of high, medium, and low. The
three core elements are 1) complexity of the elements of the

problem and the life space involved; 2) extensivity of
knowledge or technology relevant to the problem solution; and
3) normative associations with the problem.

For example, a low expertise problem would 1) require
the observation and control of many (possibly complex)
ancillary conditions, relationships, and behaviors for which
an expert cannot practically be utilized; 2) expert knowledge, even when highly developed, is present for only a part
of the problem or a particular phase, i.e., expert knowledge
is lacking in the core content of the evaluation of the
problem's emergence, definition, or resolution; and 3) there
is limited or no agreement among experts or subgroups in the
general population on the applicability of particular
expertise to the problem and on the definition of the problem
(particularly normative). Low invoked expertise problems
involve the presence of all these elements; high invoked
expertise problems, the absence or reverse of these propositions; medium invoked expertise problems will involve a
varying mix of presence and absence of the criteria. Table
II-1 elaborates on these three categories and gives some
tentative examples.

TABLE II-1

A Typology of Social/Health-Related Problems
on the Level of "Invoked Expertise"

Low Expertise
(high community variance)

Problem either lacks formal recognition in professional
taxonomies or is included with other problems. It tends
toward diffuse or non-specific etiology or symptom syndrome.
In particular it lacks a treatment modality or technology
that has been well tested, let alone refined.

Both initial and ongoing effects are closely tied to
traditional social values or norms which are created and
sustained by significant primary groups.

Specialized expertise is only ancillary to problem
definition and coping. Perception and response are highly
idiosyncratic, and not readily visible to formal social
institutions. Regulation of behavior depends heavily on
shared local values and "moral suasion."

Regardless of the perceived severity of the problem or
consensus as to longer run effects as seen by specialists,
major social values and the non-uniform character of the
problem as experienced by individuals makes concerted formal
action of limited value.

TABLE II-1 (Cont.)

Low Expertise Example
(high community variance)

1. Life cycle role transition (women entering work force after absence, retirement of male, etc.)
2. Youth-parent tensions
3. Leisure malaise (due to shortened work week, etc.)
4. Common cold effects
5. Consumer purchases by family (house, furnishings, car, appliances, etc.)
6. Family budgeting
7. Post-natal family adjustment

Medium Expertise
(medium community variance)

Problems in this category have an actively developing technology, but with widely varying success levels in application or where competing approaches show similar limited effectiveness of solutions. Differing definitions, analytical frameworks, discipline and specialization origins; various operational "models" are rampant. Little is known about long-term effects of given solutions.

Often problems in this category are in a state of flux and redefinition. The experts can't agree and formal agencies vie over proper jurisdictional lines. Rival "labels" as to the seriousness of the issue occur, although there is widespread recognition that "something" should be done in the short-run.

Non-expert elements may be significant in symptom remediation and treatment.

Medium Expertise Examples
(medium community variance)

1. Alcoholism
2. Simple Depressive Psychosis
3. Job-related emotional stress
4. Control of smoking
5. Obesity
6. Post-operative and general physical therapy
7. Career selection
8. Marital discord
9. Family planning
10. Arthritis

TABLE II-1 (Cont.)

High Expertise
(low community variance)

Problem has a well-defined and sophisticated technology associated with its detection and resolution, although debate may occur regarding its most efficient solution "design" or engineering.

Problems of social values are minimal--high consensus is present both from experts and non-experts as to the need for action. Debate centers on timing, equity, and speed of implementation of solution.

Problem is often identified with a highly specialized field within a profession and may be treated entirely within the confines of a formal agency.

Actions and efforts by non-experts or advocate groups cannot greatly change the nature of the problem or provide a solution that is at variance with the known data.

High Expertise Examples
(low community variance)

A. Health and Family Issues:

1. Hypertensive heart disease
2. Dislexia
3. Sickle Cell Anemia
4. Schizophrenia
5. Organically based child mental retardation
6. Prenatal child/mother care
7. Cancer detection

From the above discussion and Table II-1 several particularly important points should be noted. At the high expertise level there is wide agreement on the definition and labeling of something as a problem. By the same token, there is a low normative and emotional loading on most issues surrounding the problem. At the low expertise end of the continuum there is not only disagreement on definition, but even disagreement as to when a problem exists. Also, these types of problems are generally accompanied by strong normative and emotional involvements. There often exist jurisdictional disputes among professions over who has proprietary "rights" to a problem area. There may be competing claims of success and efficacy by both professional helpers and nonprofessional helpers and organizations. These situations become more manifest as one moves from high to low on the scale. In high

expertise problems these conflicts are lowest. In low
expertise problems there may be low manifest conflict but
much latent or incipient conflict. In the case of medium
expertise problems, conflicts among professionals, nonprofessionals, and various specialists are likely to be most
apparent.

Further, in differentiating problems one can note that
specialized bureaucratic or service structures exist to treat
particular types of problems using particular methods.
Specialization, standardization, and social control of this
sort is likely to be greatest with problems described as high
invoked expertise. Those problems which fall into medium
invoked expertise, on the other hand 1) often lie within a
disputed frontier of professional expertise and thus are
viewed as the "property" of several specialities; and 2) are
reflective of ambiguous or limited success when viewed in
comparison to high expertise problems. In the case of low
expertise problems, the very emergence of an issue as a
problem may be problematic when viewed from the standpoint of
either the professionals on the one hand or the lay community
on the other. Thus, the problem-labeling process could be
viewed at this level in its most diverse and fundamental
form.

Central to the problem-level-invoked concept is the
proposition that expertise and jurisdiction over a problem
area (or task area within the treatment of a particular
problem) can be highly dynamic. Problems can move both up
and down the scale. One need only observe the medical profession where historically the trend was for doctors to
assume ever increasing areas of responsibility for medical
care, and then, with either the routinization of some tasks
or the development of competing technologies, the diffusion
of some tasks to other new professions and para-professions.
An example of the conflict surrounding some medium expertise
problems is alcoholism, where both professionals and nonprofessionals using a variety of techniques claim efficacy.

With this typology in hand a selection of problems can
be made which will provide comparable stimuli for the study
of coping responses of different individuals and groups. The
problems from the same level of expertise will be those most
legitimate for comparison of coping.

THE CHOICE OF PROBLEMS FOR ANALYSIS OF HELPING PATTERNS

There are three reasons for differentiating among types
of problems: 1) the role of primary group or informal
helping systems in coping may vary considerably by problem
type; 2) some communities or population groups may be more

able to provide significant coping resources than others, depending on the type of problem; and 3) the involvement of professional helpers will vary systematically across problem type regardless of community or demographic differences. Thus, if one wants to focus on informal, nonprofessional helping (involving the widest variance due to community character) one needs to examine those problems which allow and even require the greatest involvement by informal helpers and nonprofessional community resources.

Medium and, in particular, low invoked expertise problems, may be handled entirely outside the formal helping and service delivery systems of the community. Also they cannot, by definition, be effectively dealt with solely by formal professional organizations. Additionally even where such problems have a high degree of visible and legitimate professional expertise associated with their initial labeling or identification, their treatment, remission, and maintenance are often largely functions of the informal helping systems embodied in local neighborhoods, networks of neighbors, friends, co-workers, and other community institutions.

Those problems labeled medium to low expertise offer the richest ground for examining variance in informal, nonprofessional systems of helping--and therefore of the natural helping networks of individuals. We now turn to the focal research design and its subsequent findings where the level of invoked expertise serves as a sensitizing concept to the understanding of how helping networks function.

CHAPTER III

USING HELPING NETWORKS: THE OVERALL PATTERNS

We begin this chapter by focusing on the idea that
there are many problems that do not have obvious solutions.
People confront problems in their daily lives for which it is
not clear that there is a single set solution; or that there
is, for example, a medication that will improve a health
problem.   Another example is the desire for a different job.
Individual mental outlook and the health of a community
depend on the ability of people to choose between several
kinds of resources for help in dealing with these problems.
But at the same time professional systems may not have the
best solutions for these problems.   Or the individual may
feel that he or she is unlikely to get a solution from a
professional system, and therefore will not rely on that
system but choose another helping system instead.
We use the term low invoked expertise to describe
common concerns or problems for which no one, including the
professional, could claim any "jurisdiction" or superior
coping strategy.   By contrast, a problem such as diagnosing
sickle cell anemia, where medical professionals have
objective, standardized ways of determining whether a person
has this disease and what can be done about it, is a high
expertise problem.   Thus, low invoked expertise or grass-
roots kinds of concerns are problems not recognized by
professionals as their central treatment task.   If an
individual goes to a family doctor and says, "I really want a
different job," what is the doctor supposed to do about that?
Listen sympathetically?   Refer the individual to a
professional or formal agency?
The strategy of the research was to concentrate on a
group of low invoked expertise problems.   This approach gives
the best test of the richness of helping resources; there is
no single solution but many effective pathways that can be
taken.   When confronted with such a problem the individual
may have to search among different kinds of resources in

25

order to find a solution. It may be that the search in
itself is a helping process.

In this chapter we shall explore the most general
findings of the helping network study. In particular, we
will focus on the individual as help-seeker: what types of
problems he or she experiences, with what frequency, and the
helping resources used to cope with them. As we shall discover, several outcomes revise conventional views of the role
and functions of helping and their effects on individual
well-being.

There may not be anything particularly pathological
about getting help, and it may not suggest that the person
seeking help is under greater stress. In fact, it may be
that the person would be under greater stress if he did not
seek help and thereby experience social isolation.

THE LIST OF "RECENT CONCERNS"

As part of the overall survey design a set of helping
behaviors was associated with a series of nine "recent
concerns" developed out of initial in-depth interviews.[1]
People were asked: "Tell me if this has happened to you
recently (in the last month or so), not recently, or never."
The following experiences were then listed:

   a) Wanted to change the way you and your (wife/
      husband) divide the family activities
   b) Wanted to get a completely different job
   c) Concerned about suspicious people in the neighbor-
      hood
   d) Felt it's no use trying to do things because so many
      things go wrong
   e) Thought about going back to school
   f) Thought about how it would be to retire
   g) Felt so "blue" it ruined your whole day
   h) Got so tense at work you blew your stack
   i) Thought about moving from the neighborhood because
      of the crime problem.

These problems were selected because of their low
invoked expertise (see Warren and Clifford, 1974). Such
problems are not conventionally seen as professional agency
concerns or formally recognized attributes of poor mental
health. Instead, the items are highly diffuse in shared
definition and may be seen by some value systems as serious,
by others as natural, and by still others as the early signs
of more serious mental stress. Precisely because of their
ambiguous character, the recent concerns provide a highly

significant test of the competing pathways to help and
successful coping for the individual experiencing them.
Indeed, they may be persistent and, therefore, chronic in
character. Others may be causal bases for dramatic "crisis"
episodes. Still others will be evanescent.

Most frequently experienced among the nine recent
concerns is that of "feeling blue". Nearly one in three
persons interviewed indicated that they had experienced this
during the last month. Least frequent was the consideration
of moving from the neighborhood--only seven percent of all
respondents had this as a recent concern. Consideration of
retirement, going back to school, and wanting a different job
were experienced by more than one in five of all respondents.
Slightly less than this proportion reported a recent concern
about suspicious people in the neighborhood (see Table III-
1).

The original goal of creating the recent concerns list
was to provide enough comparisons between persons with a
problem and those without it to evaluate the role of helping
networks. We developed the problem list with the expectation
that perhaps half of the sample might have at least one concern at the time they were interviewed. In fact, 72 percent
of the people interviewed reported at least one of the nine
and 46 percent reported two or more. The average is 1.7
recent concerns. Less than one in twenty persons experienced
a recent concern problem load exceeding four and no one
reported having all nine problems (see Appendix Table III-1).

TABLE III-1

Distribution of Concerns That Have Been
Felt Recently - in the Last Month or So
(Percent of Sample Experiencing Each Problem)

Felt so "blue" or "low" it ruined your whole day	31%
Thought how it would be to retire	29%
Thought about going back to school	25%
Wanted to get a completely different job	21%
Concerned about suspicious people in the neighborhood	19%
Got so tense at work you "blew your stack"	17%
Felt it's no use trying to do things because so many things go wrong	14%
Wanted to change the way you and your (wife/husband) divide the family activities	10%
Thought about moving from the neighborhood because of crime problems	7%

N = 2499

"VITAL LIFE CRISES" MEASURE

Several recent studies[2] suggest that life change is
significantly related to health change and that successful
handling of these crises is due in part to three factors: 1)
the existence of sustaining communication networks; 2) the
individual's involvement in communication networks; and 3)
the existence of social processes associated with these
communication networks.

The relationship between life change and occurrence of
disease has been a concern of medical and social researchers
for many years.[3] Specifically, much research has been
devoted to the study of individuals faced with a number of
vital life crises and the adaptive or coping behavior evoked
by these events. "Life change" in this context refers to
significant alternations in an individual's lifestyle which
result from encounters with vital "life crises." These
crises represent major areas of dynamic significance in the
American lifestyle which evolve from ordinary, and sometimes
from extraordinary, social and interpersonal experiences.
The selected vital life crises used in the present study
include family relationships, marriage, education, occupation, and health.

The relationship between life change and minor health
change was first investigated by Holmes and Holmes (1969)
utilizing the Schedule of Daily Experiences (SDE), a modification of the Schedule of Recent Experiences (SRE) used in
previous studies by Thomas Rahe (1964). The SDE was used as
a diary by respondents to record minor health changes on a
day-to-day basis. Minor health changes were defined as the
signs and symptoms of everyday life such as minor accidents,
nervousness, tension, fatigue, dizziness, lack of energy, and
insomnia that do not require a visit to the doctor and
usually pass unnoticed. Using 42 of the original 43 life-
event items and corresponding magnitudes, they recorded the
number and type of symptoms occurring for each life-change
item in the sample. Their findings indicated that
respondents were more likely to experience the signs and
symptoms of everyday life on greater-than-average life-change
days. Moreover, they observed that life change was directly
related to health change. They concluded that minor health
change may be causally related to events that require adaptive or coping behavior on the part of individuals faced with
vital life crises.

The Social Readjustment Rating Scale (SRRS), which
delineated the original forty-three life events in Holmes and
Rahe's original study, was reduced to fourteen of the
original life-event items. These particular items were
included on the basis of their representing the entire range

of magnitude estimation scores, assigned to each of the
forty-three items in the Holmes and Rahe study.

Table III-2 indicates the items taken from the Holmes
and Rahe scale and the frequency of their occurrence. The
list was introduced in the interview with the following question: "Have any of the following things happened to you or
someone in the household in the last year?" Most frequent of
the fourteen items was a "personal injury or serious illness." More than one in four respondents reported such
events. Next in order was "the death of a close family
member"--experienced by one in five respondents. One out of
every eight persons interviewed reported a "change of job."
A virtually identical proportion said they "began or ended
school or job training." One in ten respondents mentioned a
spouse "began or stopped work."[4]

Changes in household composition by adding a new member
occurred in one out of twelve cases, while having a child
leave the family home is reported in one out of eighteen
instances. Beyond these life crises are six which were
reported by less than one in thirty respondents. These
include retirement, divorce or separation, being fired, and
being arrested.

What is the frequency with which the Holmes and Rahe
life crises are experienced in comparison with the newly
created list of recent concerns? In fact, both are very
similar in problem load. Thus, 65 percent of the people

TABLE III-2

Specific Types of "Life Crises"
(During the last year or so)

Personal Injury or Serious Illness	28%
Death of a Close Family Member	18%
Change of Job	13%
Began or Ended School or Job Training	12%
Spouse Began or Stopped Work	11%
Been the Victim of a Crime	9%
New Person Added to the Household	8%
Child Left the Household	6%
Retired	3%
Divorce	3%
Death of Spouse	2%
Separation	2%
Fired from Job	2%
Been Arrested	1%

N = 2501

interviewed reported at least one life crisis during the year
leading up to the survey and about one in three persons
report experiencing at least two such events. About one in
eight individuals interviewed reported having more than two
life crisis (see Appendix Table III-2).

Clearly, recent concerns are experienced with greater
frequency in a short time interval—one month—in comparison
with the life crisis events covering a one year period. The
two experiences have a different character: the latter are
discrete and have a fixed point of occurrence or finite
beginning and end, such as serious illness with hospitalization. By contrast, recent concerns are more amorphous as to
onset and are potentially continuous and persistent.

THE RECENT CONCERNS LIST AS A MEASURE OF ACTIVE COPING WITH
THE ENVIRONMENT

In utilizing the nine problems as a major test of the
help-seeking behavior of individuals we employed, in effect,
a conceptually different type of problem than the more conventional life crisis.[5] In the former instance, individuals
are coping with problems that involve change in their life
style, including desired and not yet realized future alterations of life style. Thus, thinking about retirement,
wanting to go back to school, thinking about moving from a
neighborhood because of crime, and wanting a different job
are potential life changes. Some of these are a means to
eliminate a negative condition in the present life of the
individual; others are looking toward change without knowing
whether this is a positive or a negative adjustment.

Recent concerns, as opposed to life crises, are
experiences that individuals report that may or may not
require the use of helping resources. Such resources are
drawn upon, not in a crisis of death or the breakage of
existing social supports, but within the context of one's
existing social networks. Such help-seeking provides a
measure of the capacity of that in-place network. By contrast, life crises refer to experiences that require a
replacing of lost networks or imply an isolation from a
network—e.g., job loss, children leaving the household.

In the case of recent concerns, existing networks may
be taxed to their limit. A search for help can thus serve to
increase the variety and strength of networks available to
the individual. But the effort is a voluntary one and is not
imposed by the severing of existing resources or social
supports as is often the case with life crises.

Taken together, recent concerns and life crises both
test the strength of helping networks in different ways.

Recent concerns tend to be associated with desired improvements as well as past deprivations.

THE USE AND EFFECTIVENESS OF HELPERS IN COPING WITH RECENT CONCERNS

The major thrust of the research design is the investigation of how the individual draws upon others in coping with a range of frequently experienced problems. We have seen that the list of recent concerns provides a valid tool for pursuing the investigation. The bulk of the sample is in the middle income range. The focus on how a middle-America strata copes with a range of daily problems provides a solid methodological foundation for testing our key concepts. This strategy also serves as an important policy impact analysis since this group is such a large population segment of the total society. This group's ability to cope with problems and to use both formal and informal helping resources has a significant meaning in terms of the volume of services used and the quality of American urban neighborhood and community life.

We begin with a consideration of the size or extensivity of helping networks in terms of the variety of helpers sought out by individuals.

People interviewed were asked: "Tell me if this has happened to you recently (in the last month or so), not recently, or never." . . . (Then   proceed down the list of recent concerns e.g., "Felt so 'blue' or 'low' it ruined your whole day.")

Each respondent who indicated that any of the listed concerns had come up recently was then asked to describe who they had talked with about it. Included were the following:

Your spouse A relative A friend	Primary Helpers
A neighbor A co-worker	Proximal Helpers
A doctor A clergyman A counselor A teacher The police	Professional/Formal Agency Helpers

The definition of "relative" was specified as someone related by blood not living in the same household.

"Counselor" included a family counselor, psychiatrist,
psychologist, or social worker.

Table III-3 shows the extent of usage of each of the
ten types of helpers listed in the interview. The percentages are based on the population of respondents experiencing
at least one recent concern. Spouse helping is clearly the
most frequent and most widely available interpersonal
resource (82 percent), if we consider only those who are
married. About two out of every five respondents with a
recent concern use a friend as a helper. (Interestingly,
this is the same as the proportion of working persons who use
a co-worker in this capacity.)

Of the total number of people with a recent concern
more than one in three seeks help from a relative not living
in the same household.

Help is sought from neighbors by somewhat more than one
in four respondents.

The data presented here demonstrates the frequent and
widespread use of informal helpers in coping with recent concerns. This lay system is the major resource--if help is
sought.

When we turn to formal helpers, the usage is sharply
lower. Police and physician helping are sought out by only
one of every twelve persons with a recent concern. This
drops further to about one in twenty who use a mental health,
social work, or similar helping professional. Clergy and
teachers are called by only one of 25 persons seeking help
for a recent concern. Note that helping for life crises
shows somewhat different patterns (see Appendix Table III-3).

TABLE III-3

Use of Different Kinds of Helpers for Recent Concerns
(Percent with at least one recent concern)

Spouse	62% (82%)[*]	Police	8
Friend	41	Doctor	8
Relative	37	Counselor[a]	6
Co-worker	28 (42%)[#]	Teacher	4
Neighbor	27	Clergy	4

N = 1611
[*]Married persons only
[#]Working persons only
[a]Includes a social worker, psychologist, or psychiatrist

ISOLATION FROM HELP SEEKING

In the work of Robert Weiss and others, the "provision of social relations" becomes a major focus of the social support and helping process. The severing of a social tie or the failure to establish a helping network may be seen as a major source of risk to mental health as well as general well-being. In light of this basic assumption about the role of helping, the absence of helpers might be considered a limitation that the individual has in coping with a range of problems in daily life. Given this perspective, let us trace the extent to which individuals try to cope with recent concerns without the use of any helpers.

Table III-4 shows each recent concern and the proportion of respondents experiencing that problem but not seeking help. Problems vary in the degree to which help is sought, although overall help is sought by most respondents. "Thinking about retirement" and "feeling blue" are more likely to be coped with in a solitary fashion. Helping is sought by seven out of eight respondents for the concern of changing spouse family roles. In general, help-seeking occurs for at least two-thirds and usually by three out of four persons who experience any given recent concern.

Is not seeking help necessarily an indicator of social isolation? Could a preference for no help be simply a style of problem-coping?

There are two major reasons to consider the importance of a personality variable in relation to the study and its

TABLE III-4

Persons with Recent Concerns Who Do Not Use Any Helpers
(Percent with this concern who did not talk to anyone)

Thought about how it would be to retire	35%
Felt so blue or low that it ruined my day	35
Felt "it was no use trying" because so many things were going wrong	30
Blew your stack at work	28
Thought how it would be to go back to school	28
Thought about moving from the neighborhood because of crime problems	21
Wanted a completely different job	20
Afraid of suspicious people in the neighborhood	18
Wanted to change the way you and your spouse divide family duties	12

N = 1782

focal concerns. First, if the individual is generally with-
drawn or has a crystallized pattern of social isolation,
problem load will be less likely to alter this than for other
individuals.

A second consideration related to personality variables
is the response of the individual in terms of problem-coping
style. Here, the tendency not to use others for help or to
avoid social contact in general may shape the conditions
under which help-seeking occurs.

In order to obtain some measure of the personality
style of the individual, a series of short questions were
included as follows:

"Please tell me if these statements are true or not
true about yourself:

    a.   I prefer action to making plans.
    b.   I usually take the initiative in making new
        friends.
    c.   I am usually sure and quick in the actions I take.
    d.   I would be unhappy if I weren't around a lot of
        people.
    e.   I think of myself as a lively individual."

These items are modified or paraphrased elements of
more highly refined measures of "introvert-extrovert"
personality types.[6]

One of the personality measures does show a nonsignifi-
cant correlation with the probability of help-seeking for
recent concerns. This occurs between the number of helpers
used and the Extrovert Index (see Appendix Table III-4).

QUALITIES OF HELPING NETWORKS

A major goal of the study is to develop measures of the
differences in helping patterns which individuals use and, in
turn, how these are clustered by types of neighborhoods and
communities. In the subsequent portions of our analysis, we
have employed two general indicators of helping processes.

Extensivity of Helping

The first measure is an index of the supportiveness of
a person's helping network in terms of how extensive it is;
i.e., how many helpers are brought into play on any given
problem. It is, basically, the range of helpers a person
talks to about a problem—up to the ten types indicated in
Table III-3.

Table III-5 presents the distribution of the number of different kinds of helpers utilized for concerns. The percentages indicate individuals who use up to ten of the helpers. We note that about one in seven persons in the 1974 baseline survey did not use any helpers in dealing with recent concerns. Another one in four used only a single type of helper. A majority (three out of five) of those experiencing at least one recent concern use two or more different kinds of helpers. For the entire sample this value is 1.5 different helpers per problem.

Intensivity of Helping

The second major index of helping patterns focuses on the number of different behaviors which a helper might provide in a given helping transaction.[7]

For each helper listed by a respondent, the additional question asked was: "Which of these things happened when you talked with that person?" The following six choices were then chosen by the respondent from a card they were handed:

   a)   (They) just listened to me
   b)   (They) asked me questions
   c)   (They) told me who else to see
   d)   (They) showed me a new way to look at things
   e)   (They) took me to see someone who could take action
   f)   (They) took some action about the matter

As many of the six could be chosen as applied to each "transaction" of helping. The most typical helping behavior—the one which occurs in the largest number of helping situations is that of listening: nearly four out of five contain such help. A majority of helping includes the more active kind of social support defined by "asking questions." Re-directing

TABLE III-5

Number of Different Kinds of Helpers Used by People
Experiencing at Least One Recent Concern

None	14%	Four	10
One	24	Five	7
Two	23	Six or more	5
Three	17		
		Total	100%

N = 1782

of the help seeker's thinking--i.e., "showing a new way to
look at the problem"--is found in one of three helping transactions. Taking direct action as part of the helping process
occurs in somewhat more than one out of four situations.
Finally, the two types of referral helping--giving information about another helper or taking the person directly to
that individual--is found in 22 percent of all transactions.[8]
Exact percentages are shown in Table III-6.

For both the extensivity and the intensivity of helping
for a given problem the modal pattern is a multiple one:
more than one type of helper and more than one kind of
helping behavior.

THE CONSEQUENCES OF HELP-SEEKING ON WELL-BEING

Our discussion of the form of help-seeking has led
almost logically to the issue of the effect of such patterns
on the individual with problems. While our study is mainly
aimed at tracing the pathways of helpings--the form and
variety of resources people use to cope with a range of
common concerns--we employed several measures of self-
reported mental and physical health that can be correlated
with the use of helpers. Basically, the question posed is:
What is the effect of help-seeking on the helpee?

To address the question of consequences of helping on
the well-being of the person seeking help a set of three sub-
scales and a summary scale were devised based upon a simple
additive score for a series of interview items contained in
both the 1974 and 1975 intervals. These items were grouped
into the following categories to create three indices:
"Depressed Mental Outlook" (DMO); "Psychosomatic Complaint";
and "Perceived Ill Health." Finally, the scores for the
individual on each of these three scales were added together

TABLE III-6

Types of Helping Behaviors Received by Those Seeking Help
For Recent Concerns

"Just listened to me"	78%
"Asked me questions"	57%
"Showed me a new way to look at things"	32%
"Took some action about the matter"	27%
"Told me who else to see"	15%
"Took me to see someone who could take action"	7%

N = 1789

and utilized as a comprehensive index of "Risk to Well-Being" (RISK).[9]

A variety of helping and problem experience factors significantly alter individual RISK scores. The total number of recent concerns is one of these. It is positively correlated to a significant degree. This is not true for the problem load of life crises; there is a trend, but it is not statistically significant.

Isolation from helpers in dealing with recent concerns is also significantly associated with individual well-being, measures of Depressed Mental Outlook, Psychosomatic Complaint, and the overall RISK scores; personality measures are not. The role of recent concerns is therefore an important one. With the exception of reported ill health, age, income, education, and occupation are not significantly related to the various well-being indicators (see Appendix Table III-5).

The fact that the newly created nine-item list can play such a role suggests--apart from its conceptual utility in the framework of our specific research--that such a list (or a similar version of it) can be used as a measurement device in other studies. We can now pursue the role of helping and recent concern load as the basis of important explained variance in individual well-being.

GAUGING THE EFFECTIVENESS OF EXTENSITIVITY AND INTENSITIVITY OF HELPING

In light of the variability in patterns of helping, the question of the empirical evaluation of which pattern types affect the well-being of the individual becomes a central one. Since we have already seen that the well-being variables are affected by the number of recent concerns--the higher the number, the worse off the individual--we may split the overall question of helping effectiveness into two parts: First, is there a role which particular patterns of helping have in reducing stress irrespective of problem load? and secondly, which is more important in terms of individual well-being--problem load or type of helping?

The results of an analysis of variance test between three elements of the helping process--intensivity, extensivity, and isolation--and the four dependent variables of individual well-being under differing numbers of recent concerns indicates that each has a significant role. The intensivity variable emerges as the most important followed in turn by extensivity and isolation. Both psychosomatic complaint and perceived ill health are very weakly linked to problem- and help-seeking (see Appendix Table III-6).

The impact of helping on reducing stress associated
with problem-coping can be shown in a graphic way.   In Chart
III-1, the pattern of RISK scores--depressed mental outlook--
is shown for persons with one, two, and then more than two
recent concerns.   The horizontal axis of the chart contains
the number of problems and the number of helpers as a cumulative total building toward the right of the chart.   The
vertical axis is the RISK score.   Chart III-1 indicates the
general upward movement of RISK with problem load.   At the
same time, there are significant dips in this pattern where
the individual has one or two concerns with four or more
helpers, and for three or more concerns with three helpers.
Where there are no helpers utilized at the one-problem level,
RISK score is the highest for that level.

The fact of greater social contact where the individual
has a set of recent concerns indicates that the effect of
such a problem load is increasingly mitigated by the active
help of informal members of the person's social support
system--a minimum "critical mass" of helpers.   Utilization of
more than this number of helpers is often linked with a
higher RISK score than using fewer than three or even no
helpers at all.   Thus, we have some preliminary evidence
regarding the optimal number of helpers that an individual
with recent concerns uses where such contact is associated
with the least stress.   Moreover, problem load, while the
underlying basis for stress, can be limited as a risk factor
--where help-seeking at a fairly extensive level occurs.

In Chart III-2 intensivity is depicted in relation to
number of recent concerns.   With a single recent concern,
RISK is lowest with four different helping behaviors; lowest
with two concerns where one to three behaviors are used; and
lowest with three or more concerns if three or four behaviors
are involved in the helping transaction.   Problem load is
minimized as a source of stress but never eliminated; scores
rise with problem load.

If the role of intensivity is further delineated by
considering the largest category of such help--listening--a
more precise view of the role of helping behaviors is
provided.   When we eliminate helping transactions where only
listening is provided by the helper, a different pattern for
intensivity and problem load emerges.   We can first see this
in Chart III-3 where no help is sought (or where only
listening is provided).   RISK scores are 14.0, 18.4, and
24.9, respectively.   Where four different helping behaviors
are provided at each problem level, the RISK scores are 8.9,
15.3, and 19.8 respectively.   At the one-problem level, the
optimal helping behavior pattern is in the range of two to
four behaviors (including a combination with "just listens");

CHART III − 1

RISK Score In Relation to Problem Load and Helpers Used

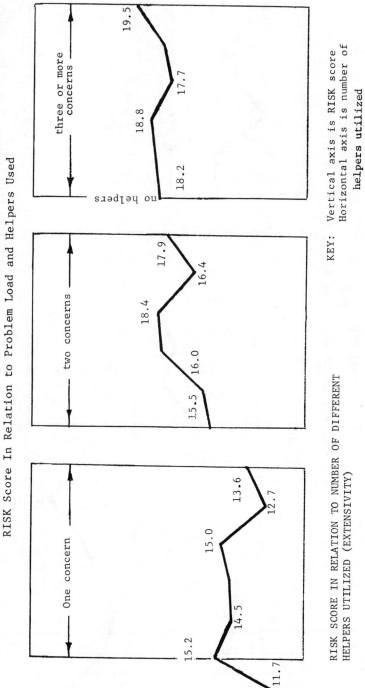

KEY: Vertical axis is RISK score
Horizontal axis is number of
helpers utilized

RISK SCORE IN RELATION TO NUMBER OF DIFFERENT
HELPERS UTILIZED (EXTENSIVITY)

CHART III - 2

RISK Score In Relation to Problem Load and the Number of Helping Behaviors

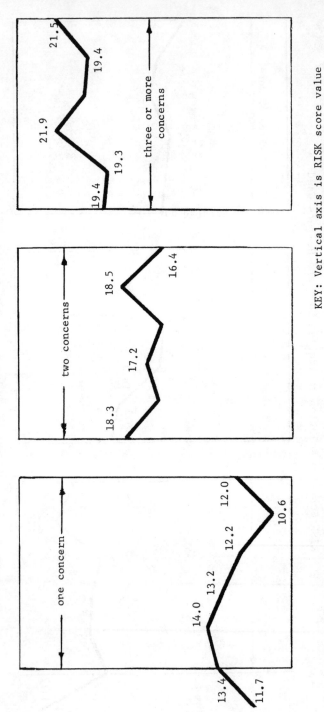

KEY: Vertical axis is RISK score value
Horizontal axis is number of
different kinds of helping behaviors

RISK SCORE IN RELATION TO HELPING BEHAVIORS

CHART III - 3

RISK Score In Relation to Problem Load and Number of Helping Behaviors
That Do not Include "Just Listens"

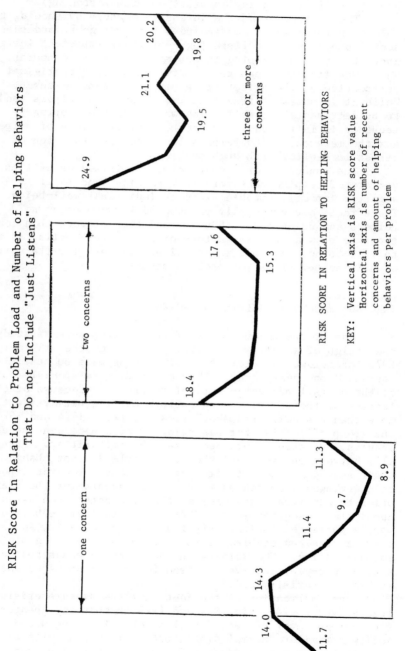

RISK SCORE IN RELATION TO HELPING BEHAVIORS

KEY: Vertical axis is RISK score value
        Horizontal axis is number of recent
        concerns and amount of helping
        behaviors per problem

with two or more concerns, the range is from one to four
behaviors (including any combination with listening).

The refinement of the intensity measure by showing the
role of helping which may include, but must go beyond passive
social support--"just listening"--provides important insights
about the role of helping in coping with recent concerns.

Our findings lead to a modification of the original
perspective on the effect of helping on the help-seeker.
While it is somewhat true that isolation from helpers tends
to be detrimental to well-being when a problem coping
sequence is initiated, neither the maximum volume of helpers
nor the mere access to helpers leads to the reduction of
stress in dealing with such problems.

The number of different helpers utilized as well as the
variety of helping behaviors they provide tend to limit the
negative impact of problem load on individual well-being.
The effects are especially pronounced between using no
helpers and using three, but the addition of more than four
tends to show a reverse pattern or no further decline in risk
to well-being. A similar curvilinear pattern for the number
of helping behaviors per problem occurs.

TRACING CHANGES IN HELPING NETWORKS

One of the unique parts of the helping network study is
the design of a follow-up survey paralleling the original
1974 interview. A total of 1,531 persons were successfully
contacted one year later. This group forms a special facet
of the overall project--"a panel sample."[10] Because of this
feature of the study, we can explore helping networks with
more than a single "snapshot" view. Between 1974 and 1975
the group of people that was reinterviewed underwent several
changes, but also maintained some key similarities. First of
all, between one year and the next people did not change
their average number of life crises. In other words, those
reinterviewed reported as many of such events for the year
prior to our first interview as they indicated when asked
about the subsequent year. Virtually identical numbers of
people increased their crisis load as decreased it, so the
average remained stable. This pattern is visually depicted
in Chart III-4. The form--a "normal curve"--means that over
a given one-year interval the sample as a group experienced a
stable life-crisis load.[11]

One implication of the fact that the average crisis
load stayed the same in 1974 and 1975 is that any changes in
the average level of mental outlook or well-being would
follow a similar "normal distribution" if coping with crises
was the key source of distress. In fact, this does not

TABLE III-4

Changes in The Distribution of "Life Crises":   1974-1975

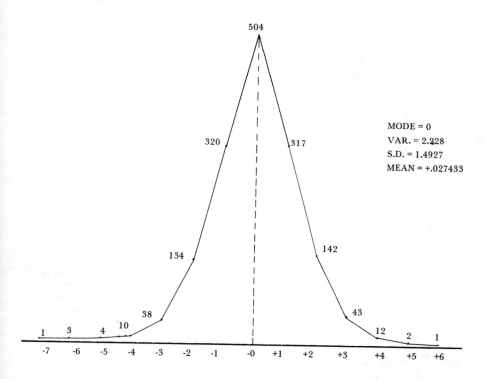

TABLE III-4 (cont.)

Changes in the Distribution of "Recent Concern": 1974-1975

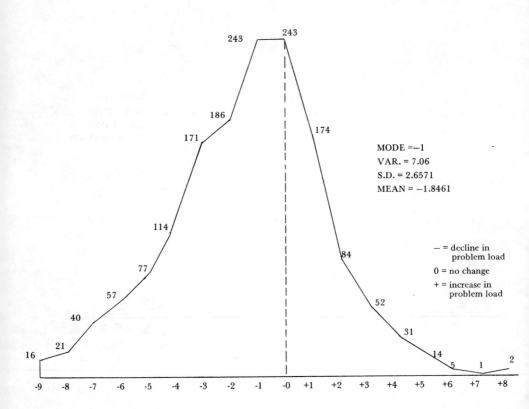

MODE =−1
VAR. = 7.06
S.D. = 2.6571
MEAN = −1.8461

− = decline in
     problem load

0 = no change

+ = increase in
     problem load

occur. Instead, there is a noticeable decline in the average score of two of the three components of the RISK well-being index despite no change in the average crisis load. Thus, Depressed Mental Outlook drops 22 percent between 1974 and 1975 and the overall RISK score by 10 percent.

What corresponds to the changes in individual mental health? It is the recent-concern problem load. This value declines from an average of 2.1 problems in 1974 to 1.8 in 1975--a decline of fourteen percent.

Another way to see the link between recent concerns and well-being is to note that 24 percent of the people interviewed in both 1974 and 1975 have an increase in the number of such experiences, while 60 percent show a reduction. Simultaneously, 21 percent increased their RISK level from 1974 to 1975, while 42 percent experienced a reduction. Thus, well-being and the load of recent concerns are highly correlated.

At the same time the average number of recent concerns drops between 1974 and 1975, there is also a significant rise in helping network activity for those people who do experience recent concerns. For the numbers of different helpers used there is a gain from 2.1 in 1974 to 2.8 in 1975 --a 33 percent rise; for the varieties of helping behaviors provided the average climbs from 2.0 to 2.5--one quarter larger than in 1974 (see Appendix Table III-9).

These changes in key measures used in the helping network study underscore the important role which recent concerns play in the lives of people and the correspondingly vital contribution of helping systems.[12]

When first contacted, one out of seven people who were subsequently reinterviewed reported they did not use any helpers in dealing with recent concerns. By 1975, people with such problems were using helpers 92 percent of the time (see Appendix Table III-12). While not for all problems, a large number of people still experience at least one recent concern without seeking any help for it.

Thus, for simple depression in 1974, one in three people sought no help. Thinking about retirement, going back to school, and "no use trying" attitude all show no help-seeking in 1974 by at least one out of four people with these experiences.

By 1975 isolation from helpers drops for six of the nine recent concerns. For the two "mental health" or mood problems there is no decline but instead a slight increase. The sharpest relative increase occur for the recent concern involving changing family role obligations--from nine to fifteen percent (see Appendix Table III-13).

The general increase in the amount and variety of helping in 1975 versus 1974 can be illustrated in a number of

ways. Table III-7 shows the particular kind of helper and
measures the rate of use in 1975 compared to 1974. Note that
it is the informal helping system that has expanded: relative helping by 27 percent, friend by 23 percent, and
neighbor by thirteen percent. By contrast, the use of formal
helpers actually declines from 1974 to 1975—specifically
doctor and counselor helping.

There is another source of change in the nature of
help-seeking in 1975 compared to 1974. Since we had
Does problem persistence mean that helpers do different
things? The answer tends to be "yes." The kind of help
rendered in 1975 is different than in 1974. See Table III-8.
While all helping behaviors have increased, referral and
"showing a new way" behaviors have the largest increase. At
the same time, the passive "just listened" has remained
almost the same as in 1974—up slightly over one percent.
Thus, helping in 1975 is more active and focuses on linkages
to additional helpers: it resembles more of a network
pattern instead of a self-contained supportive resource in a
purely social-emotional sense.

There is another source of change in the nature of
help-seeking in 1975 compared to 1974. Since we had
initially found some degree of correlation between personality style of the individual and helping, the persistence of
such a pattern would link help-seeking more to individual
factors rather than the role of social context. Does this
occur? The answer appears to be "no." The "Extrovert"
personality and "Action" personality measures are less
correlated to helping in 1975 as compared to 1974 (see
Appendix Table III-14). Consequently, while there is
evidence that the early phases of problem-coping may entail

TABLE III-7

Change in the Use of Different Kinds of Helpers: 1974-75

	1974	1975	Percent Change
Spouse	84%	92%	+ 10%
Friend	57	70	+ 23
Relative	51	65	+ 27
Neighbor	45	51	+ 13
Co-worker	44	49	+ 11
Teacher, Clergy, Police	21	21	0
Doctor	13	12	− 8
Counselor (social worker, psychiatrist, psychologist	7	6	− 14

N = 1531

an important role in terms of personality style affecting the probability of contacting others for help; by the time problems have persisted, such a correlation has diminished.

The various measures of individual mental outlook and well-being are tied to the kind of help provided over the one-year period between 1974 and 1975. "Listening" help and "asking questions", along with "taking action", were all at first related to a lower level of risk to well-being. One year later, however, listening shows a modest reverse trend: a slight positive correlation with the RISK score. However, each of the other four types of helping behaviors are strongly related to a reduction of the RISK score (see Appendix Table III-15).

PATHWAYS TO HELPING: SOME OVERALL PATTERNS

Basic to the helping network project is the view that problem-coping is not simply a random search for miscellaneous advice, social support, or concrete aid. Rather, we submit, it is a learned response to the exigencies of everyday life. It is cumulative: a "style" which an individual establishes using a set of channels that are comfortable and useful. These are fashioned out of experience, so they must work or else the individual will discard them. To this degree, help-seeking is rational if not instrumentally expedient. Such is the dynamic upon which our analysis is based. Then what are the typical approaches taken? How are

TABLE III-8

Kinds of Helping Behaviors Given for Recent Concerns:
1974-75

	1974	1975	Percent change
"Just listened"	89%	90%	+ 1%
"Asked Questions"	70	73	+ 4
"Showed me a new way to look at the problem"	36	43	+ 20
"Took some action on the problem"	31	33	+ 8
Referred by telling about or talking to someone else	20	25	+ 25

N = 1531

the various kinds of helpers mobilized? Let us summarize
what pieces of the puzzle we have uncovered thus far.

　　To approach this task we first group all helpers into
four types: primary group, proximal, formal, and professional. The first consists of spouse, friend, and relative; the second, of co-worker and neighbor; the third, of
clergy, police, and teacher; and the fourth, of physician and
counselor (psychiatrist, etc.).

　　Chart III-5 provides a way to consider each of the four
clusters of helpers as a starting point and to trace the
help-seeker's subsequent destination. Use of primary-group
helpers in 1974 tends to lead to continued use of these same
helpers in 1975; such initial help also is associated with
less use of formal and professional helpers.

　　Where the proximal system is utilized first, this tends
to be related to subsequent use of the same kinds of helpers
in conjunction with formal helpers such as clergy, teacher,
or police. There is some association with subsequent use of
professional helpers. Primary helpers may or may not be a
follow-up pattern where proximal helpers are part of initial
help-seeking.

　　In the case of the initial use of formal, non-
professional helpers, follow-up tends to occur with the same

CHART III-5

Pathways to Helping: Starting Point and Follow-Up Patterns

Help in 1975

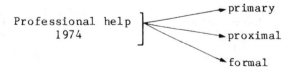

Primary helping
    in 1974   ──────────→ primary

Proximal helping   ↗ proximal
    in 1974   ←
                                          ↘ formal

Formal, Non-Prof.   ↗ proximal
    helping   ←
    1974   ↘ formal

                                          ↗ primary
Professional help
    1974   ←──────────→ proximal

                                          ↘ formal

system or proximal helpers. There are negative linkages to a
follow-up with either primary-group helpers or professionals.

When professional helping is the entry point, helping
follow-up tends to occur with any of the other three
varieties of helpers. The pattern implied is that continued
use of professionals is a relatively rare sequence. This is
the only instance where starting in a given system does not
tend to be significantly correlated with follow-up use of
that same system.

In Chart III-6 the "traffic flow" pattern shows how
each kind of helping system is linked to others. The
schematic depiction indicates that beginning or following-up
movement between the proximal and formal systems is a unique
pattern of symmetrical exchange that does not occur for other
system pairings.

The primary system has three different blockages as
shown in the diagram: follow-up with formal helpers, with
proximal helpers, and with professional helpers.

CHART III-6

Traffic Flows Between Helping Systems: 1974 to 1975

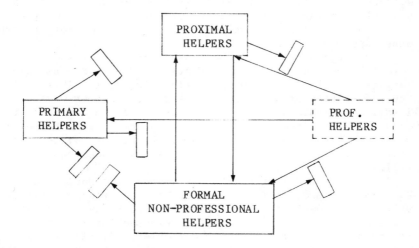

PRIMARY HELPERS: spouse, relatives, friends
PROXIMAL HELPERS: neighbors, co-workers
FORMAL HELPERS: clergy, police, teachers
PROFESSIONAL HELPERS: social worker, psychologist, psychia-
                        trist, physician.

The formal system shows two blockages: follow-up with primary helpers and professional helpers.

Only in the case of proximal helpers is there one blockage: following-up with professional helpers. The professional system is asymmetrical: starting here can result in follow-up in any direction, but the reverse is not true: each of the other systems tends not to use professionals once that other system has been mobilized.

Several implications flow from the patterns we have reviewed. First of all, we note that professional helping tends to be the basis for simultaneous use of primary, proximal, and formal helpers. But where these other systems have been mobilized, they tend to restrict the follow-up utilization of professionals. The implication would appear to be that, in general, problem-coping sometimes starts with professionals as part of a team of helpers. But if they have not been included from the outset, they will not be called upon later. If helping emerges out of primary-group helpers (spouse, friends, or relatives), it tends to be self-contained: it is an exclusive system which then mitigates the need for other systems. If help-seeking initially includes formal helpers (clergy, police, teachers), this tends to preclude going back to primary or professional helpers, but not proximal helpers such as neighbors or co-workers. Finally, the proximal system appears to be fluid and multi-facing: using helpers of this type did not preclude the use simultaneously and subsequently of helpers from other systems.

We suggest that neighbor/co-worker helpers and the formal helpers are the most versatile: they serve as gatekeepers as well as follow-up helping resources. This is less true of primary or professional helpers. Another way to describe the role of the proximal system is to see it as the crossroads or linkage between other systems. This brokerage or referral role has far reaching implications for the concept of what is a healthy support system. (See Chapter VIII.)

We have seen rather clear evidence that social contact enhances the probability that a problem experienced initially will recur. Our data do not permit us to unravel the causal nexus as to whether, for example, help-seeking implies a strong motivation to deal with a problem; or, if instead, such motivation derives from contact about the problem. The evidence from our data tends to be consistent with a theory of problem-coping in which the labeling as well as the solution emerge in a reciprocal fashion from social interaction.

Basic to our discussion of the emergence and persistence of recent concerns is the interpretation of these

problems as efforts to master or improve one's life, not
simply to restore a broken social tie or overcome loneliness.

The number of different helpers utilized, as well as
the variety of helping behaviors they provide, tends to limit
the negative impact of problem load on individual well-being.
The effects are especially pronounced between using no
helpers and using three, but the addition of four or more
tends to show a reverse pattern or no further decline in risk
to well-being. A similar curvilinear pattern for the number
of helping behaviors per problem occurs.

Help which is only "listening" and is not linked simultaneously to more active behaviors such as asking questions,
referring, intervening by taking the individual to someone
for help, or providing a "new way to look at the problem", is
not much better than the individual coping alone.

Such refinement of the intensity measure, by showing
that the role of helping may include, but must go beyond,
passive social support ("just listening"), provides important
insights about the role of helping in problem-coping.

While it is true that total isolation from helpers
tends to be detrimental to well-being when a problem-coping
sequence is initiated, neither the maximum volume of helpers
nor the mere access to others leads to the reduction of
stress in dealing with such problems. Using too many
different helpers (more than three per problem) or using
helpers who simply provide social support (good listeners
only) without taking an active role in resolving the problem
by providing information, insight, or other help, and the
ability of the individual to call on a sufficiently wide
array of helpers are the critical reasons that problem-coping
may occur with a minimum rather than a maximum of risk to the
individual's sense of mental and physical well-being.

Our findings indicate that both life crises and recent
concerns are associated with risk to individual well-being.
The first type of problem involves the loss of a relationship
or an imposed life change: such events as loss of job, death
of spouse, divorce, change in household composition, or being
a victim of a crime. A list of fourteen such events shows
these to be normally distributed over time with a modal
experience by approximately two-thirds of the total sample of
one such event per year.

The second type of problem which we label as recent
concerns are a set of nine experiences that are basically
responses to a desire to improve the quality of one's life.
These may be ways to overcome threats to that environment
such as crime fear in the neighborhood or stress in the work
place. Or they involve desired improvements such as job
change.

Recent concerns are events that are experienced within the span of one month and, as such, may be seen as frequently recurring or persistent; at a given time, approximately three out of four individuals experience at least one of these.

We have found that: 1) multiple recent concerns are more important in determining individual well-being than multiple life crises of the Holmes and Rahe type measured in this study; 2) while the number of recent concerns per se is highly correlated with stress or risk to well-being, 3) the form and pattern of help-seeking utilized by the individual can substantially reduce and, in specific instances, entirely eliminate this correlation; 4) individuals tend to use more helpers with the recurrence of a problem; 5) as problem load goes up, the apparent preference of individuals not to seek help declines; 6) using too many different helpers or 7) using helpers who simply provide social support without taking an active role in resolving the problem by providing information, insight, or other help may be of little value. Finally, we suggest that the quality of help provided and the ability of the individual to call upon a sufficiently broad array of helpers are the critical reasons that problem-coping may occur with a minimum rather than a maximum of risk to mental and physical well-being.

A SUMMARY OF FINDINGS

Let us review the path travelled in this chapter. We begin by examining two kinds of problems which have been labeled as recent concerns versus life crises. The list of the former includes wanting to get a completely different job, thoughts about going back to school, wanting to change the way the family activities are divided between husband and wife, being concerned about suspicious people in the neighborhood, feeling it's no use trying to do things because so many things go wrong, considering a move from the neighborhood because of crime problems, etc. What all of these problems have in common is that they involve the desire to make a change in one's life--either overcoming something which is undesirable, such as crime in the neighborhood, or trying to achieve something desirable, such as more education or a different occupation.

The list of life crises, on the other hand, included experiences such as personal injury or serous illness, death of a spouse, divorce, being arrested, being fired from a job, being a victim of a crime, etc. The life crises involve the severence of a relationship, the breaking of a social tie--loss of job, loss of loved one.

Our findings show that the two types of problems are different in important ways. We find that people do different things because of experiencing one of the recent concerns than when experiencing one of the life crises.

Recent concerns are measures of discontent with the status quo—family, job, or neighborhood. They are aspirations for change or the desire to alleviate an undesirable life condition. As such, they are dynamic forces for future decisions and life adjustments. They are more stressful if there is no perceived solution, help, information, or possibility for alleviating the cause.

In life crises by contrast, the question is: Can the various support systems be relied upon to work when the very basis of such crises is the severing of a close relationship via death, divorce, separation, children leaving home, etc., losing a job, or similar "loss of relationship" problems? Where life crises are involved, the severance of ties means often that the availability of helpers irrespective of their competence is more critical for reducing stress than any given behavior.

We generally find that as problem load—either of the concern variety or life-crisis type—goes up, so does stress. The former type has a greater capacity to generate depression and psychosomatic symptomology, but not reports of ill health. When problem load is multiple—two or more problems of any type—stress levels begin to climb sharply. At the third-problem level it is generally at a high level for the individual regardless of other factors in the situation.

Recent concerns appear to derive from, and are apparently sustained in their importance by, social contact. Our view is that helping networks may aid the individual in finding a new set of life priorities, either in response to a sudden crisis or in a standard, developmental sequence. But the price of a helping network is that the same system that provides new directions also reinforces the frustration and mental outlook that can undermine individual well-being. Helping networks appear to be relatively effective in giving people what they want—they are tailored resources reflecting individual patterns.

In this chapter we have seen the highly dynamic way in which helping unfolds. We have only broadly explored how types of helpers and given kinds of problems interact to produce a pathway that is effective for the individual. Given the very complex demands seemingly placed on helping networks it is clearly necessary to go beyond a single snapshot to understand them. The longitudinal approach of the helping network study was a most limited one. Yet, it does suggest the richness and texture that is in need of description and exploration, for both practical and theoretical reasons.

Our data trace a very elaborate form of human exchange and cooperation in one urban setting. The set of social ties we have called helping networks is not really an organized structure, nor is it simply a chaotic maze. It has distinct properties: size, scope, form, and content. We need to specify further what basic characteristics it does or does not share with more traditional bases of human community and social attachment. The ongoing dynamics of helping networks cannot be considered only from the standpoint of individual pathways. Our overall conceptual approach indicates that helping occurs in a social contact. To this analysis of such conditioning neighborhood and community factors we now turn our attention.

CHAPTER IV

THE NEIGHBORHOOD CONTEXT OF HELPING NETWORKS

A major consideration in both the conceptual design and
implementation of the helping network study has been the
definition of helping networks as anchored or bounded by the
local neighborhood context. In this chapter we shall provide
a review of major findings and offer several detailed
descriptions by the staff of field observers who supplemented
the systematic interviews conducted in the 59 "walking
distance" neighborhoods located in eleven municipalities in
and around the city of Detroit.

Neighborhood will be treated in terms of three variations on the theme of a local community: 1) The neighborhood as a helper for problems; 2) The patterns of neighborhood social organization, interaction, and networking that
provide for ties to resources beyond the next door helper;
and 3) The neighborhood as a perceived and subjective community of attachment. Our research shows that all three are
important and are interrelated, and yet each is a distinctive
approach to how community functions at the local level.

NEIGHBOR AS HELPER

A very natural approach to the question of "What is a
neighborhood?" is to focus on the eyeball-to-eyeball level:
the role of neighbor. Suzanne Keller (1968) has explored the
idea of neighboring perhaps more fully than any other
researcher. She points out that what a good neighbor is
depends a great deal upon the perceptions and social norms of
people. A good neighbor is not necessarily the good
Samaritan who comes over to be friendly and is very sociable.
Instead, a good neighbor may be a person who simply minds her
or his own business. Keller also distinguishes neighboring
from close friendship; a good neighbor is not usually as
close as a good friend. If you become good friends with your

55

neighbor, the friendship relation usurps the neighbor relation: ". . . good neighbors . . . are friendly but not
friends" (1968:25-26). One observer in a neighborhood in the
Detroit study put it this way:

> There is a distinction between neighbors and friends in
> the neighborhood. People will say, "I have my friend.
> She lives two blocks up--she's not just my neighbor,
> she's my friend." So there is a high mutual aid with
> the friends who are your neighbors. There are little
> groups of people in the neighborhood who are both
> friends and neighbors.[1]

But when does a person need a neighbor and not a
friend? Here is Keller's answer:

> The neighbor is one whom a person turns to because of
> proximity not because of intimacy and the resources for
> dealing with "real trouble." Small-scale, transitive,
> and emergency problems perhaps--but not therapeutic
> encounters.

> Essentially, the neighbor is the helper in times of
> need who is expected to step in when other resources
> fail. These needs range from minor routine problems to
> major crises, and the help requested may be material or
> spiritual. Moreover, the help asked for and given is
> not unlimited. It is called forth in situations that
> spell danger to a group or community, as in times of
> natural disasters and unforeseen calamities, or that
> routinely afflict any and everyone, so that the help
> you give today you may ask for tomorrow (1968:29).

There are rules for neighboring. It is not really as
casual as it appears. But what is the source for such rules?
How are the rules enforced? How does one learn about the
proper neighbor role?

Helena Lopata addresses some of these questions in her
1971 study, Occupation: Housewife. She points out that much
of the American culture stresses the "proud isolation" of the
pioneer. The definition of "privacy" is connected with the
geographical separation which characterized many communities
before the advent of the automobile. Neighbor contacts in
this earlier epoch focused on cooperative work and public
activities of church-going and marketing. The rest of the
time families functioned in "splendid independence." By contrast, the waves of immigrants who arrived in the latter part
of the 19th and early 20th centuries came from the European
peasant societies where village interaction is fostered by

the close proximity of dwellings to which people returned
after a day's work in the nearby fields. Central meeting
places--piazzas, streetcorners, and squares brought people
into intimate, face-to-face exchanges in a daily, or less
frequent, repeated routine of contacts.

Taken in its broadest context, neighboring is defined
by regional, social class, ethnic, and other cultural traditions, many of which persist in some form in American
communities. But it is this unpredictable character of the
role of neighbor which is the most basic contemporary
reality. Many different norms of being a good neighbor
exist, and they tend to reflect the shifing role expectations
which abound in our society in such areas as sex, status, and
lifestyle.

Informal Contacts in the Neighborhood

"Neighborhood sociability" embraces the number and kind
of neighboring patterns across a whole neighborhood. How
often do the people in the neighborhood have face-to-face
contact with each other? How many neighbors are in contact
with others in this way?

The existence of the sociability function between
neighbors can be an important source of social belonging for
the individual. It also serves to mitigate some of the
depersonalizing influences ascribed to the urban environment.
But this must clearly be separated from exchanges between
neighbors which represent friendship, and also from very
selective kinds of face-to-face contact based only on ready
access in its most narrow sense. It involves the willingness
of neighbors to exchange greetings or visits.

"Back fence" exchanges are the essential ingredients of
a neighborhood serving as an arena of sociability. Here,
people are willing to take advantage of the opportunity to
chat with neighbors. Moreover, they are comfortable with
such exchanges, and are encouraged to chat when the occasion
presents itself rather than merely reflecting an air of
indifferent aloofness. Here is the way this process is
described by one resident we interviewed:

> I was out there trimming the tree, you know. And
> Manny was out there fertilizing his lawn. First thing
> you know, he was offering me this saw of his and I was
> trimming everything in sight. The neighbors across the
> way saw us and we got to talking about the time Jessie
> fell off the ladder and Tom (yet another neighbor)
> drove him to the hospital to have his sprained ankle
> taped up. But, you know, things are like that around
> here. You get to talking about one thing and pretty

soon we're on each other's porches drinking beer and shootin' the breeze.

Such a willingness to exchange greetings invites the opportunity for further interaction.

Neighborhood as a Center of Interpersonal Influence

Although neighborhoods serve as an important arena of sociability for the individual, they also function as a center of influence, both overt and subtle. Prevailing styles within a neighborhood influence the people living there. The focus of influence may range from the way one decorates a kitchen or yard to methods of child-rearing and voting preferences.

The neighborhood can be the center of political attitude, change, informal advising, and exchange. What begins as simple home-improvement aid can sometimes result in more far reaching impact as witnessed in the following example taken from one observer's notes.

Mrs. Smith had come from a staunchly Republican background. When she moved into the "Historic District" she valued the "geneology" associated with her home but stayed pretty much to herself. According to Mrs. Smith, "I already had two boys but when I had Laura I just wanted more space. But that meant adding a dormer or something. Jim [her husband, an electrical engineer] seems to have started the whole neighborhood thing for us. When the (neighborhood preservation) association saw the contractors' trucks, John, Jake, and Ed came over to offer their help in encouraging us to do the building ourselves. It was then we were made aware of the strict code for home improvements here. One offered help in carpentry, another in roofing and heating, another in plumbing, and Jim already was eager to do the wiring . . . . So we all began. I love this neighborhood. Seems my whole outlook on life has changed. Don't tell my folks, but for the first time I've even voted for Democratic representatives. That shows you what they've [her new neighbors] gone and done to me."

Through the processes of continuous observation of the behavior of neighbors, the "learning by imitation" occurs. This frequently entails neighborhood peer groups of both adults and children. As one of our ethnographers summed up after looking over her field notes spanning a one-year time difference:

We were particularly interested in the Larkin family
because they moved in as we began our ethnography.
They were so different from the rest of the neighborhood. Not in the way they looked, but the way they
acted. You have to understand this neighborhood has a
fantastically involved parent group and groups of pre-
teens, teens, etc., organized for explicit, mutual-aid
purposes. Behavior is so damned rational.

When the Larkins moved in we noted in our conversations
that there was yelling--child yelling at child, parent
at parent, and all combinations. Talking with that
family (and with their neighbors) this year was a real
trip. The kids were all on various teams and the
parents had been given parties as new residents and
asked to join other groups. They (the parents)
declined but other neighbors took it upon themselves to
have the Larkins over, to invite them to monthly block
clubs. Anyway, you wouldn't recognize this as the same
family. The atmosphere actually begins to approach
rationality.

Mutual Aid in Neighborhoods

Exchange of help between those living in close
proximity in urban areas is another frequent and important
function. When the rapid response of neighbors is essential,
such aid is usually not available from other sources, either
kin or formal organizations. Thus, rescue in disaster is
made in 75 percent of all instances by neighbors. This means
exchanging goods and services of various kinds. It may be as
simple as the borrowing of the proverbial cup of sugar.
Often neighbor exchange is part of an elaborate system. The
following field work notes provide an example:

I really don't socialize with my neighbors much, but
you know you can count on them. There is the sense
that if something happened, they would be there. One
kind of thing is if somebody gets a load of gravel or a
load of dirt they are going to put on your yard, everybody will come over and sort of throw in a hand.

Or with a friend, you come home and you just bought
some beer but it's hot, you might send a kid down with
the hot beer and trade it for some cold beer. Or, if
you run out of sugar. But it wouldn't be like a
regular kind of thing. You would replace the
sugar. . . . Maybe a beer or something, but the
exchange may be generalized over a long term.

NEIGHBOR HELPING: CRISES AND RECENT CONCERNS

Our survey asked: "When someone has something on their mind that is bothering them--a personal problem--is there a person in the neighborhood who can help out?" We found that about one in three people answered that they knew of such a person. Yet when we asked about neighbor help for life crises over half of all people intereviewed--56 percent--say that they have been helped by a neighbor for at least one of these kinds of problems. Clearly, then, emergency helping by a neighbor is significant and reflects the kind of function that neighboring plays in urban society. Thus, while one in four people report they have no friends in the neighborhood, among this same group (those without neighbors who are close friends) neighbors are used for life crisis helping 36 percent of the time.

In the case of recent concerns the neighbor is not turned to as often as in the case of life crises. On an overall basis, one in four people with such an experience turn to a neighbor for help.

Considering the relatively small number of close friends people report they have in the neighborhood--five on the average--a considerable amount of neighbor helping goes on. There appears to be no close link between the potential of a neighbor to be helpful for a personal problem and the actual use of neighbor helping.

What kind of help do people want from a neighbor? Although 80 percent of the time "just listening" (see Appendix Table IV-1) is the kind provided, simply having a good listener is not enough. Asking questions, suggesting who else might be contacted, and concrete actions are most positively linked to what is implicitly a definition of a "good neighbor" (see Appendix Table IV-2).

What is the effect of neighbor helping on those seeking it? One approach is to take the general measure of individual well-being--actually the risk to or amount of stress reported by the respondent. This scale is built by the adding together of several interview questions dealing with depressed mental outlook, psychosomatic symptomology, and perceived ill health. The higher the score, the more the respondents indicated these patterns of attitude and experience which may be seen as a risk to their well-being in both a mental health sense and in terms of a broader rubric of their quality of life.

There are two kinds of neighbor help associated with lower risk scores. For recent concerns, referral and to some extent "taking action" are associated with lower RISK levels. A different profile emerges for life crises. Here behavior such as "asking questions" shows an opposite relationship to

the RISK than occurs for recent concerns. Life-crisis
helping and "taking action" are also associated with lower
RISK scores. Thus, what neighbors do for a problem, not just
help of any kind, determines its positive effect on the well-
being of the help-seeker. Moreover, what helping behavior is
considered positive may vary by the type of problem. For
both types of problems, when the neighbor serves a referral
function, a similar result is apparently generated--
well-being is enhanced by such help (see Appendix Table IV-
3).

     Neighbor helping is therefore not simply an extension
of close friendships, but is rather a more socially distant,
yet nevertheless valuable relationship of mutual aid and
problem-coping. Considering the large proponderance of
friends people tend to have living outside of their
neighborhood--five in the neighborhood versus 31 outside of
it (see Appendix Table III-4)--the volume of help provided
within the neighborhood setting is indeed significant.

     The ability of an individual to know where to find help
and the anticipation that it can actually be helpful are
themselves signs of the health of the community in which that
individual lives. The general analytical strategy is to
focus on the extent to which the individual's well-being--as
measured by psychosomatic health complaints, the individual's
evaluation of his/her physical health, and some measures of
simple depression--is influenced by the interaction between
the problem load or the number of problems that the
individual seeks help for and the kinds of helper they
ultimately utilize for these crises or concerns. It was
hypothesized at the beginning of the study that certain kinds
of neighborhood and community environments would be important
in determining the shape and significance of the helping networks in that locale; and by implication, it was expected
that how well an individual deals with a given problem would
also be affected by the settings and helping resources
available.

Neighborhoods and Helping Networks

     A major step in the analysis of empirical findings from
neighborhoods is the tracing of "modal" problem-solving pathways. In the integral area the overlap between lay helping,
quasi-institutional, and formal service systems is extensive.
All of these systems are available if social norms sanction
them. Depending on the persistence and severity of a
problem, individuals are likely to use all three systems.

     In some neighborhoods an extensive network of
indigenous informal and quasi-formal resources are most

likely to be used in problem solving. Access to formal
service systems is restricted both by normative barriers and
by lack of organizational links that cross the local
community boundary. In other neighborhoods the immediate
system of informal and quasi-formal helping is developed to
only a limited extent. The potential is great but actual
utilization is low. Instead, individuals employ selected
helpers, such as friends or family not living in the local
area. Access to and utilization of formal services, if
located nearby, are liable to be limited, while less proximate agencies will be selectively sought out depending on the
attitudes and judgments about what constitutes good service
professionals.

In still other neighborhoods use of local informal and
quasi-formal resources will be sporadic and inconsistent
depending on who are the newcomers to the community, trans-
ferring of allegiance from older agencies, or the presence of
professional helpers in one's social circle.

NEIGHBORHOOD REDEFINED

A comprehensive definition of neighborhood should
embody both the reality of loose-knit and close human
relationships. A definition must be universal and encompass
neighborhood in terms of different organizational patterns--
the fixed elements and the dynamics as well--of the neighborhood process. To be useful, our description must say what
goes on, who does it, and how they function. The framework
for such a task is the following:

*A neighborhood context refers to the social organiza-
tion of a population residing in a geographically proximate
locale. This includes not only social bonds between members
of the designated population but all of that group's links to
non-neighbors as well.*

This "larger than geographical neighborhood" definition
has several advantages over more conventional efforts to
demarcate neighborhood. First, it permits us to look beyond
the geographical boundaries that define the people who
provide help for problem-coping. It permits comparison of
resources and connections. The "neighborhood context"
approach communicates a very important idea: that people are
affected in a neighborhood by more than their individual
actions as neighbors.

Neighborhood Versus Community

What distinguishes neighborhood and community are often
political jurisdictions or notions about natural boundaries.

The neighborhood itself may contain a series of meaningful units. The micro-neighborhood is operationally defined as a next-door neighbor, the person in the next apartment, or the most immediate set of adjacent households. It is defined when a mother yells out the window to young people playing in the street, "Go play in your own neighborhood!" That notion in turn leads us quickly into the notion of the residential block.

Beyond the residential block begins the walking-distance neighborhood. The administrative definition of a walking-distance neighborhood is usually the elementary school district. In our own research on neighborhoods, the elementary school district has been utilized because it is a compromise between the notion of the very small micro-neighborhood and larger definitions such as "the west side," the "black community," "my part of town," and so forth.

In this research the question of neighborhood as community is an open one: its answer requires some diagnosis and comparative analysis of empirical patterns. In many cases, a person's community is no larger than their neighborhood. For some people, the neighborhood and the community are the same thing.

Class and Community

A large number of studies have shown both class and suburban-urban differences in social interaction and participation. Some, such as the work of Gans (1967), Shuval (1956), Bell and Boat (1951), and Fava (1958), have found that differences in personal social associations tend to be along lines of class and ethnicity. For instance, these studies tend to agree that while working-class people have more intense relationships with kin and neighbors, middle-class people have higher rates of participation in the larger society and are quicker in establishing social relationships (even if superficial) with others.

Blum (1964), in his definitive review of the literature on social class and participation in primary relationships, identifies a number of widely supported research observations on social class. Drawing upon the work of Bott (1957), Berger (1957), Young and Willmott (1957), and Gans (1962), among others, he concludes with a number of propositions about working-class social supports:

> The working classes should be less likely to make new friendships than the middle classes because such friendships must be incorporated into their social networks. In close-knit networks such incorporation requires the tacit assent of a community of others,

thereby reducing the control which the individual
exercises in his selection of new friends.

The working classes are less likely to become involved
in primary relationships with co-workers and others,
because such relationships serve as potential sources
of normative conflict with their social networks. . . .

The working classes are more likely to be isolated from
activities, issues, and associations at the level of
the community and larger society because their
close-knit networks minimize their contacts with others
different from themselves. . . (Blum, 1964:198).

Vance Packard (1964) and others have expressed the view
that the highly mobile middle class has destroyed their sense
of community and isolated themselves from important social
relationships with kin, friends, and neighbors.

These observations agree with the more scholarly works
of Maurice Stein (1960) who has summarized the major American
community studies and observed a growing "eclipse of
community" and the growth of a "mass society." These
observers of steady deterioration of primary relationships
among the mobile middle classes are in sharp disagreement
with Adams (1968) who, in his study of middle-class kin
relationships, found strong maintenance of mutual-aid
relationships between parents and children despite occupational mobility.

The research of Litwak (1960a, 1960b) and his
colleagues has also affirmed the continued existence and
importance of close primary relationships, including mutual
aid for a wide range of problem areas, despite both geographic and occupational mobility by large segments of the
population. The meaning of this body of research for helping
includes the implication that working-class people will
likely have a narrower range of helpers but more intense and
readily activated helping relationships. Middle-class
people, in contrast, will have a wider range of helpers and
access to a wider range of community resources. It also
argues that primary social relationships are largely homogeneous as to class and often also along lines of ethnicity.
Thus, even within a community one could expect major
differences in the amount of helping along class lines.

Community represents a pattern of relationships,
associations, settings, and cultural nuances that exist and
define social reality for the people living in a particular
community. It represents this as well or better than does
the demographic profile of the population. Certainly, having
a particular level of income or education, belonging to a

particular religious group, or having a particular ethnic
background has consequences for where people are likely to
live and the range of their life experiences and values. But
a community is the stage upon which these people play out
life's drama and the sets, props, and presence of other
actors has a strong effect on how they can play their role.

Communities have histories, experiences of success or
failure in political action, change and succession in population, growth and decline, cultural norms, institutions and
physical settings which either enhance or limit different
types of behavior. These factors are only a limited sample
of those which affect the character of a community. That
they operate is evidenced in this research and elsewhere.
That so little is understood about their causal interaction
and effect on people's lives is testimony to the limited
state of knowledge of, and research on, communities as an
important social entity.

In the sample investigation, eight different municipalities provide a sample of both white- and blue-collar
communities in the Detroit metropolitan area. By taking
account of the variance ascribed to selected neighborhoods
within each of these larger sampling units, the combined
effects of community and neighborhood will be examined. The
geographical distinction in the two units of analysis is
complemented by the conceptual approach which considers
neighborhood as going beyond specific territorial boundaries.
To this degree, the community as a helping system is not
identical to the neighborhood as a helping system. While
help from neighbors may be a way to separate the two, access
to the neighborhood and utilization of it may, in fact, be a
characteristic pattern of a total community.[2]

The relationship of the major variables described by
the conceptual approach we have outlined is shown in schematic fashion in Chart IV-1. Individual social class and demographic characteristics are viewed as equally significant
vis-a-vis the contextual variables of neighborhood and
community. Each cluster of independent variables then
relates to the intervening variable of problem-coping. Help-
seeking as a consequence of problem experience is influenced
in turn by the social context and by individual demographic
variables. Well-being as the dependent variable is therefore
shaped by the direct influence of helping systems--"social
supports"--and by each of the two clusters of independent
variables.

Neighborhood Variations in Social Fabric

A key focus of the analysis of helping is the role of
different social structures of the localities in which

individuals reside. This focus directs attention to the
context within which given problems are developed and what
kinds of resources are used or perceived as valuable. As we
shall subsequently discover, neighborhood is not simply an
objective physical setting, but involves a set of actual and
potential social anchoring points in terms of pathways to
helping.

Based on a series of earlier studies[3] three dimensions
are employed to define significant neighborhood variations
that are important to help-seeking and problem-coping: 1)
The extent of individual identification with the area, 2) the

CHART IV-1

Relationships Among Major Concepts of the Helping
Network Study

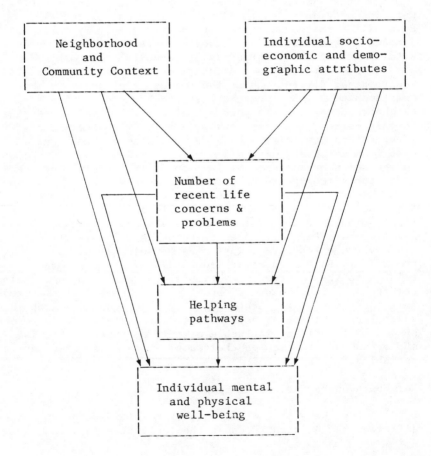

degree of social exchanges within the neighborhood, and 3) the extent to which the area is explicitly linked to the larger community. Additional work with this classification scheme has led to modifications in an effort to treat the typology sufficiently to cover divergent social class, ethnic identification, and location within the metropolitan area (see Chart IV-2). Using measures of neighbor contacts, associational patterns, and local area ties, the 28 areas sampled in the study were originally divided into the following six types of areas:

The Integral Neighborhood: A locale with 1) high levels of formal and informal interaction with one another, 2) manifest high levels of contact with local government, 3) high levels of reported voting in the last national election, 4) strong commitments to remaining in the neighborhood, and 5) strong positive attitudes toward the area.

The Parochial Neighborhood: A locale with 1) extensive formal and informal interaction with one another, 2) positive attitudes toward the neighborhood, 3) not high levels of political participation outside of their local area.

The Diffuse Neighborhood: A locale with 1) relatively limited formal and informal contacts, 2) positive views toward the neighborhood, 3) no extensive ties in the political structure of the larger community, and 4) possibly hostile or indifferent to the values of the larger community.

The Stepping-Stone Neighborhood: A locale with 1) extensive formal and informal contact, 2) no pronounced positive

CHART IV-2

A Typology of Neighborhoods Based on Social Organization
and Reference Group Orientation

Neighborhood as a Reference Group	Type	Formal and Informal Organization	Orientation to Larger Community
Neighborhood is a Positive Reference Group	Integral	+	+
	Parochial	+	−
	Diffuse	−	−
Neighborhood is not a Positive Reference Group	Stepping-stone	+	+
	Transitory	−	+
	Anomic	−	−

reference group orientation in the local area, and 3)
extensive participation in the political process of the
larger community.
The Transitory Neighborhood: A locale with 1) low reference
group identification with the local neighborhood, 2)
little formal or informal interaction, and 3) participation in the larger community to a moderate or high
degree.
The Anomic Neighborhood: A locale which 1) lacks formal and
informal ties to the local area, 2) does not have a
high level of participation in the larger community,
and 3) lacks strong positive identification to the
neighborhood.

Because the helping network study developed both
standardized survey data and observational reports for each
neighborhood, the latter creates an added qualitative
description of the various local areas. Using both interviewer evaluations and the observation reports of the two-
person teams of observers, the flavor of each type of setting
can be discerned.

DESCRIPTIONS OF THE INTEGRAL NEIGHBORHOOD

Eleven of the 59 areas studied fall into this pattern.
Our findings show that relative affluence and higher educational levels are often associated with this type of
neighborhood. What is most unique to this kind of locale is
its dual character--internally cohesive and yet also having
effective ties and relationships with the larger community
outside of the neighborhood.
Here is one description of a moderate income integral
neighborhood:

There is a distinct sense of neighborhood
identity in Oakland. When asked to demarcate their
neighborhood on a map of the city, informants outlined
an area that coincided exactly with the bounds of the
elementary school district.
The residents are aware of living in an area
considered to be poor by the rest of the city. They
jokingly refer to themselves as "the slums" of the
city. One resident said, "I lived here five years
before I found out it was a slum." Residents have a
tremendous commitment to the neighborhood. Several
women stated that their husbands had wanted to move,
but that they talked them out of it.

Some people stated that the neighborhood acts as a surrogate family.

There is a very high level of helping in Oakland. When people are new to the area, the neighbors offer tools and advice regarding home repairs, and often help out. When someone is building an addition or improving their home in other ways, the neighbors come over and assist in the construction.

One man, who is a medic, gives free assistance to his neighbors if someone is injured. Another, an electrician, fixes neighbors' televisions at the cost of the parts. When one resident broke his back, all the neighbors assisted the family. One woman said that her neighbor, who has a green thumb, volunteered information on how to care for her plants that weren't doing well.

The school is probably the most important focus for organizational activity in the neighborhood. In addition to a very active PTA, there is an extensive volunteer program. There are five components of the volunteer program: 1) Bookies--those who make blank books in various shapes and decorations for use in the classroom; 2) Bucket Brigade--where volunteers work on a one-to-one basis with children having reading difficulties for 1/2 hour/week; 3) Roomies--volunteers involved in classroom activities; 4) Resource mothers-- who work in the school media center; and 5) Preschool-- run by the volunteers and open to any child whose parent volunteers 1 hour each week to the school in any of the above capacities. According to the principal, there are 350 families attending Oakland elementary. 67 volunteers are active. It is the largest volunteer program in the city of Royal Oak and serves as a model for other schools in the area.

Another example of life in a classic integral neighborhood:

Even with the high rate of residential movement in and out of Hill, people moving in do not find it difficult to become integrated and involved in neighborhood activities. The Newcomer's Club welcomes every new family to the neighborhood and invites them to join the organization. Joining results in the opportunity to become participants in garden clubs, sewing clubs, and golf and swimming activities, etc. If the greetings of the neighbors are not returned, the new family is left alone.

Parties, picnics, and bridge are a part of
neighborhood life. Privacy is not of critical
importance, although there is a "rule" that children
should not visit neighbor's homes before 9:00 in the
morning or after 6:00 at night.

People help out with neighbor's children. For
example, a severe storm occurred. One mother wasn't
home and couldn't get to the school to pick up her
children, but she knew she didn't have to worry because
a neighbor would look after her kids until the crisis
was over.

Residents of Hill are deeply involved in the
neighborhood elementary school. Out of 270 parents
eligible to come to one parent-teacher conference, for
example, 267 attended, and the other three could not
come because of illness.

There are 150 parents (mostly female volunteers)
who participate in school helping projects such as
acting as teacher assistant's in the classroom, working
on the library check-out system, or sitting in on the
lunch hour "counseling" sessions where children who
have worries can "just come and cry and the parents
will act as mothers and help them with their problems."

DESCRIPTIONS OF THE PAROCHIAL NEIGHBORHOOD

This kind of setting is a rather unusual form of contemporary neighborhood--only seven of our 59 areas were
grouped into this category. In some ways it is the nostalgic
ideal of a self-contained and internally cohesive community
that many ethnic groups traditionally formed. What is most
distinctive to the parochial area is the capacity to keep the
outside world away when values or threats are perceived by
residents. This means that it is a "defended" neighborhood
discussed in the work of Gerald Suttles (1968). Privacy may
sometimes even outrank collective identity in the parochial
setting. Self-reliance and independence are the marks of a
resident of such a neighborhood. Stability and modest economic value are common correlates of the parochial locale.

A Classic Black Parochial Neighborhood

All residents are black, but both whites and
blacks own and operate the commercial establishments in
the area. Most residents are in their 30's and 40's
and have children in elementary and junior high school.
Most adults have a high school education and are
factory workers. A few hold office jobs.

The school district is bounded on two sides by
commercial highways, but on the other two sides by
residential streets. The businesses along the
boundaries provide a full range of services and cater
to both outsiders and residents of Hig.

Most homes in the neighborhood are single
dwelling units that were built in the 1950s. They
range in size from small one-story to tri-level structures, but most are medium-sized, having one and two
bedrooms. They are constructed half of brick and half
of aluminum siding.

For the most part the homes are very well cared
for and there are quite a few lampposts and trimmed
hedges decorating the yards. In the middle of the
neighborhood is a recreational center that is utilized
by neighborhood residents. There are six churches.

There is quite a lot of organized neighborhood
activity. The recreation center has a pool and
sponsors organized baseball and football games. There
are block clubs that meet at each other's homes and
have a yearly picnic. The library sponsors story-
telling hours for children, has speakers, and allows
community groups to use the library auditorium.

A recent flyer distributed throughout the area
read, "Now the library isn't just a place to get books.
It's a place to get help. What to do if your basement
is flooded. How to pick a good nursing home. Who to
call if your street light is out. . . . Anything you
need to know about just call."

A White Parochial Neighborhood

The vast majority of the residents of Carr are
predominantly white, Michigan-born children of mid-
westerners. Most come from surrounding neighborhoods
within the City. Although a range of occupations can
be found, most of these fall into different types of
skilled and semi-skilled labor.

People in Carr are warm and friendly. Mothers
often sit out on the front porch to supervise the
children and sometimes bring out coffee. Men talk with
each other in the driveways and on front lawns. These
interactions were seldom observed to move into the
living room, however. It was reported that children
are not allowed to run freely in and out of neighborhood homes either. Typical remarks of Carr residents
included: "Everybody feels that what happens in your
family is your family business . . . but they will
help you if you come to them."

Residents of Carr were reported to buy gifts for
neighbors and their children on occasions such as
birthdays, high school graduation, and the arrival of a
new child, and to collect money in the event of death
for the bereaved family, etc. One resident reported
that she often relied on her neighbors for transportation as well as for help in almost any kind of
emergency.

Another Typical Parochial Locale

Many of the people living in the older homes
moved into Raupp at about the same time and are about
the same age. These people have gotten to know each
other well over the years, and newcomers have a difficult time breaking into this established social network. There is no formal mechanism (such as Welcome
Wagon) to integrate newcomers. If newcomers do break
into the structure, it takes a long time and it comes
through connections made by their children with other
kids from established families in the neighborhood.

The established social network has many rules
about appropriate neighborly behavior. Borrowing, for
example, is reserved for emergencies, such as running
out of a particular food item, and then it is returned.
A woman who borrowed shampoo from a different neighbor
every time she needed to wash her hair was eventually
refused. "If you run out and you don't have time to
get more, then you borrow; but you don't borrow something all the time."

Neighbors share advice about cars and gardens,
etc., when they are asked for it, but not regarding
personal things such as marital problems and child
delinquency.

Neighbors will help out in a crisis situation.
For example, the husband of a woman who was active in
the PTA was killed by a motorcycle gang. The neighbors
immediately raised $1,000 just by calling around in the
neighborhood for her. "Your neighbors are really there
when somebody dies."

Many people in Raupp are seriously concerned
about urban renewal and organize to give citizen input
into decisions about any renovations or new construction. For example, there was a plan for low income,
integrated housing to be built within the neighborhood.
People protested the plans, took out petitions, went to
city council, and successfully presented their case.
They argued, "If you want to do something for these ADC
people, then subsidize scattered kinds of housing, but

don't concentrate them all in one spot." The low-
income housing project was not built.

DESCRIPTIONS OF THE DIFFUSE NEIGHBORHOOD

In the sample of 59 areas this neighborhood type is as
frequent as the integral type--eleven areas are designated in
the grouping. What is most pronounced about the diffuse
neighborhood is the strong identity with the area often based
on the initial similarity of residents--all moving in
together or all sharing similar values or other status
attributes. Despite a potential for much neighborhood
contact, however, the setting often never attains a level of
activity that might be expected. Largely this is a product
of the external commitments and lack of threats which might
tighten local organization. Overall there is a
"togetherness" based on relatively direct contact and much
assumed common interest.

Some Examples of Diffuse Locales

"Neighbors tolerate a great deal, but there isn't
much variation to have to tolerate."
There aren't any messy housewives; of course,
there aren't any norms to say it is normal to have a
clean house. They tolerate a lot. There really isn't
that much variation in the neighborhood to have to
tolerate a lot. It is an older neighborhood and things
are built up. There is a history there. Why would
anybody want to move into such a neighborhood? Somehow
the recruitment into the neighborhood has been effective to the point where people with different life
styles and views aren't coming into it. They are
selecting themselves out.

Very nice upper-middle-income area. Houses very
similar to one another with maybe four or five
different housing layouts repeated throughout the sub-
division. Although the people were friendly enough to
the interviewer, they did not associate with their
neighbors. They selected their friends from outside
their immediate neighborhood. In many cases the
respondents even remarked that they did not understand
why neighbors weren't more friendly toward each other
as they had been in the neighborhood in which they had
previously lived.

A Classic Diffuse Neighborhood

> "I plan to die in this house," said the member of
> the LeBlanc PTA firmly. This is one example of the
> strong commitment that residents have to their
> neighborhood. There is minimal turnover in LeBlanc.
> Newcomers to the block are apt to be native born in the
> area. There is a strong extended family pattern. One
> finds brothers, sisters, parents or children living
> down the block from one another. The neighborhood is
> viewed by most residents to be a safe area. In addi-
> tion, most people are very close to their work. This
> also contributes to the residents' strong commitment to
> the area.
> Helping behavior in LeBlanc generally revolves
> around ritual gestures, such as furnishing pots of food
> or contributions of flowers when somebody dies. A
> chronically ill woman depended on her male next-door
> neighbor for frequent rides to the hospital until his
> wife protested to him that he shouldn't get involved
> because he might be responsible should anything happen
> to the neighbor in his car.

A Second Classic Diffuse Area

> Policemen are working at night, firemen have long
> shifts, one guy works ten hours a day as a supervisor
> at Chrysler. People's schedules are all different.
> But every time that we pressed people, they talked
> about at least one neighbor that they were pretty close
> to. In this one family the guy told the kids how to
> repair cars. People usually had at least one close
> friend within the neighborhood. One woman was in the
> hospital, and she had three little kids, and a neighbor
> came in to take care of the place. . . .
> In some neighborhoods where there are a lot of
> policemen, you don't call the police. You go down and
> tell someone and it is taken care of informally. It
> never really goes through the official channels. But
> you get the feeling in this neighborhood that right
> away you call the officials. When the kids were on top
> of the school they called the police. . . .
> In general, there is a feeling of alienation from
> all kinds of organizations and institutions. We dis-
> covered, for example, that the neighborhood is right on
> the edge of one of the parishes. When we first went to
> the priest and asked him if this was part of his
> parish, he called the archdiocese and they didn't
> really know. He said he thought maybe part of it was

in the parish, but he thought more of the people wanted
to go up north to St. Monica's. So we went up to St.
Monica's, and they didn't have any idea about this
neighborhood. . . . They weren't sure of their own
boundary, because this is sort of a nebulous zone where
people aren't centrally attached to anything. It's on
the edges of the parish, and on the edges of a lot of
things that are going on, on the edge of Detroit.

DESCRIPTIONS OF THE STEPPING-STONE NEIGHBORHOOD

While it is a fairly atypical kind of urban area, it
has some unique characteristics that make the six areas found
in the 59 neighborhood sample distinctive. Although
originally found in the community literature to be
characteristic of white, affluent, and mobile executive
families, in the Detroit area survey stepping-stone neighborhoods were typically black, central-city locales. What distinguishes this often highly organized neighborhood from the
integral type is the lack of long-term commitment residents
may feel to the locale. This lack of strong identity means
that leadership turnover is common as social mobility
provides new, more attractive neighborhoods to move to, or
where job transfers take many active residents out of the
area after a few years. The welcoming of new residents often
becomes highly institutionalized, although many residents
have themselves prepared to enter and re-enter many neighborhoods as part of their career pathway. In stepping-stone
neighborhoods residents look to the larger community for many
activities and organize locally as a function of that commitment.

Some Descriptions in White Areas

Nice moderate neighborhood--mixed ages--homes
seemed to be well taken care of. Comfortable inter-
viewing here. People seemed to be friendly--down to
earth--lower middle class. Homes seem to change hands
frequently. People don't seem to stay too long.

In Normsville, neighbors exchange services and
help each other out in times of crisis. For example,
it was reported that when a neighbor's home was damaged
by a fire, the women of Normsville got together and
made curtains for the kitchen, and many people gave the
family clothes. There is a man in the neighborhood who
paints cars very well. He also likes to fish, but he
doesn't own a boat. So sometimes this man will paint a

neighbor's car in exchange for the use of the
neighbor's boat. Women in the neighborhood frequently
exchange baked goods and recipes. Men often work on
the church grounds for free.

People go out and pick up voters and take them to
the polls and back home.

Normsville has some links to groups and institutions outside the neighborhood (in addition to outside
churches). One group in particular, the Visiting
Nurses Association (VNA) has reportedly had considerable influence in the area. One of the primary concerns of the VNA is child abuse. Through connections
with the Protective Services, the VNA is able to find
temporary housing for abused children if hospitalization is not required. It was also involved in a
program to educate unwed mothers and others about how
to care for their infants in an effort to decrease the
infant mortality rate. In addition, the association
provides some counseling and family planning for people
in the neighborhood. It was reported that residents of
Normsville also utilize other clinics and counseling
agencies in the downtown Detroit area, including
Detroit General Hospital and the Northeast Guidance
Clinic.
The Community Center provides many services and
sponsors a lot of organized activity in the neighborhood. For example, it has offered classes in cooking
and dance. The Center has a basketball court and a
bowling alley, a medical clinic and a dairy food co-op.
The Center also rents tools to the neighborhood,
including rakes, hoes, lawnmowers, ladders, and paint
brushes. They also have a program which involves
taking people in the neighborhood to shopping areas
downtown and bringing them back later in the day.
Other organized activity is centered around the church.
For example, the block church will often have a summer
picnic and almost everybody will attend. It was also
reported that senior citizens in the area have
organized themselves and are starting to help each
other.

Premature births are really high in the area we
are talking about. Because of this, the schools and a
lot of the agencies got together with unwed mothers and
with their parents. Somehow the group got aid from the
business association so they could teach the young
adults how to care for their kids. Assistance has

dropped tremendously. They had 1,000 babies who
reached their first birthday, whereas in 1973 there
were only 800.

DESCRIPTIONS OF THE TRANSITORY NEIGHBORHOOD

Some of its unique attributes: the current lack of
activity is often a result of rapid population turnover. In
an earlier period the neighborhood was often strong, but is
now weak. Individuals are often tied into somewhat separate
cliques--newcomers versus oldtimers, renters versus owners,
etc. Ties to the larger community are utilized on an
individual basis but are not diffused or shared through
neighborhood contacts so it is not linked as a community to
external institutions or organizations.

The paradoxical qualities of a transitory neighborhood
is reflected in this observer commentary:

> This is a very considerate neighborhood. You
> call first before going over. Another woman mentioned
> that neighbors try not to call between 4:00 p.m. and
> 7:00 p.m. because people are likely to be eating during
> that time, and that people don't visit after 10:00 p.m.
> But some people did not think the neighborhood was so
> considerate. One woman described a block party on her
> block. They had come to collect $1.00 for beer from
> everyone, then her family hadn't been invited.
> Needless to say, she felt left out. In fact, several
> residents complained that there are cliques of neigh-
> bors that are "in" and are friendly with each other,
> but that the rest are left out.
> Some people in Twain say they depend on their
> neighbors if they have a problem or need help. One
> woman said, "I wouldn't bother my family. I'd have to
> go to my neighbors. Neighbors would know more about it
> than family." But another resident said, "If it comes
> down to an emergency, they'd help. Otherwise it's dog
> eat dog and cat eat cat." There seems to be an exten-
> sive system of mutual aid between men in the neighbor-
> hood. People say men help each other in building and
> house repairs. There is an expressed feeling that one
> should have construction, etc., done by a neighbor.
> "He'll do a better job," residents say.

Another Classic Transitory Area Reflects the Erosion of Past
Cohesion

There is very little organizational activity
within the neighborhood boundaries. The homeowner's
associations that were active when the neighborhood was
new have disbanded.

Because of the different values and lifestyles,
the people need a neutral helper they can trust. In
the Hill area everybody is on about the same economic
level, but that is not the case here.

Amount of diversity . . . One lady said that the
kind of person coming into the area now is not as good
as it used to be, and she said that she thinks some of
the women are setting up "business." The principal
said that some of the mothers are topless dancers and
high-class waitresses. There seems to be quite a bit
of diversity, given the income. There are a lot of
people moving in that the older residents are not used
to, like people who aren't concerned with the maintenance of their property and don't take care of their
children to the standards of the older residents.
There is diversity within the old town. There are ADC
people. There are racial differences. And there are a
lot of southerners who are very foreign to the older
residents.

SOMERSET APARTMENTS (Liberal, young, transient,
population): It seems that in the Somerset area, there
is a high premium on privacy. They want the management
to do everything. Like one woman said, "A few ladies
stop by, and I let them know where I'm at and just keep
doing my work." So maybe they want to be left alone.

OLD TOWN (Older people who have lived in Troy for
many years): We spoke to a woman who had lived in this
area for 18 years, and these were some of her comments.
"I feel like a stranger in my own community. At one
time people would interact with each other, they would
share. They would share tools and food with each
other. You would know everybody in your community.
People would invite you in when you walked down the
street. But none of this happens anymore. The sub-
divisions have ruined all that. Those people keep very
much to themselves. Somerset Mall people are strange.
I don't get on with them. They wanted a beer party for
parents after a school event. That's not appropriate."

A woman from Somerset had a different view. She said, "Those darn people have been doing the same thing for 25 years. They don't want to try anything new."

DESCRIPTION OF THE ANOMIC NEIGHBORHOOD

We come now to what is virtually a "nonneighborhood." Anomic means individuated. People simply go their own ways. They do not belong to organizations. They may not see much of each other in an informal way. The neighborhood lacks a sense of community.

Individuals may choose to live in the anomic neighbor-hood in order to have the kind of anonymity that they consider necessary for their own lifestyle. But the fact remains that the anomic neighborhood cannot really mobilize to respond to common interests. Often families have no choice but to rely on a neighborhood which is isolated and lacks linking resources.

"Anomic" often means barriers between neighbors. Here's an example in one such area in relation to personal hostility and crime problems:

There are a lot of individual hassles. Their children get into fights or problems. After they clear it up the parents continue to feud. That is still on an individual basis. There is indication that when these feuds take place they are not really long-lasting, permanent things. . . . The Jones are on the black list this week. Next week it might be the Smiths, and the Jones will be okay again. . . . The church has been robbed at least once. . . . They have five or six buses whose gas tanks are constantly being siphoned. Windows are broken in the buses. . . . There is the neighborhood fence. Frank's Bar and Lounge was robbed. The car wash is where they dis-tributed the drugs. And then there is the one house that has been robbed three times and a couple other homes have been broken into.

There is a lot of crime there for such a small area. People talk about it, but they don't talk about it in terms of what shall we do about it, they just talk about it to note the fact. You get the feeling that people think, "Well, it hasn't happened to me, so I don't really give a damn. When it happens to me, I will be concerned." We know at least on person who works closely with one of the detectives on the drug squad. She's worked with her family because of her situation. Her son is involved and she wants to deal

with it.   But you get this noncommital, non-
involvement attitude.

The observed contacts we saw were friendly but superficial: meet at the mailbox and talk for five minutes about
generalities; but we also heard of hostile things: neighbors
feuding. . . .

Households are generally very privacy oriented.
One woman said she had never been in her neighbor's
house, she had only been in another neighbor's house
across the street twice in five or six years.   Back
yards are fenced in; some people invest a lot of work
in the back yard just for their own enjoyment.   This
dimension is a little different for the different
streets.   The northern part is more open in terms of
interaction and people go back and forth.   Here you
find the coffee klatches.   In the southern part you
have all these fences and several houses are like
fortresses, completely sealed off.   They have "beware
of dog" signs.   There is no way to get near the house
with all the fences; they have to unlock the fence to
drive up in the garage.

Residents of Edgedale expressed feelings of
alienation from the school.   They complained that
parent's groups are seen as fund-raising organizations
and nothing else.   Many residents dislike some of the
teachers, and they don't like having to share their
principal with another elementary school because theirs
is so small.   Some parents tried to organize so that
they could have some influence.   One lady who was a
part of that organization said that many people asked
her, "Why are you knocking your head against a stone
wall? You can't get anything out of the school
district; you might as well not try."   There was also a
group of mothers who were tutoring children with
reading problems.   But they were not encouraged by the
teachers, and the group eventually died out.

DESCRIPTIONS OF THE MOSAIC NEIGHBORHOOD

In this study we have employed an additional, seventh
neighborhood type which emerged from analyzing the results of
observational and survey data.   This form is characterized by
an individual's naming only their immediate neighbors as the
boundary of their neighborhood.   When averages for the
walking distance area are calculated, the neighborhood form

is low on all three of the basic indicators so that it might
be classified as anomic. However, the "small island"
definition of neighborhood is somewhat distinctive. Here,
the individual may have close social ties to a small number
of immediate neighbors, although the locale as a whole (its
average) is not high.[4] In effect, collective action is
unlikely, but small-scale social networking is. This new
form of neighborhood we called "mosaic"--fragments of a
larger neighborhood that are each unique and separate. Here
are several descriptions of mosaic neighborhoods:

> The amount of interaction and helping behavior
> observed between neighbors was found to vary by the
> street and age of residents on each street. These
> differences were thought to occur because the streets
> are physically isolated from each other, and it was
> reported that most people in Deadwood Plains identify
> with the street they live on rather than with the
> entire neighborhood or community. Among younger
> residents, there was a lot of helping behavior in terms
> of watching each other's children, helping with yard
> work such as sodding, and lending of tools and
> materials to neighbors. On some streets young women
> get together frequently for coffee and gossip. Much
> less interaction was observed between older residents
> on the streets south of Fairline.

A Classic Mosaic Neighborhood

> Little activity was observed in Lincoln, and it
> varied from block to block. On a few blocks people
> were observed visiting in their front yards and
> children were riding bikes. Few people were observed
> in any of the parks, however. People in the neighbor-
> hood sometimes congregate at the centrally located
> Burger Chef. Women sometimes meet there for coffee;
> families frequently dine there. An article on
> privatism had been published in the Detroit Free Press
> previous to interviewing some of the Lincoln residents.
> The article was cited again and again by residents who
> insisted that the kind of privatism described in the
> article was true of their neighborhood. Some of the
> people interviewed expressed a faint desire for the
> neighborhood to be more cohesive, but saw no way of
> achieving this.
>   There is little mutual aid in the neighborhood.
> People may borrow a coffee urn or a frying pan in
> exceptional circumstances, but those children with no
> one to feed them at noon are taken in by neighbors only

for pay, and infrequently at that. One resident said
that she had asked her neighbors to look after her
children at times, and they had done so, but that she
stopped asking when they did not reciprocate. Most
people do not place much confidence in the behavior of
their neighbors. They fear sending their children to
the local parks when they are not supervised. They
mentioned that their "nice suburban children" would
vandalize anything if they had the chance.

NEIGHBORHOOD TYPE AND DEMOGRAPHIC PATTERNS

Use of the neighborhood types with the addition of the
mosaic form replicates the analysis conducted in 28 neighborhoods in the 1969 study of black and white neighborhoods (see
Warren, 1975). Thirty-two additional suburban neighborhoods
were added to complete the 59 areas used in the helping networks project.

In terms of types, neighborhoods located in the city of
Detroit tend to be five times as often in the anomic category. Non-Detroit neighborhoods are more than twice as
likely to be integral, three times as likely to be parochial,
compared to Detroit neighborhoods (see Appendix Table IV-5).

Race composition plays a major role in determining
neighborhood type.[5] Integral settings are twice as frequent
in white locales. Stepping-stone, parochial, and transitory
neighborhoods are found more often among black than white
neighborhoods. The diffuse form occurred only in a white
population locale. The mosaic occurred more often in white
than in black neighborhoods (see Appendix Table IV-6).

In terms of family income level and individual education the integral type of setting is distinctive: half of
the residents in such locales had family earnings of $20,000
or more in 1974; this is true of only one in twelve residents
of anomic neighborhoods. It is still true, however, that 43
percent of families with incomes over $25,000 do not live in
integral neighborhoods, and only 19 percent of those families
earning $6,000 or less (the poverty level) reside in anomic
locales (see Appendix Table IV-7).

Nearly half of all the residents of integral neighborhoods have attended some college compared to one in five
residents of anomic areas (see Appendix Table IV-8).

SURVEY FINDINGS: NEIGHBORHOOD TYPES AND HELPING BY THE
NEIGHBOR

Earlier discussion has established that the direct
helping function of neighborhood via the role of neighbor
helping is the fourth most frequently utilized type of
helper--behind spouse, relative, and friend. Moreover,
neighbor help is more frequent for life crises in comparison
to recent concerns--56 percent in 1975 versus 41 percent.
How does this vary by types of neighborhoods? In fact, there
is much less variation than might be suggested by the large
differences in the social structure and functions of
different kinds of areas which the survey and descriptive
patterns have illustrated.

For life crises only the integral locale stands out:
neighbor help is utilized by two out of three persons with
such an experience. Parochial neighborhood helping is
sharply lower--47 percent. All of the other forms of
neighborhoods show rather similar patterns hovering at the
average level. In regard to recent concerns there is again
no sharp difference in help sought from a neighbor, and this
small amount of variation is not correlated with the strength
of the neighborhood as a whole (see Appendix Table IV-9).

While the amount of neighbor helping is similar across
types, what the neighbor provides in the way of help differs
in some systematic ways. Referral and action intervention
helping is found more often in the stronger neighborhoods:
integral and parochial. Although the stepping-stone provides
a great deal of referral, it ranks lowest in providing active
problem intervention in coping with recent concerns (see
Appendix Table IV-10). In the case of life crises, the
integral is highest in providing referral helping by the
neighbor, and the anomic area is lowest.

Even though referral behaviors are relatively
infrequent--averaging eight percent for recent concerns and
six percent for crisis helping--they serve as a critical
measure of the linking function of the neighborhood. Anomic
and mosaic settings are least likely to provide this kind of
help: The transitory, integral, and parochial settings are
the most likely to provide this bridging form of problem-
coping (see Appendix Table IV-10).

THE NEIGHBORHOOD AS A HELPING CONTEXT: THE SURVEY FINDINGS

In stressing the role of local community as a key
mechanism for well-being, there is hypothesized (or assumed
to be) a capacity for either self-sufficiency or networking
functions rooted in the proximate social ties of the

individual. Both ideas convey more than a simple mechanistic
view of the neighborhood as a one-to-one relationship. In a
broader view of neighborhood, the total pattern of social
ties and helping is seen as filtered and shaped by the context of local community. In terms of each neighborhood type
we have used a definition that begins with the physically
demarcated area of a population and then proceed to measure
the social ties of the population living in that setting.
This is what we mean by neighborhood context.

Does the strength of social fabric of the neighborhood
context correlate with the well-being of individual
residents? To address this question we must compare the
various indices of self-reported depression, mental outlook
and reported overall health of the people interviewed. These
indicators--summarized as the RISK score--show some correlation with neighborhood social forms. Thus, residents in the
integral setting have the lowest averages of RISK scores,
while those located in anomic and transitory settings are
highest. In the initial 1974 survey transitory had the
highest RISK scores; by 1975 this distinction went to the
anomic locale. In fact this neighborhood context was the
only one to reflect an increase in average RISK score for
residents while all others showed a decline (see Appendix
Table IV-11).

Neighborhood context does appear to be of importance in
the well-being of residents in each differentiated setting.
The reasons for this effect are clearly manifold, although we
mainly focus on helping resources and problem-coping.

ISOLATION FROM HELPERS AND THE NEIGHBORHOOD CONTEXT

Much of the literature on social support as well as the
specific correlational findings in the helping network study
indicate that having no help in coping with recent concerns
is a significant source of self-reported stress and a higher
RISK score.

How much is the context of neighborhood a factor in
shaping the individual's total range of helping resources?
Wide variations by neighborhood type occur. The stepping-
stone, transitory, and integral show high ranks on extensity
--variety of helpers used. By contrast mosaic and parochial
show few helpers used for each recent concern experienced.

Do neighborhood contexts differ in the probability that
an individual will be socially isolated in dealing with
problems? Overall, fewer than one in six individuals who
have at least one problem--a recent concern--used no helpers
in coping with that problem. In the anomic neighborhood context this rises to one in three persons. Only eight percent

are isolated in this way in stepping-stone neighborhoods.
The other types are arrayed in between (see Appendix Table
IV-12).

EFFECTIVE HELPING AND THE NEIGHBORHOOD CONTEXT

In light of the important role which the specific
behaviors of the helper play in what is considered helpful
and, in turn, what is associated with higher risk to well-
being, changes in the kind of helping as well as the type of
helping system used become a measure of effectiveness.

For each of the five types of helping behaviors--from
"just listening" to "taking action" correlations were made
with the extent of helping and the RISK score in each
neighborhood context (see Appendix Table IV-13). Reduction
in the RISK score between 1974 and 1975 is associated most
closely with increasing amounts of referral and asking questions. "Just listening" helping is negatively related to
reducing the RISK score.

Neighborhood types which have shifted most in the
direction of those behaviors most associated with reducing
the RISK score include the integral and parochial setting in
regard to "asking questions" and the stepping-stone and
transitory settings in terms of referral behavior.
Neighborhoods which have adopted helping behaviors that tend
to increase the RISK score are the ordinary anomic and
diffuse in terms of listening behavior.

In order to summarize the change trends between 1974
and 1975 in regard to the helping process in each neighborhood context, two global dimensions of helping can be used:
extensivity and intensivity. The first measures the number
of different types of helpers used in dealing with a problem.
Intensivity refers to the variety of helping behaviors. In
practice, this means "just listening" in combination with one
or more of the other kinds of helping behaviors.

We find that major shifts in the rank of neighborhood
contexts on each of the two key dimensions of helping networks occurred between 1974 and 1975. In terms of the number
of helpers used, the stepping-stone context shows a change
from a first rank to a seventh rank; parochial has gone from
sixth to second; the anomic mosaic has increased from a
seventh rank to a third rank. On the intesivity scale, the
transitory context shows a change from third to seventh.
This same context has declined from second to fifth on the
extensivity dimension (see Table IV-1).

These patterns suggest that such a shift reflects the
rather superficial but wide net cast in such a setting of
turnover and social mobility. By contrast the privacy

implicit in the parochial setting and its inward directedness
may limit initial wide searching for help and subsequently
channel it in accordance with locally legitimated referrals.
The mosaic setting may show low initial range of helpers used
due to the small scale of neighborhood size and the resulting
constriction of early referral linkages. Relative decline in
both numbers of helpers and variety of helping behaviors for
the transitory context may reflect the lack of access individuals have to ongoing relationships within their neighborhood
and their need to continue to search for help outside rather
than any coherent development of helping ties over a given
period of time.

The relative increase in 1975 of extensivity for integral, parochial, and anomic mosaic neighborhoods suggests the
capacity of helping networks in such contexts to adapt to
effective problem-coping. The decline in extensivity of both
stepping-stone and transitory context suggests the strained
capacity of resources of problem-coping in these contexts.
Table IV-1 therefore summarizes the strength of helping
systems as they occur in different neighborhood contexts.

TABLE IV-1

Rank Order Patterns for Types of Neighborhoods in Relation
to Numbers of Helpers and Helping Behaviors for Recent
Concerns

	1974		1975	
	Exten-sivity[a]	Inten-sivity[b]	Exten-sivity	Inten-sivity
Integral	(3)	(2)	(1)	(1)
Parochial	(6)	(1)	(2)	(2)
Diffuse	(4)	(5)	(4)	(3)
Stepping Stone	(1)	(4)	(7)	(5)
Transitory	(2)	(3)	(5)	(7)
Anomic	(5)	(7)	(6)	(6)
Mosiac	(7)	(6)	(3)	(4)
Correlation with RISK score	+.29	-.71	-.71	-.77

[a]Number of helpers per problem
[b]Number of different helping behaviors for each problem

THE PERCEIVED NEIGHBORHOOD CONTEXT

In a study which attempted to distinguish between the psychological and cultural models of community (Sanders, 1966), it was suggested that the psychological perspective involves an abstract attachment of the individual to her/his community. Individuals identify with their community in order to gain a sense of belonging and security, both emotional and physical. On the other hand, the cultural perspective argues that individuals identify and interact with their community because community members share common values, norms, and goals. The psychological perspective is similar to the notion of "symbolic communities" (Suttles, 1968) which suggests that community is really "in the mind of the beholder" (Warren, 1975)--a sense of belonging and sharing. The cultural perspective views community in more utilitarian terms, as a help-giving resource which defines and is defined by several important parameters of social interdependence and thus social integration (Warren, 1971).

Each of these models of community suggests two approaches to defining "community": 1) community is an idea or perception of an individual that implies some feeling or attitude about the social network in which the individual is a member; 2) community is a real group of people who share common goals and possess resources which may be utilized to handle individual or group problems. We agree with Sanders and Suttles that community is an abstract idea or feeling of belonging. It is a perception of common ties or bonds which are developed and sustained through social interaction. These ties or bonds may or may not actually exist in the neighborhood, but if the individual perceives them to exist, then a sense of community exists for the individual. An individual's perceived sense of belonging is the proper measure of whether a neighborhood is a community for that individual.

PERCEIVED NEIGHBORHOOD CONTEXT AND HELPING

We have employed a set of three questionnaire items which provide a multivariate definition of each neighborhood type as perceived by respondents.[6] The items are as follows:

I'd like you to think about the people who live in this neighborhood, the area within walking distance of your front door.

    a) Do people in this neighborhood have many things in common, some things in common, or a few things in common?

    b) During the year, do people in this neighborhood get together many times, a few times, or hardly ever?

    c) Do many, a few, or hardly any people in this neighborhood keep active in groups outside of the local area?

There are important differences in the role of individual helpers associated with each neighborhood setting. Thus, where the individual says they are in an integral neighborhood, neighbors are mentioned nearly twice as often as in anomic settings; while relatives are mentioned less (34 compared to 47 percent, respectively). For the diffuse setting, friends and relatives rank above the average of other neighborhoods, but so do doctors and counselors (including psychiatrists and psychologists) and teachers. Transitory settings resemble diffuse in terms of reliance on help from relatives and doctors, but differ in not using other formal and professional helpers to the same degree. Police are used most often in parochial neighborhoods. Friends are used most often in diffuse settings; relatives, most often in anomic areas; neighbors, least often in diffuse and anomic contexts (see Table IV-2). Given these trends, we can now usefully explore what can be learned from a combination of the two forms of measuring neighborhood context: the objective and subjective versions of the various types.

THE COMBINING OF REAL VERSUS PERCEIVED NEIGHBORHOOD CONTEXT

The data presented in this chapter on perceived neighborhood type and the variety of findings shown earlier for real neighborhoods have indicated two conclusions: 1) each operationalized typing produces important differences in both help-seeking and well-being, 2) many of the patterns noted for the same perceived and real types emerge with similar helping and well-being levels.

For many people interviewed their perceived and real neighborhoods diverge. We show that the two sets of measures have relatively little overlap (see Appendix Table IV-15). That is, individuals who perceive they are living in one type of neighborhood are, according to the aggregated measure of the sample in which they live, often classified as residing in some other form of neighborhood context. In the case of the integral-integral, diffuse-diffuse, and ordinary anomic-ordinary anomic pairings, a higher compatability between real and perceived types occurs. For the parochial and

TABLE IV-2

Type of Helpers Used in Relation to Perceived Type of Neighborhood Context

	Primary			Proximal		Formal			Professional	
	Spouse	Friend	Relative	Co-Worker	Neighbor	Teacher	Clergy	Police	Doctor	Counselor
Integral	78%	52%+	34%-	36%	36%+	8%+	6%+	10%	9%+	6%
Parochial	78%	45%-	29%-	35%	26%	7%+	1%-	12%+	3%-	5%
Diffuse	76%	54%+	40%+	37%	19%-	6%+	5%	6%	10%+	8%+
Stepping-Stone	78%	49%	32%-	35%	30%	3%	3%	8%	5%	5%
Transitory	76%	49%	44%+	29%-	25%	1%-	3%-	1%-	10%+	3%-
Anomic	71%-	49%	47%+	29%-	20%-	1%-	5%	9%	8%	4%-
Total Sample	76%	50%	39%	33%	26%	5%	4%	8%	8%	5%

stepping-stone types, there are disproportionately higher
numbers of respondents who correctly perceive themselves in
these than in other contexts; for the transitory and mosaic
types they do not.

Given that most individuals are perceiving an arena of
neighborhood different from that which actually prevails,
what are the consequences of such misperceptions? In a very
oversimple way, individuals may over- or underestimate the
strength of their neighborhood. If they see many resources
and a great deal of interaction this can lead them to utilize
such resources as helpers more than if they view their
neighborhood as noncohesive, lacking in sociability, and with
no links to the outside world. By the same token, if the
individual tends to perceive great activity and identity
among neighbors, the result may be to enhance the probability
of seeking help even when the results of such aid may be less
than satisfactory. It is then useful to consider four situations: 1) where a strong neighborhood exists and is also
perceived as such, 2) where the strength of the neighborhood
is present but not recognized, 3) where the neighborhood is
weak but perceived as strong, and 4) where it is accurately
seen as weak.

Where perceived and real neighborhood types are cross-
tabulated, patterns indicate that if the neighborhood context
is perceived by an individual as weaker than in fact it is,
utilization of neighbors is significantly lower than average
in thirteen cases and above average in only five. By contrast, where the neighborhood is viewed as more effective
than it really is, there are ten instances of above-average
use of neighbors for helping and seven below-average
coordinates (see Appendix Table IV-16).

The same cross-tabulation analysis strategy of perceived and real neighborhood context in regard to shifts in
the use of neighbor as helper between 1974 and 1975 shows
that where perceived neighborhood skews the neighborhood type
toward a stronger neighborhood, there are more above-average
gains in neighbor helping between 1974 and 1975 (see Appendix
Table IV-17).

The link between well-being scores and the combinations
of real and perceived neighborhood is an important one. The
RISK scores for persons who perceived their neighborhood as
weaker than in fact it is, show significantly more above
average RISK scores (see Appendix Table IV-18).

USING NEIGHBORHOOD RESOURCES

Several analyses have illustrated the critical inter-
face between perception and reality in terms of the

supportive role of the neighborhood in two ways: first, in terms of actual help sought from neighbors; second, in terms of the sense of community implied by the perceived neighborhood measurement. The separation of these two facets of neighborhood context is both methodological and conceptually difficult at best, impossible at worst. By having sought an external validation measure of the neighborhood context we have, in addition, found a need to reconceptualize the meaning and importance of that core idea of this research.

Several implications derive from the dual labeling and separate concepts which are measured in the study. First of all, it is possible to construct a somewhat oversimple fourfold table dealing with the correlation of perceived and actual neighborhood resources (see Table IV-3). Many individuals are in a dissonant situation with respect to the use of the neighborhood and its potential as a source of help in time of trouble or problem-coping.

TABLE IV-3

Real and Perceived Neighborhood Resources

	High-Helping Resources	Low-Helping Resources
High Resource Perception	Consonant +	Dissonant ±
Low Resource Perception	Dissonant ±	Consonant +

"At rest" (no need for help-seeking) certain perceived neighborhoods may be comfortable social contexts to be living in because one recognizes a close bond to one's neighbors and sees the neighborhood as a lively and well-insulated setting from external intrusion (parochial), or a place where there are influential people with close ties to a City Hall or to the larger world of community and power. Even without a specific current problem load, an individual will benefit from such a sense of local community. In a second sense, the perceived resourceful neighborhood is good in that as problems occurred one has been able to get help from neighbors which has paid off--via direct aid or through referrals.

The neighborhood that is high in perceived resources can aid well-being by its intrinsic banishing of, or insulations against, a sense of isolation or alienation apart from its utilitarian role in giving help or getting a person to outside helpers. Actual neighborhood types measure mainly the access to an availability of helping networks and their resources. As such, actual neighborhood type is not as powerful a prophylactic against stress and alienation as perceived neighborhood type.

If individuals fail to recognize or accurately assess the resources of their actual neighborhood setting, they may tend to underutilize its resources. In addition, being in a strong resource neighborhood but perceiving it as a weak one will reduce whatever social attachment value one is able to draw upon. That is, even if one uses the help of the neighborhood, it will tend to be devalued.

When the individual views the local neighborhood as more of a resource for helping than it is, the consequent dissonance may increase stress when help is obtained since that help may not turn out to be as useful as anticipated. It does not solve the problem. Perhaps it may only gloss over the need for action or change. In addition, if the individual continues to use the help of neighbors, the result is a straining of whatever resources of helping already exist and thus creates frustrations by both helpers and helpees akin to an overloaded hospital ward where patients demand help, but the staff simply cannot do the job.

If individuals perceive their neighborhood as weak in resources, and in fact it is weak, the result is a realistic perspective which may reduce frustration and the alienation due to unrealized expectations. But it also means that unless some other contact or base of linkage to helping networks—such as a job or family or organizational memberships—is present, individuals will be highly burdened by their isolation in coping with problems. They may resist any effort to change their lives or may suffer greatly at the loss of any close relationships or other life crisis.

Thus, three factors influence the role of local neighborhood: the consistency of perceived and actual resource capacities, the positive or negative evaluation of the neighborhood, and the capacity of the actual neighborhood setting to generate helping resources. In general, the perceived neighborhood significantly influences the individual mental state—the frequency of depression, psychosomatic symptoms, reports about physical well-being. The actual neighborhood context is more closely related to the kinds of helping resources and the kind of helping behaviors that are available. While perceived neighborhood also affects these

factors, it is clear the community and actual neighborhood
are also critical for pathways to helping.

The probability of using the neighbor for a helper is
not the most critical dimension around which either perceived
or actual neighborhood context must be evaluated. For in
this regard weak and strong, actual and perceived neighborhoods show equal and sometimes higher levels of use of
neighbors. *The critical point to bear in mind is that we are
examining the capacity of actual neighborhoods to link the
person to helping resources, and in this sense, the degree to
which that context can be truly described as a helping network itself.* Use of neighbors often measures the degree of
isolation the individual experiences relative to other kinds
of helpers and nonneighborhood resources. Clearly, continued
reliance on neighbors in a weak neighborhood may lead to an
early and more determined search for other kinds of help if
such neighbor contacts turn out unless--lacking in variety,
pay off, or referral potential. Being locked into the
neighborhood context in its narrow and more neighboring sense
then may be detrimental to effective problem-coping and to
the reduction in risk to individual well-being.

NEIGHBORHOOD CONTEXT AND ITS SIGNIFICANCE

There are two aspects in the measurement of local
community (neighborhood) in the helping network study: one
is the description and perception by individuals of the kind
of identification and social patterns of their neighborhood;
the other is the aggregated pattern of an actual neighborhood
area using the elementary school district as the sampling
unit. While, to some extent, each may be a substitute for
the other (in terms of a common set of underlying dimensions
which create the different forms which are present), each is
also significant in its own right.

The perceived type of neighborhood description is very
close to a measurement of the quality of local community--the
degree to which a sense of community is strong or weak,
including varieties of each. This is, in effect, a measure
of "symbolic community" to use Suttles' term. Actual
neighborhood patterns are largely a set of resource descriptions. Both share a common element of reference group
commitment, but they differ in that in one instance
individuals are aggregated to provide a "critical mass" of
resources while, in the other instance, each individual
within any neighborhood holds a perspective on what are the
available resources and patterns independent of the actual
resources available. The issue with respect to this concern
implies a distinction between what sociologists alternately

refer to as community and neighborhood. In many instances, these two concepts have been used interchangeably with little regard for specifying any substantive differences which exist between them.

The critical distinction between community and neighborhood is that the former is partially a perception on the part of the individual regarding the existence or non-existence of common bonds; neighborhood refers to an area in which people live in close proximity to one another and share a common life provided by the functional capacity of the neighborhood network.

Consequently, there are always two sides of neighborhood that must be kept in mind. The first side is the subjective or perceived side which we call community and that determines how one perceives the social relationships intrinsic in that neighborhood network. This perception may affect the way one seeks help when problems are encountered. The other side is the objective or real neighborhood which consists of the helping resources and the neighborhood helpers. Thus, the concept of neighborhood has a double impact--it affects the way one experiences a problem because of the resources that are available and because of the sense of belonging (community) which will determine how these resources will be used or if they will be used at all. When the two coincide, we speak of neighborhood as community.

This double-barrel approach suggests four situations which may determine resource utilization, and by implication the degree of identification and integration of residents into the functional neighborhood network. These four situations can be described as follows:

Neighborhood Resource Identifiers

These individuals perceive their neighborhood as having many things in common, extensive formal and informal interaction, and a sense of common ties with their neighbors. These perceptions will lead them to identify strongly with their neighborhood and utilize existing helping resources quite heavily. These individuals find the neighborhood's information-communication to be accurate and effective, and they accept and use it. Neighborhood identifiers will usually actively seek to establish extensive lines of communication and draw others into the network thereby increasing the number of identified individuals.

Neighborhood Resource Exploiters

These individuals also perceive their neighborhood as having many common ties and extensive lines of communication

among neighbors. This perception will affect the way
intrinsic helping resources may be utilized. In strong
neighborhoods where helping resources are plentiful, these
people would be neighborhood identifiers. In neighborhoods
where resources are quite meager, however, these people may
exploit those resources. They are committed to those
resources or exhaust them. If neighborhood exploiters
experience a problem or crisis they will actively seek to
utilize whatever resources are available in the neighborhood
to cope with the problem.

Neighborhood Resource Avoiders

Having no great sense of local community, these individuals will most likely not take advantage of the helping
resources available within their neighborhood. If the
neighborhood is rich in helping resources and information-
communication about these resources, these individuals may
get help for problems but they would not actively seek this
help and tend to underutilize existing help resources since
they lack a sense of community. Moreover, these individuals
would not even be aware of the availability of indigenous
neighborhood helping resources.

Neighborhood Resource Isolates

These are individuals who do not utilize the neighborhood's information network. They have no sense of community,
and the functional neighborhood lacks any form of helping
resources. If these people experience problems they will not
cope with them within the helping context of their real
neighborhood. Since they lack any sense of community and
limited resources exist in their neighborhood, they will
either have to seek help outside the neighborhood or rely on
their own resources and not seek any additional help.

TO SUM UP

Our research offers evidence that the "neighborhood
context" is a multiform basis of helping that goes beyond the
extent of direct neighbor help. The patterns we find suggest
that the kind of help provided interacts with the problem in
determining the value of the help.

Given our initial conceptualization of the neighborhood
context as a base for utilization of and access to a variety
of helping resources--informal and formal--the data described
in this paper have supported such a view in empirical terms.
While neighbors are not the most frequently used helpers,

when called upon to help their referral role can be very
significant in reducing stress and the risk to well-being
presented by both life crises and recent concerns.

We have also seen from this analysis that usage of the
neighbor does not insure what kind of help will be tendered.
Neighborhood context apparently shapes the role of the
neighbor who is turned to for help. In some neighborhood
settings--particularly the ordinary anomic and transitory--
greater reliance on neighboring helping occurs than had been
theoretically predicted. But the usefulness of such help
appears to reflect less the preference for employing such
individuals as helpers than the barriers to utilizing other,
nonneighbor helpers. In short: a portion of neighbor help
is ineffective in reducing the risk to well-being. Turning
to a neighbor in a time of need does not always reflect
choice but necessity. The outcome in such instances is less
than satisfactory.

From our conceptual base of differentiating neighborhood contexts, we have identified patterns of neighbor help
that are not seen as especially valuable or whose effectiveness may be less than impressive. The explanation lies, we
suggest, with the role of the neighborhood as a means to link
the individual to the resources of others in the neighborhood
and beyond--not simply as an expression of sociability or as
a self-contained system. Instead, neighbors are gatekeepers
to the outside world in at least two ways: directly, via
referrals to organizations and nonneighbor experts and
helpers; indirectly, via the passing on of information gained
from the knowledge and experience of other neighbors which
are, in turn, disseminated throughout the neighborhood where
interaction is broad-based and diffuse in its character.

Neighborhoods appear to differ, not so much in their
ability to provide a few key helpers in a time of need, but
in the linkages which such contacts can provide. These may
open up a wide base of additional helping resources or serve
as the end-process in problem-coping, or simply be ineffec-
tual sources of temporary emotional uplift or solace without
providing directions for problem solution or amelioration.

A strong sense of community in a residential locale may
help to banish isolation, and a corresponding feeling that
one is part of the group is a way of becoming socially
integrated. More specifically, a strong sense of belonging
may help prevent stress and be conducive to a healthy mental
outlook.

The benefit of community is not simply utilitarian.
The value of considering both the perceived neighborhood
relationship network and the actual neighborhood lies not
only in our ability to track problem-solving resources but,
perhaps as importantly, it allows us to examine the

expressive notion of sense of community or community
belonging. It is belonging and the sociability--seeing
others interact--that means it is a worthwhile thing to
belong. It can be a good community because "we keep to
ourselves--we keep the larger community out" or it is a good
community because "we are tied in." Either of these perceptions can be considered by its members as signifying their
view of what is a healthy community.

     We now turn to a more geographic base of community,
that of the municipality forming a political-administrative
unit of residency.

CHAPTER V

COMMUNITY PATTERNS AND PROBLEM-COPING

In this chapter an analysis is provided of the eight communities that form a major component of the helping network survey sample. Essentially, the communities selected provide important comparisons of the helping networks which individuals within each setting utilize.[1] The doctoral dissertation of David L. Clifford ("Comparative study of Helping Patterns in Eight Urban Communities"), extensively develops the theme of the specific municipality and helping systems.[2]

The first stage of sampling for the study was the purposive selection of eight Detroit suburban municipalities. These cities--Warren, Livonia, Pontiac, St. Clair Shores, Royal Oak, Mt. Clemens, Troy, and Lincoln Park--were selected using two criteria: 1) they cover each of the three counties: Wayne Co. (three); Oakland Co. (two); and Macomb Co. (three) in the Detroit SMSA; and 2) they represent a socio-economic and historical cross section of Detroit suburban communities (see Figure V-1).

In this second stage, a one percent random sample of households was selected in each of the communities.[3] This created some 766 initial interviews.

The representative cross-section sampling of addresses used for the eight communities does not attempt to represent the Detroit Metropolitan area or the SMSA. Instead, the purposive criteria were derived from an effort to compare larger and smaller municipalities, older and newer communities, and those with predominantly blue- and predominantly white-collar populations.

The communities are located in each of the three counties composing the Detroit SMSA and include the fourth largest city in Michigan--Warren--as well as Mount Clemens with a population of only a tenth as great. The sample includes one of the fastest growing communities of the State --Troy. Largely blue-collar setting are represented by

99

FIGURE V - 1

Map of the Tri-County Areas with the
Eight Sample Communities

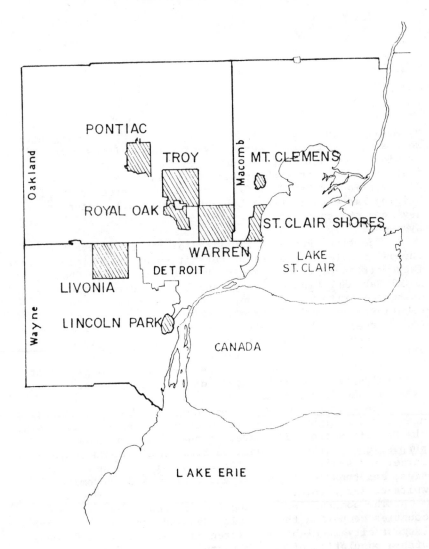

Lincoln Park, Pontiac, and Mt. Clemens. Mainly white-collar
communities include Livonia, Royal Oak, and Troy. St. Clair
Shores and Warren are mixed blue- and white-collar settings.
Six of the eight communities might be classified as suburbs
of Detroit. The two which are more geographical distant from
Detroit--Pontiac and Mount Clemens--are also the only cities
with a significant number of black residents. (Summary demographic data for each of the municipalities is shown in
Appendix Table V-1.)

AN INDEX OF THE STRENGTH OF COMMUNITY HELPING SYSTEMS

      In this part of the analysis we seek to develop some
basic views of how one community may differ from another in
terms of the helping roles found within each. Our strategy
will be to select the measures of volume and content of
helping as the way to define relatively "healthy" communities
in regard to helping capacity. In effect, the question we
explore at this point is: "Given a recent concern, how well
it is coped with in community 'A' versus community 'B'?"
      We employ a total of four measures to construct our
barometer of community-helping health. First, we compared
the number of helpers per problem found in each locale. This
is the extensivity index used in earlier chapters. There are
rather sharp community differences here. The highest
community--Royal Oak--averages twice the number of different
kinds of helpers per problem as the lowest community--Mt.
Clemons.
      The second comparison is that of total numbers of the
same or different helpers for each recent concern
experienced. Here a similar doubling from highest to lowest
occurs.
      A third community comparison in regard to helping is
that of intensivity--the average number of different kinds of
helping behaviors that occur for recent concerns. On this
measure the eight municipalities do not differ in any marked
degree. The highest level is found for Lincoln Park--1.8 per
problem versus the low of 1.3 for Pontiac (see Appendix Table
V-2).
      The fourth indicator of community health is the
probability of having a recent concern without the use of any
helpers whatsoever. This "isolation" measure shows some
important variation for the eight municipalities sampled.
The high is 19 percent in Warren, Michigan; the low ten percent in both Royal Oak and St. Clair Shores (see Appendix
Table V-3).
      What happens if we put the four indicators together to
form a community helping scale--a way to define the strength

of helping systems in one locale versus another? In fact,
communities show a fairly consistent pattern from one index
to the next. When added, a clustering of three groups occurs
with rather large intervals between. At the high end of the
barometer is Royal Oak, followed closely by Lincoln Park and
St. Clair shores. These three are similar to one another and
when ranked are a significant distance away from the next
community on the scale (see Appendix Table V-4).

THE HEALTHIEST COMMUNITIES

Royal Oak

        Scoring at the top of the health or helping strength
index, this community is a rather densely settled older
suburb of Detroit. Royal Oak is approximately one-third of
the area of the largest sample city--Livonia; it had a 1970
population of 85,000, about twice as dense. First settled in
the 1820's, growth came very slowly to the Royal Oak area as
dense woods and marshes made it extremely difficult to reach
from Detroit. In 1891 it was incorporated as a village with
400 people. Thirty years later it was incorporated as a city
with a population of 6,000. In the twenties the city boomed
with the rest of the economy as more prosperous Detroiters
migrated straight out Woodward Avenue (Detroit's "main
street") which runs through the middle of the city. By 1930
the population had grown to almost 23,000, an increase of 280
percent for the decade. During the depression growth slowed
to a near halt, but since then it has shown steady growth up
to the 1960s.
        If Royal Oak and Livonia are similar demographically,
this difference in age and size gives them different
"climates." Royal Oak has a more urban feel than many of the
other newer suburbs such as Livonia, Warren, and Troy. Royal
Oak has many commercial strip developments along, and running
off, the Woodward corridor. There are numerous long residential streets with older houses, some of which might be termed
stately. The tree-lined streets and neighborhoods have
strong identities. They give the appearance of being well-
manicured. Royal Oak has a greater number of poor people in
older housing than does Livonia. Such a community thus has
more social diversity as well.
        In spite of its being a middle- to upper middle-class
community, Royal Oak's median family income of $13,600 places
it almost $2,000 below Livonia and about equal with the more
blue-collar suburb of Warren; 62 percent of the work force
are in white-collar occupations and half of these in professional or technical fields.

Royal Oak can claim some national prominence. Although Catholics make up a little less than one-third of the population, their presence in the community is felt to a disproportionate degree. The Shrine of the Little Flower, built by Father Coughlin--the demagogic "radio priest" of the 30s--is located in Royal Oak. The Shrine is a major attraction in the city and this period of the community's history is still vividly remembered. While Father Coughlin is no longer active in the shrine, its art-deco carillon tower and parochial school serve to underscore its prominence as a community institution. In a close second position to Royal Oak is the community of Lincoln Park.

Lincoln Park

Located just nine miles southwest and downriver from downtown Detroit, Lincoln Park is the second smallest community in the sample with a population of 53,000 packed into slightly less than six square miles. Although not incorporated as a city until 1925, Lincoln Park was one of the earliest of the French settlements outside of Fort Detroit. It remained a small, largely rural community until the 1930s, when Henry Ford's offer of $5 per day for working in the auto plants brought in workers looking for a pleasant residential area near the factories (Lincoln Park is less than three miles from Ford's huge River Rouge complex). The next spurt of growth cam in the 1940s with the mobilization for war production and the postwar upswing in the auto industry.

Although proximate to a large portion of West Detroit's industrial complex, Lincoln Park is largely residential. Only one-fifth of the 24 manufacturing plants located inside the city employ over twenty people, making it the least industrialized city in the sample. In recent years the growth of the city has halted, and between the 1960 and the 1970 censuses the population actually declined 1.8 percent.

The city has a diversity of white ethnic groups including Canadians, Poles, Hungarians, Italians, southern whites, and some Greeks. Catholics are the largest religious group, representing 42 percent of the people in the sample. They are organized in several closely knit and well-organized parishes. In number they are followed by mainline Protestants (36 percent) and Fundamentalist sects (16 percent). Blue-collar workers, 60 percent of the work force, predominate in the community. Many work in nearby plants for either Ford Motor Company or Great Lakes Steel Corporation.

Although Lincoln Park is heavily blue-collar, it is a relatively prosperous community with a median family income in 1970 of slightly over $12,000 a year. Based on 1970

census figures, approximately four percent of the families in
the city are below the poverty level, ranking it third
highest in this category of the eight communities, although
still well behind the ten percent in Pontiac and seven percent in Mount Clemens.

St. Clair Shores

Completing the triumvirate of healthiest communities is
St. Clair Shores. This small lakeside suburb (nearly the
same size as Royal Oak) is dominated by comfortable homes and
a dense development of marinas and lakeside recreation areas.
Incorporated in 1951, St. Clair Shores parallels Livonia in
its explosive growth during the 1950s when its population
increased 287 percent to 76,000. This was followed, however,
by a rapid deceleration of growth, only a 15 percent increase
in the sixties, as the relatively small land area was quickly
developed to capacity. In 1970 the population stood at
88,000, larger than Pontiac but on a little more than half
the land area. The city is predominantly residential in
character--there are only 73 industrial establishments and
only one out of five of these employs more than 20 people.
While the city's growth has paralleled that of Livonia,
there are some strong differences in character. While a
majority--53 percent of the work force--are in white-collar
occupations, fewer of these are in the professional and
technical areas than any other of the white-collar communities in the sample. Much of the city's early growth was
based on the upward mobility of skilled blue-collar workers.
The median family income of $13,598 places it in the middle
range of the communities in the study.
St. Clair Shores has a great deal of ethnic diversity
with a quarter of its population having at least one foreign-
born parent. Unlike the other white-collar suburbs, these
ethnics are not mostly Canadians and Britons. The largest
ethnic group is Italians, followed by Canadians, Poles, and
Germans. This ethnic heritage is organized, and St. Clair
Shores is the home of an Italian Culture Center which opened
a little over a year ago. Religiously the community is
predominantly (60 percent) Catholic.

TWO MEDIUM-STRENGTH COMMUNITIES

Two communities that are grouped as medium healthy are
clearly differentiated from the top cluster on the four
helping system measures. Both are among the most affluent in
the sample of municipalities. Ranked fourth among the eight
locales, Livonia is the shape of a perfect square, being

constituted by a single northwest-ordinance 36-square township.

Livonia

This sprawling suburb lies west of Detroit. Incorporated as a city in 1950, it is a product of the post-World War II suburbanization of cities. Between 1950 and 1960 its population increased 280 percent, from just over 17,000 to almost 67,000. In the decade of the 60s it increased another 65 percent to 110,000. The city is composed predominantly of large, relatively expensive housing developments. In style it is very much a middle- to upper middle-class, white-collar suburb. Although largely residential, there are about 140 manufacturing establishments in the city making it, in this respect, very comparable to Troy, more industrialized than Lincoln Park, but well below Warren.

People of this community are largely of northern European extraction. Although twenty percent of the people in the community have foreign-born or mixed parentage and six percent are foreign-born themselves (both figures about average for the sample communities), 41 percent of the first category are either Canadian or British. Fifty-one percent of the respondents in the sample are Protestant, 37 percent Catholic.

The median annual family income in Livonia in 1970 was over $15,000, making it the wealthiest of the eight sample communities. It is also one of the highest in formal education: with fifteen percent of the adults having completed four years of college. This level of education and income is reflected in the occupational structure with 60 percent of the work force in white-collar jobs. Among the sample communities it also has the fewest people below the poverty line: only two percent of the city's families.

Troy

If Royal Oak is an example of the older, stable, and somewhat modest yet dignified white-collar suburb, Troy is just the opposite. It is one of the youngest and fastest growing suburbs in Detroit, with a reputation for fast economic expansion and for a life style just as fast due to the many singles and young marrieds that have dominated its recent growth. Incorporated in 1955, Troy more than doubled its population between 1960 and 1970, from 19,402 to 39,412. In 1972 the population stood at 46,800, an increase of almost 19 percent in just two years.

Troy is a large, formerly rural farming area, covering 13 square miles. Located about a 30 to 40 minute drive from

downtown Detroit, it embodies, in many ways, the abandonment
by business of the central city for the promise of rich
suburban markets, fewer social problems, and comparatively
little crime. New office buildings dot the major arteries of
the city.

Companies such as S. S. Kresge, the third largest
retailer in the United States, have recently moved their
headquarters from Detroit's inner city to Troy. Similarly,
Budd Company, one of the largest and oldest auto supply
firms, has moved its headquarters here. The Somerset Mall,
boasting some of the most exclusive and expensive stores in
the country--Saks, F. A. O. Schwartz, Bonwit-Teller, Lord and
Taylor, Abercrombie & Fitch--has located here in the midst of
suburban wealth and growth. Many of Troy's new residents are
emigrants from the city of Detroit and from older suburbs.

Of the eight communities in the sample, Troy has the
largest proportion of white-collar workers (65 percent) and
the largest proportion in professional and technical occupations (40 percent). To match this occupational structure,
census figures show that 40 percent of the adults have
completed four years of college. This is two and a half
times the percentage of any other city in the sample. Median
family income is $13,399 which is not as high as one might
expect of such a well-educated population, but which may be
accounted for by the high number of younger families and
single people.

Of the eight communities in the sample, Troy has the
lowest percentage of foreign-born population and the second
lowest percentage of those with foreign-born or mixed parentage. Of the ten percent of the population having foreign or
mixed parentage, the vast majority are from Canada or Great
Britain. It is more diverse religiously than any of the
other eight communities. Of the survey respondents, 41 percent are mainline Protestants, 31 percent Roman Catholics,
nine percent fundamentalist, and 12 percent other religions--
largely Jewish and Greek Orthodox.

LOW HELPING STRENGTH COMMUNITIES

Below the middle cluster of communities, three cities
form a group in the helping index values widely separated
from those we have just described. These three municipalities are largely blue-collar, but have a number of characteristics that make each unlike the other in several important
ways. The first of these "least healthy" communities ranks
sixth on the average of the four indicators. This is
Pontiac, Michigan.

Pontiac

The city is solidly blue-collar with 65 percent of the work force in manual occupations. Named after a rebellious Indian chieftain, this city has a unique mixture of inner-city slums (where the black population tends to be clustered) and a rural periphery intertwined with lakes and recreational facilities. Its major industry is a large General Motors automobile assembly plant (its namesake is one of the five GM offerings) and truck-bus manufacturing facility.

The median annual family income in Pontiac in 1970 was $9,681, the lowest in the sample. Only five percent of the adults have completed four or more years of college. It also has the least stable family life of any of the sample communities with nearly ten percent of the adults either separated or divorced--by far the highest in the communities studied.

Pontiac is one of the two communities in the study with more than a barely discernible nonwhite population; over one-quarter of the city's population is nonwhite. Additionally, although only about eight percent of the population has foreign or mixed parentage, over half of these people are Spanish-speaking. Thrown into this ethnic mix is a heavy concentration of southern whites who moved here seeking work in the auto factories. (This latter population group is identifiable in part by the fact that 46 percent of the survey respondents identified themselves as belonging to fundamentalist Protestant denominations.)

Pontiac was one of the very first cities involved in the rebellion against forced busing to achieve racial balance. Irene McCabe, a city resident, was the founder of the National Action Group (NAG) which grew, however briefly, to national prominence and crystalized the opposition to forced school busing as a means of achieving racial balance in schools.

Of the communities in the study, Pontiac is probably the least like a suburb and the most like an autonomous city. Indeed, in the last few years Pontiac has been spawning suburbs of its own. Located in the middle of Oakland county, north of Detroit and more distant from it than any other community in the study, it is still held firmly in the orbit of Detroit by the auto company decision-makers located in Detroit, Highland Park, and Dearborn.

The dominance of auto operations has brought Pontiac a great deal of wealth, but has also tied it to the economic ebb and flow of the automobile industry, which often means a cycle of boom and bust for the entire economy of the city. Although there are relatively few industrial establishments in the city (68 according to the 1970 census) these are huge

auto parts manufacturers and assembly plants employing tens
of thousands. Exact estimates of size are not made available
because of laws protecting individual companies from having
to disclose the exact size of their work force.

The growth of the city in recent years has almost come
to a halt. Its days of glory and greatest growth came in the
early part of this century with the birth and early development of the auto industry. Between 1910 and 1920 the population increased 135 percent. In the twenties it jumped
another 90 percent, but with the depression growth came
almost to a halt, followed by modest or very low growth since
then. In 1970 the population was 85,279.

Closely following Pontiac and ranked next to the lowest
of the eight communities is Warren, Michigan.

Warren

Another large suburb (36 square miles) is the fourth
largest city in Michigan. Warren was allegedly built in part
by the flight of auto workers from Detroit's industrial
plants, the flight of the plants themselves from the perceived racial and crime problems of Detroit, and the need
for large tracts of land by manufacturing plants. For six
straight years in the late fifties Warren was the fastest
growing city in the United States. It doubled and even
quadrupled its population every year in this period. In the
fifties its population jumped 1,000 percent from a village of
727 to a city of 89,246. In the sixties its population
slowed but still managed a 100 percent increase to 180,000.
Industrial expansion followed space. The newer long-line
processes and single-story manufacturing operations flocked
to Warren's open expanses. Chevrolet, Fisher Body, Bundy
Tubing, Chrysler, the U.S. Tank Arsenal and the G. M.
Technical Center are just a few of the more than 1,000 manufacturers that have made an investment of more than $300
million in this city over the last two decades.

Relative to other communities, neighbor interaction
appears to be low and limited. In a number of areas chain-
link fences with locked gates close in the front yards as
well as the back. A pervasive attitude seems to be that
"I've made it and now I've got to fight to prevent others
from taking it from me." There seems to be a view of Warren
as a safe haven, but one which is under siege from the outside. In 1970 the city became the first in the U.S. to turn
down ($10 million) urban renewal funds at the polls. A sub-
sequent federal court case initiated by some Warren citizens
charged that the plebiscite on renewal funds had been biased
by a "racist climate" and asked that the decision be set
aside, but the courts ruled against this suit.

Although about 55 percent blue-collar, Warren is a relatively affluent city with a median annual family income of about $13,500 in 1970. It is predominantly Polish and Roman Catholic with other large contingents of people of Italian, Canadian, and German parentage.

Mount Clemens

At the bottom of the rankings of the eight communities --but only by a small margin compared to Pontiac and Warren-- Mt. Clemens is the most distant from Detroit, lying on the northeastern side of lake St. Clair 25 miles from the city's political boundary.

Mt. Clemens is the smallest city in the study with just over 20,000 people and a declining population. Although dwarfed in population by its neighbors to the south, St. Clair Shores and Warren, it is the seat of Macomb county by virtue of its being the oldest city in the country (incorporated in 1879). Settled by French trappers and woodsmen in the mid-1700s, the village grew slowly but fairly steadily from the mid 1800s through 1940s. Mount Clemens was an early and important logging and trading center which entered upon what natives refer to as its "Golden Age" in the late 1800s when its mineral waters and mineral baths attracted people from all over the country to take "the cure."

The physical and demographic decline that set in during the past 25 years has not been turned around despite the heavy investment in urban renewal in the late fifties. The population in 1970 had declined about 3 percent from the 21,000 of 1960.

The $11,000 median family income (1970 figures) makes Mount Clemens the second poorest city of the eight in our sample. With seven percent of its families below the poverty line it stands near Pontiac at the lower end of the economic rankings. Its population is predominantly blue-collar. There is a relative lack of ethnic diversity, except for the fact that blacks account for 17 percent of the total population of Mt. Clemens.

WHAT EXPLAINS THE DIFFERENCES IN COMMUNITY HEALTH?

The descriptions of the physical patterns of the eight communities along with the socio-demographic characteristics we have mentioned may suggest a basis for understanding why one locale has a stronger helping network pattern than another. For example, if a community is large, perhaps that causes it to be less of a helpful community. If it is small

it will be intimate and therefore the strongest type of
community. Thus, Lincoln Park--second in helping--ranks
seventh in size; Royal Oak first in helping is tied for fifth
in size with St. Clair Shores. These patterns might suggest
that the smaller the locale the stronger the helping networks. Yet this hypothesis does not hold, since Mt. Clemens,
the smallest of the communities, is also weakest in helping
structures. Pontiac, of medium areal size, is weak in
helping; Troy and Livonia, while the largest of the eight
communities, are not the weakest in helping networks. Overall, then, only some inconsistent trends suggest that a
smaller geographic community has a better change to develop a
strong helping system.

On the question of actual population size, the pattern
again shows no correlation in terms of helping network
strength. The most populous community--Warren--is similar in
terms of health to Mt. Clemens--which has the smallest
population of the eight communities.

In the recent anthropology and community psychology
literature several theories of the role of density as a
source of human stress have emerged. The work of Claude
Fischer (1978) argues that the greater density of urban life
creates barriers to close social ties and causes a
fractionalization of community into complex subcultures. The
withdrawal from community as a function of the very crowded-
ness of urban life is, of course, best evaluated in terms of
the very large urban centers which are not part of the eight
community sample with which we are dealing. Nevertheless,
the communities vary in density from the high of 8,830
persons per square mile to the low of Troy, which in 1970 was
1,176. Pontiac, a rather settled and "urban" place, has a
density half that found in Lincoln Park.

When each community is ranked by population density,
those places with higher density tend to have stronger
helping systems (the rank order value is +.50). Lincoln
Park, St. Clair Shores, and Royal Oak are all communities
with over 7,000 persons per square mile. These are medium
densities when compared to large urban centers (New York has
over 26,000 persons per square mile, and Chicago has over
15,000). At the same time, the healthy communities in the
survey resemble a density found in Los Angeles (about 6,000
persons per square mile). The nearest urban center--
Detroit--had a density of nearly 11,000 persons per square
mile as reported in the 1970 U.S. Census.

Perhaps the patterns we have noted suggest that moderate density is most conducive to a healthy helping network--
enough behavior settings and chance contacts to stimulate
helping exchanges, but not such a high density as to reduce

privacy options that are conducive to keeping one's helping confined to known intimates and primary group members.

What about socio-economic attributes of residents--do these factors explain the basis of strong versus weak community helping networks? The information available gives some support for this view. Family income rank of a community in 1970 correlates +.49 with a community's health rank as measured in the 1974 data. Using a measure of family buying power--net disposable income--which was obtained from a market survey one year prior to our interviews we find a similar correlation of +.43. In terms of the percentage of people in a community who are in white-collar occupations there is a similar positive link between strength of helping networks and occupational status (+.48).

While the overall patterns suggest that economics plays a clear role in community health, there are important discrepancies that suggest more than a simplistic determinism. Thus, Lincoln Park is ranked sixth on the percentage of persons employed in white collar jobs, sixth on median family income in 1970, and sixth on family buying power measured in 1973. While Troy is second in family buying power, it is fifth in helping network strength. Warren is ranked fourth in median income for 1970 but seventh in network health. Livonia is first in both median income in 1970 and family buying power in 1973 and yet ranks fourth in helping system strength. The three strongest communities in terms of helping networks all rank lower on the index of 1973 family buying power (see Appendix Table V-5). Thus, an economic or social class explanation can go perhaps half of the way to an explanation of community helping strength; with moderate density added in one can begin to gauge the potential for one locale being more effective in helping than another.

SOME CORRELATES OF STRONG HELPING: INTEGRATION INTO THE
LARGER SOCIETY

Community helping capacity appears to be a factor in explaining the extent to which people have positive or negative orientation to the problems of the larger society. We can illustrate this point in terms of events and issues independent of the survey of helping itself. At the time of our initial interviews, the Arab oil embargo and the subsequent shortages that created the first "energy crisis" occurred. A number of questions were asked about attitudes regarding these events--how the problem had come about and what should be done to deal with the situation. Included in the questions asked was the following:

> Some people say the whole energy problem is nothing but
> a trick by the oil companies and the government
> officials in Washington. Other people say it is a real
> problem that we have had energy shortages. How about
> you, how much of the problem is real and how much of it
> is phony?

A virtual 50-50 split occurred in people's perceptions--as
many believed the crisis was deliberately created as thought
the problem was a genuine one. When the average attitude in
each of the eight communities is tabulated, and then each
locale ranked on the extent to which people say the energy is
real, a strong correlation is found. Those communities with
the best helping systems are most likely to say that the
crisis is real--in Royal Oak 63 percent, compared to only 35
percent in Warren. The correlation value is a high +.74
across the eight cities: the stronger the helping system,
the more people believe the energy crisis is real.

Voting behavior is a second instance of how healthy
networks are associated with residents responding to events
beyond their borders. Information on the 1976 presidential
election was gathered one year after the helping network
study was completed. In Royal Oak 75 percent of the eligible
registered voters went to the polls in November, 1976, compared to only 52 percent in Pontiac. A rank correlation
occurs between the amount of voting in the 1976 presidential
election and the communities' health level that is strongly
positive (+.76)--the stronger the helping system the greater
the probability that people voted (see Appendix Table V-5).
These patterns illustrate the tie between community helping
networks and various other ways to describe a community as
healthy.

WELL-BEING SCORES AND COMMUNITY HELPING

To what extent do we find a relationship that links the
levels of individual well-being measured in the survey
directly with the health rank of the community in which a
person lives? While there are clearly many factors that
shape the response of the individual to the problem load--
including neighborhood and individual social attributes--we
also find that the municipality plays a separate role of its
own. When we took all of these factors into account simultaneously, community ranked midway in the list of "explana-
tory variables."[4] Which community a person lived in shaped
his or her mental outlook and amount of reported distress-
depression independently of any other considerations of sex,
occupation, income, and neighborhood.

To illustrate the role of community in the well-being of the individual, we ranked each of the eight sample cities using the percentage of people who had a RISK score that was above the median for the entire group of people interviewed in all of the locations. Using the 1974 pattern there is some indication that strength of helping systems reduces risk to well-being. The healthiest community in terms of networks (Royal Oak) in 1974 ranked in a tie for the second lowest RISK score of all of the communities. In addition, Mt. Clemens which has the weakest helping system, had the third highest RISK score in 1974. By 1975, a clear pattern emerged among the eight communities: those with stronger helping systems are lower in risk to well-being (the rank order value is -.74). Thus we find that Royal Oak ranks first on helping and last in terms of the proportion of people who have more than the mid-point level on the RISK score; also, the exact opposite is true for Mt. Clemens--first on RISK and last on helping strength (see Table V-1).

TABLE V-1

Risk to Well-Being Score in Relation to the
Eight Municipalities
(Rank orders for 1974-1975)

		1974 RANK ON RISK SCORE	STRENGTH OF HELPING RANK	1975 RANK ON RISK SCORE
High strength	Royal Oak	(6.5)	(1)	(8)
	Lincoln Park	(1)	(2)	(4)
	St. Clair Shores	(6.5)	(3)	(7)
Medium strength	Livonia	(5)	(4)	(6)
	Troy	(4)	(5)	(3)
Low strength	Pontiac	(8)	(6)	(2)
	Warren	(2)	(7)	(5)
	Mt. Clemens	(3)	(8)	(1)

COMMUNITY AND UNIQUE HELPING PATHWAYS

Clearly the specific nature of helping in each community is shaped by a variety of influences. Each system has in fact its own unique attributes--a local style of

helping which includes the number and kind of helpers turned
to. Thus, we find that Royal Oak stresses the use of friends
and co-workers along with married couples relying on each
other heavily for problem helping. St. Clair Shores is
similar in terms of spouse and co-worker helping, but adds a
distinctive role for neighbor helping. Lincoln Park
emphasizes relative helping and deemphasizes the use of a
friend; Livonia stresses spouse helping and avoids neighbor
help. Troy is average for the use of various helpers, but
also is below average in using the neighbor. This is also
true for Warren and Mt. Clemens. However, the former
community also is limited in terms of spouse, relative, and
co-worker helping. Mt. Clemens is below average in the use
of every helper but that of co-worker. Pontiac stresses
informal helpers such as relatives, friends, and neighbors,
but tends to shun co-worker and formal helpers.[5]

Not only do communities have specific preferred
helpers, but the existence of special combinations of helpers
is unique to each locale. In Royal Oak it is a relative-
friend and relative-neighbor pairing that is preferred; in
Lincoln Park a relative is teamed up with formal helpers,
neighbors, and friends; in St. Clair Shores it is a relative
grouped with neighbor, friend, and co-worker. Mt. Clemens
has no significant helper links. Pontiac has a cluster
involving the neighbor that includes formal helpers, friends,
and relatives. In Warren formal helpers are linked to the
use of neighbor helping, although both tend to be rare; if
they occur at all, they are clustered. In Troy--the fast-
growing, affluent suburb of Detroit--friend helping forms a
pathway linking co-workers, neighbors, relatives, and formal
helpers (see Table V-2).

Just as we can note locally unique linkages between one
kind of helper and another, so there are also several idiosyncratic barriers to helper ties. These are situations
where the use of one type of helper is negatively correlated
(to a significant degree) with the use of another helper: in
effect, each is mutually exclusive of the other. Where are
some of these patterns manifested? They tend to predominate
in the unhealthy communities: Mt. Clemens has four of these;
Warren, three; and Pontiac, one. In the case of Mt. Clemens
there is a barrier between use of spouse for problem-coping
and the use of friends, co-workers, or formal helpers; a
barrier between relative helping and co-worker or formal
helpers; and between neighbor and co-worker helping. Warren
manifests barriers of helping between spouse and formal
helpers, between co-workers and relatives, and between
neighbors and co-workers.

Even the more healthy communities display blockages in
the use of various combinations of helpers. Thus, Troy has

the most complex set of boundaries surrounding the spouse as
a helper. Here the almost exclusive choice is the use of
that one helper and no others, or the obverse. Formal
helpers, relatives, friends, neighbors, and co-workers are
all "repelled" by the use of spouse as a problem helper.

THE CONTENT OF HELPING IN EACH COMMUNITY

We have explored the variety of links and barriers
among various helpers that provide a unique map or path of
helpers that are more evident in one community than another.
Although the average number of different behaviors for
problem-coping did not vary as much as the number of helpers
used, this intensivity describes special helping qualities
that distinguish particular cities. For example, referral
helping is stressed in both Royal Oak and Lincoln Park, but
it is restricted in both Warren and Mt. Clemens. "Taking
action" on a recent concern is stressed in both Troy and
Livonia, but not in St. Clair Shores and Pontiac. "Showing a
new way to look at a problem" is not the preferred helping
style in Warren, Mt. Clemens, and St. Clair Shores that it is
in Lincoln Park. However, "asking questions" is one style of
helping that both Lincoln Park and St. Clair Shores emphasize
compared to other cities (see Table V-3).
There are, of course, many other ways in which the
helping process is different in each of the eight sample
communities. Thus, in both Warren and Mt. Clemens, the weak
overall helping system is linked to a person going directly

TABLE V-2

Types of Helpers Stressed in each of the Eight Communities

	Spouse	Relative	Friend	Neighbor	Co-Worker	Formal System
Royal Oak	+		+		+	
Lincoln Park		+	−			
St. Clair Shores	+			+	+	
Livonia	+			−		
Troy				−		
Pontiac		+	+	+	−	−
Warren	−	−		−	−	
Mt. Clemens	−	−	−	−		−

to a formal helper without any contact from an informal helper. Such a pattern is very unusual in Pontiac where many formal helpers are screened via neighbor or relative contacts.

Clearly, one of the most important factors about the eight municipalities is the role of social isolation. While neighborhoos types and community pattern interact to determine who people turn to for help, it is particularly in the larger municipality that isolation may occur in regard to the use of formal helpers.

Yet even a neighborhood-level explanation of neighbor helping cannot be understood unless the norms of the wider community are taken into account as well. Moreover, while the neighborhood types heavily shape where help begins and ends, the wider community serves as the target of much neighborhood-based referral and gatekeeping. If that larger system is lacking in effective formal services, or if the speed with which one can gain access to any set of helpers varies, the effect on individual well-being is doubly affected.

TABLE V-3

Types of Helping Stressed in Each of the Eight Communities
(Above and below average patterns)

	"Just Listened"	"Asked Questions"	"Showed a new way to look at the problem"	"referred by telling or talking to someone else	"took action on the problem
Royal Oak				+	
Lincoln Park		+	+	+	+
St. Clair Shores		+	-		-
Livonia			+		+
Troy	+				+
Pontiac					-
Warren	-	-	-	-	
Mt. Clemens			-	-	

COMMUNITY HELPING SYSTEMS: AN OVERVIEW

The objective of this chapter was to explore a method for describing variances in the helping systems existing in sampled communities. We gave considerable attention to the correlation between the quality of these support systems and individual coping, and from there to individual and social health. In addition a health barometer was created to classify communities in terms of their helping resources and problem-coping. This was a general classification of the quality of a community's human support system.

The helping network project focuses heavily on the context of helping rather than on differences in the individual who seeks help. Helping is seen as the process of mobilizing resources for solving problems. In the community analyses presented in this chapter we examined who acted as helpers in each of the eight communities, the pathways to these helpers, and the kinds of helping behaviors that people engaged in and found helpful to them. There were significant differences by community type in who the helpers were, the uses of professionals, and the kinds of helper behaviors that were sought after and offered.

It appears that the risk of not getting any help for a problem is more a function of the community structure than it is of neighborhood structure.

Being located in different types of municipal communities affects not only the average number of different types of helpers a person uses to cope with problems, but also the kind of helping behaviors that occur. Some communities provide for a wide range of helping behaviors; others concentrate simply on emotional support; still others have helpers to take action or to refer the individual to others. These critical differences in helping behaviors are linked to individual well-being.

Helping analysis is not simply looking at the direct contacts that an individual makes with a helper. An individual is part of a system of networks that can provide resources or pathways to them. The individual may not know directly about a resource, but he or she may be in a context in which other people know about a resource and can provide that information. It is an issue of community social integration--patterns in which people relate to each other and to the community as a whole, and ways in which resources are coordinated and used for the common good--which can be contrasted with the disintegration of resources and linkages.

Measuring the helping systems of communities is one major way to define what is meant by a "good community" in the sense implied by Roland Warren's work (1970). Or perhaps it is the very essence of community itself: its capacity to

provide an environment of social support and to encourage the
individual to participate, to grow, to learn, and to draw on
the resources of the whole society.

WAYS TO USE THE HEALTH BAROMETER ANALYSIS

The major point we have tried to make is this: it is
possible to evaluate the social health of a community.
Several kinds of tools can be used. They can be applied to
such issues as the planning and evaluation of citizen voluntary programs. For example, if the neighbor is less used in
some communities than others, and the formal agencies are
used a great deal, wouldn't we want to focus our attention on
strengthening the neighborhood and the way in which neighbors
help each other, rather than on adding more agencies? By
contrast, if we find that a community shies away from using
professional helpers, wouldn't we want to discover why that
is happening, what the barriers are? Are they in the attitudes of the individuals in the community, are they in the
way in which the services have been given, or is it just that
not enough funding has been given to such programs?

TO SUM UP

Community diagnostic tools of the kind we have
described can help pinpoint weaknesses of a community. It is
in essence very much like a general medical checkup. We can
identify some of these problems before they reach the serious
stage. And this, perhaps, is one of the most valuable roles
for the kind of analysis presented here.
Once the community is in the throes of a recession,
once it is beset with a multitude of problems that are beyond
the capacity of its citizens alone to deal with, it is clear
that preventive action simply will not make any difference.
If the opportunity were offered of anticipating the
needs of a community before tensions became crises and
problems developed in ways that increased individual stress,
there is still no assurance that the economic investment in a
preventive strategy could occur in all but the most affluent
settings. Instead, the indicators utilized in this discussion of helping networks must be seen as promising leads
to aid in the best design of human services and cost
effectiveness.
Communities can compare themselves to others by means
of the network patterns that typify their residents.
Diagnostic strategies of this kind may initially serve only
as exercises for thinking about the goals and effectiveness

of helping in a given locale. While the differences we have
noted are useful to planning and other professional agencies,
the central fact is the predominance of informal helping that
cannot be directly altered by formal organizations. Such
organizations can gain a great deal of insight about how they
are reaching clients and serving their constituency by using
the techniques suggested in this chapter. But the municipal
community is a reality shaped by many social and political
factors. What we have described here may be more properly
seen as a resultant matrix drawn and placed as an overlay on
the map of a complex set of causes whose effects we have
traced.

CHAPTER VI

THE HELPING NETWORKS OF DIFFERENT
SOCIAL GROUPS

In this chapter we shall describe several patterns of problem-coping networks that occur for whites versus blacks, men compared to women, different age and income groups, and other social clusterings. These findings reflect the fact that strength and character of networks are not random phenomena. In particular, we seek to determine if sex, race, and age influence the number of recent concerns and life crises a person is liable to experience and the access he or she may have to help. It is therefore critical to the research we have conducted to review some of the major trends in these dynamics that our study reveals.

SEX AND RACE PATTERNS

The helping network survey included a range of central city and suburban neighborhoods whose ethnic composition reflects that of the Detroit metropolitan area. A total of 530 black residents cutting across 23 different neighborhoods in five separate cities is a significant portion of the total of approximately 2,500 persons interviewed in 1974. 1,333 of the individuals were women and 1,147 men. Four major groups will be compared for their separate patterns of problem experiences and helping: white men, white women, black men, and black women.

Does sex or race play a major role in determining the amount of life crises or recent concerns that an individual experiences? The trends are small but do show the following: women have a slightly higher average number of reported life crises than men of the same race, with black women having the greatest probability of experiencing at least one of these events during the preceding year--73 percent versus 63 percent for white women. For black men the figure is 67 percent and for white men 63 percent. However, in the case of recent

121

concerns race and sex differentials are reversed: more
whites--both men and women--report at least one such event
than do blacks of the same sex. The differences are small
and yet are statistically significant (See Appendix Table VI-
1). Yet the average number of recent concerns does not vary:
white men report such events with an average of 1.8 per
person compared to 1.7 for the other three groups.

Several differences in the kinds of helpers that are
most used are linked to race and sex. Both black men and
black women report us of neighbor help more than do whites of
either sex. At the same time, independently measured amounts
of neighboring show blacks slightly less likely to see a
neighbor more than once a month (see Appendix Table VI-2).

In an earlier study comparing black and white neighborhoods (Warren, 1975) the theory was proposed that blacks tend
to be "locked in" to neighborhoods because of housing
discrimination. At the same time, blacks also tend to be
"land-locked" more than whites--i.e., to have a smaller geographic base of community. Taken together, these patterns
lead to greater use of neighbors not by preference, but by
necessity. The findings in this helping network study tend
to confirm this more important neighbor role for blacks compared to whites.

There are additional differences when blacks and whites
are compared. Relative helping is more frequent for blacks
than whites, and it is especially high for black women (50
percent compared to 28 percent (See Table VI-1).) In terms
of formal helpers both black men and women are more likely
than whites to seek the help of clergy. This trend is also
found for use of police for helping with recent concerns. In
terms of professional helpers, white women use a doctor more
than other groups, with blacks using counselor help (social
worker or mental health professional) somewhat more than do
whites.

In terms of the total variety of helpers used, black
men rank higher than other groups, while white men rank
lowest. This difference occurs for formal and informal help
alike.

There is another differential: spouse helping for
married black women is lower than for white women: 72 percent compared to 82 percent.

When we turn to the kind of help provided several
significant differences also can be found. Males--regardless
of race--are more likely to obtain helping that includes
"asking questions" by the helper than is the case for women.
Black women receive a significantly lower amount of "just
listening" than do black men. Blacks regardless of sex are
more likely to report that their helpers "show a new way to
look at the problem" than whites do. The same trend also

occurs for referral helping: blacks receive more than whites (see Table VI-2).

TABLE VI-1

Race and Sex of the Individual in Relation to the Use of Each Type of Helper in Coping with Recent Concerns

	White		Black	
	Female	Male	Female	Male
Spouse*	82%	82%	72%	85%
Friend	41	39	45	52
Relative	40	28	50	41
Co-worker#	41	44	38	41
Neighbor	25	22	35	43
Clergy	3	2	9	8
Teacher	3	5	4	4
Police	7	8	10	16
Doctor	11	6	6	6
Counselor@	5	5	9	8
N =	1040	902	285	245

*Includes married persons only
#Includes employed persons only
@Includes social worker, psychologist and psychiatrist

TABLE VI-2

Race and Sex of the Individual in Relation to the Kinds of Helping Behaviors Received

	White		Black	
	Female	Male	Female	Male
"Just listened"	79%	76%	70%	82%
"Asked questions"	54	60	50	64
"Showed me a new way to look at the problem"	32	28	34	35
Referred by telling about or talking to someone else	20	21	26	27
"Took action"	28	25	23	27

Overall, the major impact of sex and race on helping tends to be in terms of the extensivity of helping for black men and the restricted social support helping for black women. Do these trends have any bearing on the well-being (RISK) scores discussed in Chapter III? Regardless of race or other factors, women tend to show higher RISK scores than men. This pattern has been found in other research dealing with mental health symptomatology and has been a point of some controversy as to whether women find it more acceptable to report psychosomatic complaints and depression than do men.[1] But beyond this "universal" difference, our survey finds that race is a further consideration in reported well-being. Thus, only 32% of black males are above the median for RISK, while 70 percent of black women are. The difference between the sexes in the white sample is smaller: 39 versus 61 percent.

The helping patterns we have discussed point to weaknesses in the social support role of helpers of black women, and show that both a wider variety and a more balanced range of helping behaviors for black men may explain why these two groups have even greater patterns of the basic male-female differences in RISK to well-being than we noted for whites.

FAMILY INCOME AND HELPING

While a common-sense view might give great weight to economic level as a major source of differences in problem load and helping, in fact, our data show a more limited role in terms of the measures we have utilized in the helping network study. Life crises do not rise with declining family income—the highest levels are for people with family incomes in the middle range: fifteen to twenty thousand dollars. For recent concerns, the highest average occurs for the group earning ten to fifteen thousand dollars. However, as income goes up, there is a pattern in which having at least one recent concern does increase in probability—56 percent for low-income and 82 percent for high-income families (See Appendix Table VI-3). Moreover, risk to well-being is clearly higher for low-income families—63 percent are above the median level. However, for other income groups there is virtually no variation.

While there are some important trends based on income level, the largest contrasts occur for persons of the same family income category but of different race. There are significant differences for black and white groups at the same income level in 25 times out of a possible 50 comparisons (shown in Appendix Table VI-4). However, both spouse and co-worker helping is clearly related to family income level apart from the role of race: both go up with economic level. In the case of white respondents, only help-seeking from relatives goes down with rising family income--from 49 percent for those earning less than $6,000 a year to 30 percent for those with earnings of $25,000 or more. By the same token, co-worker help-seeking--which goes up with income regardless of race--rises more steeply for the black respondent: the differential is ten to forty percent for blacks compared to 17 to 34 percent for whites.

Blacks tend to rely on neighbors for helping more than whites do regardless of family income level. Differences are large and statistically significant for all comparisons.

In all but the low-income comparision, blacks rely on friend helping more than whites do.

Clergy help is higher for blacks than whites at three of the five income intervals; it is particularly evident in the middle income categories of between $10,000 and $25,000.

Use of police as helpers is higher for blacks at all income levels, but does not attain statistical significance in the lowest and highest income groupings.

Teacher, doctor, and counselor helping reverses direction by race at given income levels. Lower income whites tend to use both teachers and doctors more, while among blacks with less than $6,000 income counselor (which includes social worker) is used twice as much as whites. The direction of this differential holds for counselor at all but the income level $6,000 to $10,000. Doctors are used more by whites at all income levels up to $15,000 and then again at the $25,000 and above level.

The total range of extensivity (variety of helpers) does not consistently increase with family income level. This is especially true for whites. For blacks, there is a steady rise to a high in the income group $15,000 to $24,999 and then a decline for the highest income group.

Our overall conclusion is that race is a more important variable in the shaping of helping and problem-coping than is income. Another way to describe the situation is to say that it is misleading to compare level of income as it affects helping networks unless one also divides the group evaluated into white and black segments of the population.

FORMAL EDUCATION AND HELPING PATTERNS

In contrast to family income, the role of education level seems to impact problem load and helping patterns rather directly apart from racial composition. In terms of life crises there is virtually no differential level based on education. The exception is that persons with one to three

years of college have a higher average--1.4--than do other
groups. However, in regard to recent concerns there are very
large differences based on educational level of the individual. Thus, four out of five college graduates have at least
one recent concern compared to only 54 percent of those with
eight years or less of formal schooling. At the same time,
however, the group with the highest average of recent concerns is the segment having one to three years of college--
the same group with a high life-crises average (see Appendix
Table VI-5). Clearly this group is often carrying a higher
problem load than either less educated or more educated segments of the population.

Does the level of education affect the kind of help
people receive? The answer to this is affirmative in terms
of the active forms versus the more passive or socially
supportive forms of helping. The major split occurs between
those who have at least some college education and persons
who do not. Those with college experience are more likely
than others to have a helper who "takes action on the
problem" and gives referrals. The persons with a four year
degree is higher than average on four kinds of helping:
"asking questions," "showing a new way," referrals, and
"action" helping. Persons with eight years of education or
less get significantly below average "asking questions" and
"action" helping (see Table VI-3).

TABLE VI-3

Educational Level of the Individual in Relations to
the Kind of Help Received

	"just listened"	"asked ques- tions"	"showed a new way"	"referred"	"took action"
8 or less years of educa- tion	76%	44% –	28%	20%	17% –
9 to 11 years of educa- tion	76	53	29	20	24
high school graduate	80	57	32	19	23
1-3 years of college	81	65 +	36	25	36 +
college graduate	75	66 +	40 +	33 +	35 +
post-graduate education	80	68 +	36	29 +	36 +

While greater formal education tends to increase the variety of helpers a person uses, the pattern is neither consistent nor dramatic. As education rises, for example, relative (kin) help-seeking declines. Professional helpers such as physician, psychologist, psychiatrist, or social worker are used most often by people with some college who did not receive a degree. Teacher helping goes from one percent for those who only completed primary schooling to eleven percent for individuals with post-graduate education. Co-worker helping is highest for those at the extremes of low or high education. Friend helping has a clear boundary: people who went to college use friends more often than those who did not (see Appendix Table VI-6).

The educational levels which are associated with a greater emphasis on active helping are also those which show significantly lower RISK scores. Thus, college graduates have the smallest proportion of people above the median level—37 percent compared to 59 percent for persons with 9 to 11 years of education. People with one to three years of college and those with postgraduate educations also show lower RISK scores compared to individuals with less formal education.

HELPING NETWORKS AND MARITAL STATUS

A basic consideration in the role of helping networks is the central role played by the spouse. Our earlier findings indicate that an individual who is married tends to rely on a spouse for helping with recent concerns 82 percent of the time. The spouse is implicated in over half of all helping transactions. In terms of well-being, it is not unique in this study to find that the divorced or separated person has a greater distress level. Thus, 68 percent of the former and 75 percent of the latter are above the median for the RISK index. The widowed segment of the population is between the married and single groups and the separated and divorced groups in terms of high RISK scores. In terms of recent concerns, both the never married and the divorced have the highest averages, with the widowed and the separated the lowest (See Appendix Table VI-7).

Does the kind of help provided differ by marital status? Single individuals show a higher than average level of "action" helping but a deficit in terms of "just listening" social support. Married persons show average levels on all five categories of helping behaviors. Divorced are below average in three kinds of helping: "just listening," "asking questions," and referral. Widowed persons are also below average on three forms: "asking

questions," referrals, and "action" help. The separated
persons in the survey show below average help in all but
referrals (See Table VI-4).

RACE, SEX, AND MARITAL STATUS: THREE KEY FACTORS IN SHAPING
HELPING NETWORKS

    Several large differences emerge both between same-sex
respondents of different race and across race groupings. In
terms of spouse help-seeking, black females are unique in
their lower reliance on spouse; black men are highest in
their reliance on spouse. Relative help-seeking is significantly higher for married blacks regardless of race; at the
same time, white married women use relative help more than
white men. Black married men are the highest in the probability of help-seeking from relatives--43 percent compared
to only 27 percent for white married men.
    Neighbor helping is highest among married black men,
although both male and female married blacks use neighbor
more than either sex of married whites.
    Friend helping is significantly higher for married men
and women who are white than neighbor helping, but all
married blacks use a friend helper more than whites.
    The patterns for co-workers are misleading because of
the differences in employment between white women and black
women, but the differences noted are not entirely due to
working status.
    Married black respondents, both male and female, use
clergy, police, and counselors significantly more than do
whites. In particular, the married black female uses clergy
and the married black male turns to police. By contrast, it

TABLE VI-4

Marital Status of the Individual and the Type of Helping
Behavior Received

	"just listened"	"asked ques- tions"	"showed a new way"	"referred"	"Took action"
Now married	80%	58%	32%	22%	27%
Never married	68 -	56	38 +	33 +	31
Divorced	71 -	52 -	34	17 -	24
Separated	64 -	51 -	26 -	24	18 -
Widowed	74	48 -	28	18	16 -

is the married white female who most often uses the doctor
for helping.

Overall, our findings indicate that the married black
respondent has the widest helping network, while the most
limited one is found for the married white female. At the
same time, married blacks of both sexes use a wider variety
of helpers than married whites of either sex (See Appendix
Table VI-8).

What about the use of helpers for the nonmarried portion of the sample? This includes separated, widowed,
divorced, and never married individuals. By implication the
important role of spouse helping may be compensated for by
the use of other helpers. Among the separated or divorced
(particularly black men and white women) some help-seeking
still includes the spouse. Relative help, particularly for
blacks, is far higher among nonmarried than married
respondents. Thus, we have noted earlier that white married
women rely on relatives 36 percent of the time, while for
their unmarried "sisters" the percentage is 51; for black
women, the increase for non-married is fourteen percent; for
white males, twelve percent; for black nonmarrieds it is
seven percent.

Friend help for nonmarrieds is highest among men
regardless of race. White nonmarrieds show a gain of friend
helping of 22 percent compared to 36 percent for marrieds;
the gain for the nonmarried blacks is thirteen percent.

Co-worker help is highest for both male and female
nonmarrieds among blacks. However, the highest level of
help-seeking from co-workers is found among white male nonmarrieds. Compared to married white males this level is
slightly lower. By contrast, nonmarried white females seek
help twice as often from co-workers as their married counter-
parts. Co-worker helping for nonmarried blacks is lower than
the level for married blacks. These findings tend to reflect
the retirement status of many older black respondents.

In regard to formal helpers, nonmarried white females
show the highest use of the physician as a helper. White
males and black females both have high levels of help-seeking
from a counselor. Nonmarried black males use police for
helpers significantly more than other nonmarried respondents.
Clergy helping is significantly higher for blacks compared to
whites.

For nonmarried compared to married white males,
counselor, relative, and friend help-seeking are significantly higher; for nonmarried white females, relative,
friend, and co-worker show significantly higher levels; for
nonmarried black men, friend and police help-seeking is
higher compared to marrieds; while for nonmarried black

women, only relative help-seeking is significantly higher
(see Appendix Table VI-9).

We can conclude that the role of spouse helping is not
compensated for by the use of formal helpers but rather by
informal ones. While there is evidence of greater use of
selected informal helpers such as kin, in general, the
variety of help sought by nonmarried persons regardless of
sex or race is less than that sought by married individuals.
The decline in such help-seeking is especially evident for
blacks and for white males.

A comparison of the help-seeking of black and white
housewives underscores the race differential in spouse
helping. In general, the variety of helping sought is less
for white than black women. Neighbor helping is markedly
higher for black housewives as is relative helping. Clergy,
teacher, and counselor helping are twice as high for black
compared to white housewives, while doctor helping is higher
for whites. Help-seeking from the spouse is nearly twice as
high for white housewives as compared to black. The
differential in marriage rates by race accounts for little of
this difference (see Appendix Table VI-10).

Let us now compare the helping network for different
sex, race, employment, and marital characteristics of the
survey sample. A simple additive index is constructed by
adding the percentage of use for each of the ten types of
helpers that a person could report utilizing for recent concerns. The range goes from the highest for employed black
men to the lowest for unemployed black women--305 versus 136
respectively (see Table VI-5).

Of the various groups above the average in helping network extensivity--number of helpers per problem--men are
found in seven of the eleven clusters, while women are found
in eight of the below-average eleven groupings. Blacks are
found in six of the upper eleven groups and four of the
bottom eleven.

Retired status is the lowest for all groups except
black unemployed women. The most extensive helping networks
for white women are used by those who are formally employed.
Employment status is also associated with the greatest network extensivity for black men and women alike.

TO SUM UP

The trends we have noted in this chapter suggest that
helping is shaped by, but is not a simple function of, social
or economic position. Individuals may have many significant
cultural or ethnic preferences for seeking help which are
only somewhat modified by geographic locale or problem

circumstances. However, the extent to which any helping
transaction will occur and the form it will take can be seen
as partly shaped by the demographic profile of the person and
partly by the perceived and real community (neighborhood or
municipality) in which he or she functions.

Regardless of social grouping, networks of help-seeking
are largely informal. At the same time, these natural
systems are neither uniform nor self-contained.

To round out our perspective on helping we now will
turn to formal and professional helpers and identify the
major patterns of their use as shown in the comprehensive
survey findings.

TABLE VI-5

Summary Measure of the Variety of Helpers Used for Dealing
With Recent Concerns for Selected Combinations of
Employment/Marital Statuses of Respondents

Employed black men	305%*
Married black men	298
Employed black women	277
Employed white women	268
Married black women	262
Unemployed black men	261
Unemployed white women	250
Unemployed white men	244
Employed white men	239
Not married black men	234
White married men	230
Black housewife	225
Married white women	224
Not married black women	203
White housewife	201
Not married white male	199
Not married white female	198
Retired white men	172
Retired black men	166
Retired black women	164
Retired white women	147
Unemployed black women	136

*Percent is computed by adding helping for each of ten
possible helpers used for recent concerns.

CHAPTER VII

HELPING NETWORKS AND THE USE OF FORMAL SERVICES

The previous chapters have reviewed the patterns of help-seeking and some of the dynamics involved in obtaining help from a variety of sources. If a problem is recognized as being serious enough to warrant professional attention, a person is often faced with a bewildering array of possibilities. Such decisions have been linked by researchers to the existence of past experience, knowledge, cultural bias, and the availability of particular professional helpers.[1] The chain of supporters and bearers of information about professionals can be referred to as a person's lay referral network.

In Gurin's national survey (1960) of those individuals who said they actually went to a professional for help, a majority reported that they did so on their own. Yet several other studies show that most people require some external support in seeking professional help.[2] Studies of admissions to mental hospitals indicate that lower status people are likely to be more severely "afflicted" at time of admission to professional care, and therefore are more likely to need a great deal of assistance.[3] Individuals from weak social settings are less likely to have informal networks of support referral. Individuals in such settings are more isolated and alienated from a wide variety of informal and formal community institutions. For them the referral process is much more subject to change, fragmentation, and unreliability.[4]

In this chapter we shall document the role of formal helping as it relates specifically to the physician, mental health professional, social worker, and such intermediate helpers as clergy, police, and teachers. We shall explore how the probability of formal system usage is conditioned by informal helping patterns. The relationship between problem load and use of formal helpers will also be explored. Finally, we shall attempt to place in perspective a concept

of the range of formal service agencies and professionals as
complementary, competitive, or coordinated counterpoints to
informal helping.

WHO IS PERCEIVED TO BE HELPFUL?

A major theme of much past research on the use of
formal helpers is the issue of barriers to obtaining help.
This problem was recently highlighted in a study of auto
workers conducted as part of the United Automobile Workers
analysis of the use made of contract fringe services in the
health and mental health sphere. In a report from the
director of the National Institute of Health in 1976 the
study by Glasser and others was cited in terms of workers in
Pontiac, Michigan. A variety of blockages to using UAW benefit mental health services was identified including lack of
"belief in the usefulness of mental health treatment
services."[5] Thus, the NIMH director's review of the Pontiac
study concludes that "despite the trend toward including
mental health benefits in insurance programs--perhaps one day
including a national health insurance program--the distribution of mental health care may not become more equitable"
(Brown, 1976:9).
In the helping network study several questions were
asked about the professional services and their effectiveness
which are pertinent to the problems described in the NIMH
report. To measure the potential for using various kinds of
helpers--and also to evaluate indirectly the past use of a
given helper--all people interviewed in the follow-up 1975
panel were asked the following question:

> How helpful are the (listed) kinds of people when there
> is something on your mind that you need to talk over--
> something personal that you are concerned about?

For each named helper respondents could select the following
responses:

> "a great deal of help"
> "some help"
> "little help"
> "no help at all"

On the average each of the eleven helpers is ranked
very helpful by 27 percent of the sample, while two out of
five people said the helpers are of little or no help. There
are dramatic differences in who is considered most or least
helpful among various kinds of helpers mentioned. Spouse

ranks first and is far ahead of any of the others with over
seven in ten persons saying very helpful. A distant second
is the physician with two out of five people saying very
helpful and one in four persons saying little or no help.
Clergy, relatives, psychologist, and teacher are grouped at
intervals of two percentage points as helpers who are above
the average in terms of being very helpful. Police, friends,
and the social worker are all just below the average level.
At the bottom of the list in terms of perceived helpfulness
are co-workers and neighbors (see Table VII-1).

What is most striking about the ranking is that a
number of helpers are highly rated, but in fact they are used
relatively rarely. For example, we found (in Chapter III)
that teachers are not used often for recent concerns or life
crises and yet they are relatively high in terms of perceived
helpfulness. This is also true of the psychologist.

If we group all helpers into four categories—those who
are used often but not highly rated, those used often and
highly rated, those not used often and not highly rated and
those with high evaluation but low usage—we can note some
overall discrepancies (see Table VII-2). Spouse, relative,
doctor, and clergy all show consistent patterns: they are
seen to be helpful and they are used relatively often for
problems. The social worker and police are not used very
often and are below average in perceived helpfulness. There
are several inconsistant helpers. First we find that
neighbors, friends, and co-workers—while used quite often
for problem-coping—are not seen as being as helpful as many
kinds of people used far less for helping. In a second
discrepant cluster we find the psychologist and the teacher;
highly rated, but seldom sought out for help.

TABLE VII-1

The Perceived Helpfulness of Different Kinds of Helpers
(Percent "very helpful")

Spouse	72%	Police	28%
Doctor	40%	Friends	26%
Clergy	37%	Social worker	25%
Relative	35%	Co-worker	16%
Psychologist	33%	Neighbor	14%
Teacher	31%		
		Average	27%

N = 1663

MENTAL HEALTH SERVICES: SATISFACTION AND USAGE

In the case of the psychologist, the high evaluation
seems to reflect deference to a professional role and not an
evaluation of actual services provided. Only four percent of
the survey sample reported using a private psychiatrist or
community mental health clinic. By contrast, thirty percent
of the population used a hospital or clinic service to deal
with recent concerns or a life crisis in 1974. In other
words, the attitudes about mental health professionals appear
to be largely shaped by hypothetical rather than real situations. Actual users are a small group, with many people who
have never used professional mental health services appearing
to rate the individuals in such occupations rather
positively.

Are there specific expectations about mental health
professionals that could influence how people evaluate such
helpers?

As part of a series of questions that sought to measure
how individuals feel about their treatment at the hands of

TABLE VII-2

Perceptions of Helpers and their Usage

	Perceived as helpful above the average	Perceived as helpful at or below the average
High Usage	Spouse Relative Doctor Clergy	Neighbor Friend Co-worker
Low Usage	Psychologist Teacher	Social Worker Police

formal helpers, a set of questions about six dimensions of
the users' experience was developed. These include "trust,"
"understanding," "concern," "respect," "competence," and
"helpfulness." For every kind of service agency contacted
the people surveyed in 1975 were asked whether it was "true"
or "not true" that "the people they dealt with" treated them
this way or could be judged to have the particular attribute
listed. Overall, all agencies tend to have 80 percent
positive scores. The fact that 62 percent of the panel
interviewed in 1975 had some contact with a hospital or
clinic makes this the most frequently used service. Very
high ratings result: 95 percent on trust, competence,
respect, and helpfulness are reported (see Table VII-3).

For the small number of people using either a private
psychologist or psychiatrist—one in 25 persons interviewed—
five of the six evaluation criteria are lower than for contact with clinics or hospitals. In the case of the even
smaller group of individuals reporting they have used the
services of a community mental health clinic—less than three
percent of the entire sample—evaluations of the experience
are still lower. In terms of helpfulness mental health
clinics receive a 76 percent positive rating compared to 95
percent for hospitals and 89 percent for private mental
health services (see Table VII-3).

These patterns suggest that when mental health services
are involved they are not as positively evaluated as the

TABLE VII-3

Evaluation of Health and Mental Health Services
that are Used

"Which of the following is true about the people you deal
with:"

	Clinic or hospital	Private psychologist or psychiatrist	Community Mental Health Clinic
You can trust them	95%	89%	82%
They show under-standing	93	85	86
The show concern	89	85	86
They show respect	95	96	88
They are competent	92	85	80
They are helpful	95	89	76
	N = 1092	N = 71	N = 45

global assessment of the "psychologist" category used to compare different kinds of problem helpers. To further underscore this trend a question was asked about services sought,
but not obtained: It shows a high complaint rate relative to
other professional and health services. Thus when people
were asked:

> In the last year or so, has this happened to you or
> your family: "Tried to get in touch with someone in an
> agency or organization to get some help, but didn't get
> any help?"

Overall one out of ten people interviewed in 1975 said they
had indeed been through an experience implied in the question. A range of governmental agencies was mentioned as the
chief offenders (see Appendix Table VII-1). Of the 169
people reporting the frustration of blocked help-seeking from
a formal agency, four percent mentioned a hospital or clinic
and five percent mentioned a mental health facility.
Considering that under three percent used such services at
all this is an above average reporting of a help-seeking
barrier. By contrast, since 62 percent of the sample used a
clinic or hospital in the same period of time and the complaint rate is only four percent, there is further evidence
of the relative dissatisfaction with community mental health
services versus general health services.

These patterns of perceptions and question responses
suggest the reasons for the underutilization which was discussed in the Pontiac survey of UAW workers. If mental
health professionals are used very rarely to deal with a
range of potentially stressful problems, it tends to underscore the view that general social stigma and other barriers
mentioned in the President's Report On Mental Health (1978)
are not the only ones to be considered in gauging the need or
demand for professional services.

While most people do not use professional mental health
services until a problem is very serious indeed (see Appendix
Table VII-2), the major import of the patterns we have
described is to see what happens when help is in fact sought.
Whether such services are perceived to be potentially helpful
may be less important than the actual experiences of
individuals in using such resources.

PATHWAYS TO FORMAL SERVICES: REFERRAL AND FILTERING

A major consideration in our analysis of formal helpers
is the fact that such contact must be understood within a
specific rather than a general social context. In other

words, much of the discussion about barriers to service
utilization described very broad social forces and perceptual
dynamics such as problem "labeling" which are useful starting
points for understanding how people react to symptoms and
when they are motivated to seek help. But the helping network study examines a more delimited set of "conditioning
factors" in the social environment of the problem
experiencer. Here, we are speaking of such considerations as
the neighborhood and community context. Use of formal
helpers is affected by the real and perceived neighborhood
context: individuals in anomic settings are three times as
likely--18 percent versus six percent--to report trying
unsuccessfully to get help from an agency than individuals in
integral neighborhoods (see Appendix Table VII-3). Residents
of different communities (in Mt. Clemens eight percent compared to 20 percent in St. Clair Shores) have significantly
greater or lesser probabilities of seeking help from
professionals and formal agencies. We also noted earlier
several demographic, racial, age, and educational factors
(see Chapter IV) which alter the probability that a person
will use formal helping in dealing with a recent concern.
     One major process which helps explain the contextual
differences that lengthen or shorten the pathway to formal
service utilization is the filtering and referral role of
informal helpers. This basic principle about the use of
formal services can be derived not only from the helping network study but a wide variety of other research as well:
*formal (or more particularly, professional) help for problems
occurs within a framework of ongoing social relationships.*
People rarely use a professional service without first being
referred to it or recommended to use it by someone else. But
it is important to also emphasize a corollary to this
principle: *helping is not a self-conscious and independent
process from normal information exchange.* To conduct the
helping network study we had to artificially distinguish
help-seeking from social support and a "web of social
fabric." This methodological and heuristic requirement of the
research should not disguise the overlap which makes so
invisible the "social service" role of neighbors, friends,
relatives, and other informal helpers.
     The pathway to formal services may involve referral by
word-of-mouth or actually taking someone to the service. In
still many other instances it is a very indirect learning and
screening that is built into a given local neighborhood value
system, an ethnic culture, or a social group "grape vine."
Individuals hear about agencies and professionals and form
opinions as to which community organization can be of most
help.

Let us illustrate this filtering process by once again taking a look at the people who reported they used health or mental services for recent concerns in the year prior to their being interviewed. In fact, we have included a range of various services including civil rights groups, legal services, and welfare agencies. For each of nine different services--public and private--people were asked to say if they had "a friend who works in this kind of organization." This is a very indirect basis of a helping network tie or pathway to using such a service.

We find that all of the services indicated are used more if a person knows someone in that kind of work. In terms of hospitals and clinics, 25 percent used such services for recent concerns or life crises if they knew friends working in such settings compared to fourteen percent usage for those who did not. Using a private psychiatrist is eleven times more likely with a friend working in such a place than when there is none. For use of a private social service agency the ratio is over thirteen to one. For a community mental health clinic the probability is more than two to one that such a service will be used if a person already knows someone who works in this kind of organization. For a civil rights group the odds are twenty to one that a person will use this agency more if they have a friend working there (see Table VII-4).

But there is a more direct version of the filtering concept. This is the simultaneous use of other helpers where help is sought from a formal or professional helper.

Of the total volume of helping that occurs for recent concerns, only a relatively small fraction--twelve percent-- implicates formal service agencies or professionals. In other words, for every helping contact that occurs for a

TABLE VII-4

Having a Friend Who Works in a Given Kind of Agency
and Use of that Form of Service

Percent Who Use

	Has friend who works there	Does not have friend
Hospital or clinic	25%	14%
Community mental health clinic	8%	3%
Private psychologist or psychiatrist	22%	2%

formal helper, there are eight contacts made with informal helpers.

We have already seen that who is used for helping and what is provided differs significantly by neighborhood, community, and individual social circumstances. Not only is the total volume of helping greater for informal helpers compared to formal, but the probability that an individual will use the latter for a recent concern without the simultaneous contact with an informal helper as well is quite low. On the average--for the entire sample of 2,500 people we interviewed in 1974--about two percent of those who had a problem and sought any help at all used a formal system helper exclusively.

To describe more vividly the normal way in which helping occured in the sample interviewed, Chart VII-1 depicts each of three systems of helping as overlapping circles: primary--spouse, friends, and relatives; proximal--neighbors and co-workers; and the formal system--doctor, clergy, police, social worker or mental health professional, and teacher. The radius of each circle is proportional to the amount of helping for recent concerns that is contributed by each type of system. The formal includes twelve percent, the proximal 46 percent, and the primary 68 percent. These do not total 100 percent since each kind of helper can be used simultaneously. The segments that overlap--AB, AC, BC, and ABC define the linkages between one system of help and another. The total is 85 percent since fifteen percent of the individuals with recent concerns seek no help at all. Of the helping which does occur, 35 percent overlaps systems, while 50 percent does not. In effect, two out of every five helping transactions cross a system.

Just as the probability of using a formal helper varies by neighborhood and community, so does the use of formal helpers as part of a "filtering" process--i.e., simultaneous use of other helpers. Thus, in the community of Royal Oak only six percent of professional help occurs without the use of a primary or proximal helper or both. By contrast, in Mt. Clemens two-thirds of formal helper use is exclusive of any other helping system. In Warren this is true of over one-third of formal helper usage (see Appendix Table VI-4). The anomic neighborhood ranks first in the proportion of people using formal helpers without also using primary or proximal; the integral neighborhood ranks sixth (see Appendix Table IV-7).

On an overall basis, ignoring neighborhood and other variations, the role of the formal/professional helper is a relatively constant one in the two periods of data collection--1974 and 1975. There is approximately a one in seven probability that a formal or professional helper is

CHART VII - 1

Venn Diagram Depicting the Interrelations
of Community Helping Systems
Based on the Data of the
Helping Network Study

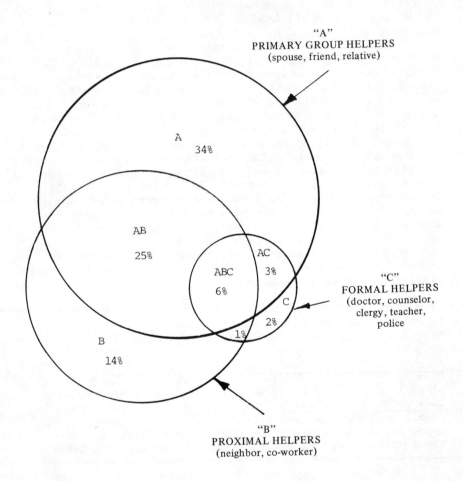

"A"
PRIMARY GROUP HELPERS
(spouse, friend, relative)

A
34%

AB
25%

AC
3%

ABC
6%

C
"C"
FORMAL HELPERS
(doctor, counselor,
clergy, teacher,
police

2%

1%

B
14%

"B"
PROXIMAL HELPERS
(neighbor, co-worker)

implicated in a helping transaction. (Refer to Charts V and VI in Chapter III.) Moreover, it is also true that we find initial use of formal helpers tends to be highly correlated with their subsequent use. This is not however the case for professional helpers--doctors, social workers, psychiatrists, etc.

While initially (in the 1974 interviews) use of professional helpers tends to occur independently of the linkage to primary, proximal, and formal helpers, a markedly different pattern is found in the follow-up interviews of 1975. Here, use of professionals is highly correlated with the use of other kinds of helping systems. At the same time, we also find that starting off by using other than professional systems tends to mean continued minimum use of professionals for helping.

The patterns we have noted suggest that, in general, problem-coping may start with professionals as part of a team of helpers. If they have not been included from the outset, they are not likely to be called upon later. But if they are used it is seldom without an implied "filtering" or simultaneous use of other helpers.

As helping emerges from informal sources it tends to be self-contained, especially if primary group members are the key resources. This in turn mitigates the need for formal or professional helpers. Formal helpers are more likely to be drawn in at a later point or not at all. If help does initially include formal helpers--clergy, police, teachers-- this tends to preclude going back to primary helpers on the one hand or professionals on the other. Proximal helpers-- co-workers and neighbors--can be utilized more readily along with the formal ones.

PREDICTING THE DEMAND FOR FORMAL SERVICES

An explicit focus of our entire analysis is the question of how a variety of informal social bonds increases or reduces the probability that an individual will utilize formal/professional service systems in coping with a range of problems related to quality of life, life stress, and health. Putting the issue another way:

> What is the relationship between self-help or informal problem-coping resources and the demand for professional services?

Essentially we are arguing that system reporting and information seeking (along with actual utilization of a range of social health services) is inextricably bound up in the

individual's "community attachment." Moreover, in contemporary urban society, a variety of forms of such attachment produces differential effects whose totality creates a
demand on professional helping that is mediated via the role
of screening and referral processes of these same natural
social ties. This linkage to professional services and programs is conditioned as much by the level of attachment of an
individual to informal systems of helping, by the trust level
in formal versus peer advice, and by the expertise in help-
seeking as by the level of problems and crises that are
experienced.

We are not using the term "demand" in a literal
economic sense. We are not able to translate the various
primary, proximal, and even formal helpers' services into a
dollar-and-cents formula. Rather, we are seeking to describe
how the various systems of social support or what we refer to
as helping networks filter or facilitate the use of specific
kinds of human resources for problem-coping.

To build our model of formal service demand we shall
consider the following five key factors: how many life
crises a person has experienced, how many recent concerns,
the extensivity (number of helpers) and intensivity (number
of helping behaviors), and the amount of helping that is
based on "just listening." Taking the various health and
social services listed—nine in all—we can ask the question:
"What is the probability that a person will use at least one
of these services?" In turn, this question can be modified
to the query: "What is the probability that a person will
use one or more services given that they have a set of problems and that they use informal helpers to a given extent
and with particular kinds of help received?" When this hypothetical question is applied to the actual data of the
helping network study we find a particular set of values that
emerge to respond to the inquiry. Thus, as life-crisis problem load goes up, a sharp increase in the use of formal
services occurs. For no crisis one-fourth of the sample uses
at least one of the services. With one crisis the level rises
to two out of five people and climbs steeply to nearly four
out of five where a person experiences five life crises in
one year.

Problem load for recent concerns shows a similar but
somewhat less precipitous climb in formal service demand with
number of events. Thus with no recent concerns there is a 31
percent usage of one or more of the nine formal services and
a rise to 50 percent with five recent concerns.

How does the helping pattern for recent concerns affect
formal service demand? We find that it tends to be moderate
—it rises to 44 percent when three helpers are involved but
then stabilizes and then declines somewhat. Where the amount

of helping which is the most common form is taken into
account--"just listening"--demand does not exceed 40 percent
until five recent concerns are experienced. When the full
range of helping behaviors is taken into account--listening
and other, more active helping--then the role of informal
networks suggests a leveling of demand for formal services
despite an increase in recent-concern problem load. Thus,
with one concern and all forms of helping included there is
actually less use of formal helpers--28 percent--than when an
individual does not experience any recent concerns--33 percent. At the two-concern level the demand for services has
increased to the same level as the situation of an individual
not having any concerns. Even with eight recent concerns--a
rare occurrence--demand for at least one formal service does
not reach beyond 43 percent. (Chart VII-2 shows the trends
in the use of services that we have described.)

        What happens if we carry out the same analysis of
recent-concern problem load and the helping patterns for such
specific services as hospitals, private mental health
services, or community mental health clinics? We find that
the problem load factor is very significant. Thus hospital
usage goes from 28 percent with no concerns to 38 percent
with five concerns; private mental health service demand
rises six-fold from zero to five recent concerns; community
mental health usage increases five-fold (see Chart VII-3).

        When the extent and form of helping is taken into
account the impact of problem load on demand for each of the
three kinds of health services shows a clear mitigation due
to the role of informal helping. This is particularly the
case where the intensivity scale is employed. Here, even
with seven recent concerns, demand for hospital services has
risen only one percent compared to the situation of an
individual having no recent concerns. Taking into account
the variety of informal helping behaviors used by
individuals, the demand for both public and private mental
health services increases from two to four percent with three
recent concerns compared to none.

        Chart VII-4 depicts, in a schematic fashion, the model
of demand for formal human services which emerges from the
research conducted in the Detroit metropolitan area. The
role of community support systems as the informal problem-
coping systems serves three functions: 1) take over some of
the load of formal agencies in strong communities; 2)
increase the demand for services through referral and problem
surfacing; and 3) compete with the formal service system in
terms of styles of problem-solving due to ethnic, cultural,
and other normative constraints on the use of formal service
agencies.

CHART VII - 2

Use of Nine Formal Agencies in Relation To
Problem Load and Helping Patterns

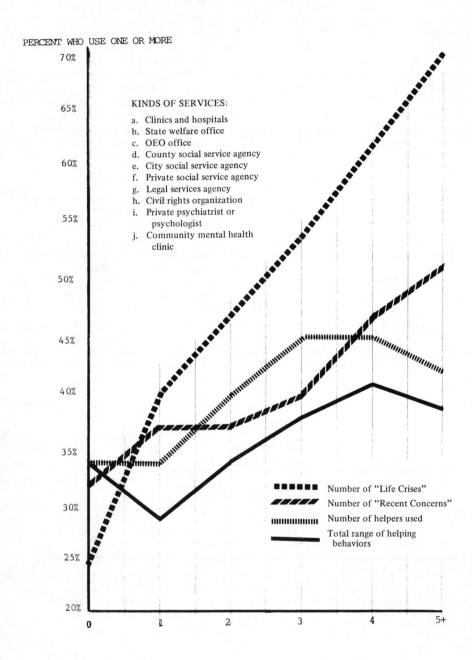

PERCENT WHO USE ONE OR MORE

KINDS OF SERVICES:

a. Clinics and hospitals
b. State welfare office
c. OEO office
d. County social service agency
e. City social service agency
f. Private social service agency
g. Legal services agency
h. Civil rights organization
i. Private psychiatrist or
   psychologist
j. Community mental health
   clinic

Number of "Life Crises"
Number of "Recent Concerns"
Number of helpers used
Total range of helping
behaviors

CHART VII - 3

"Demand" for Hospital, Private and Public Mental Health Services

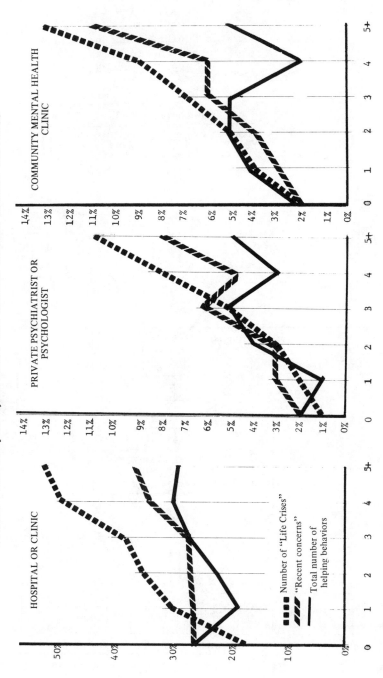

CHART VII - 4

Schematic Depiction of the Relation of Formal and Informal Life Support Systems

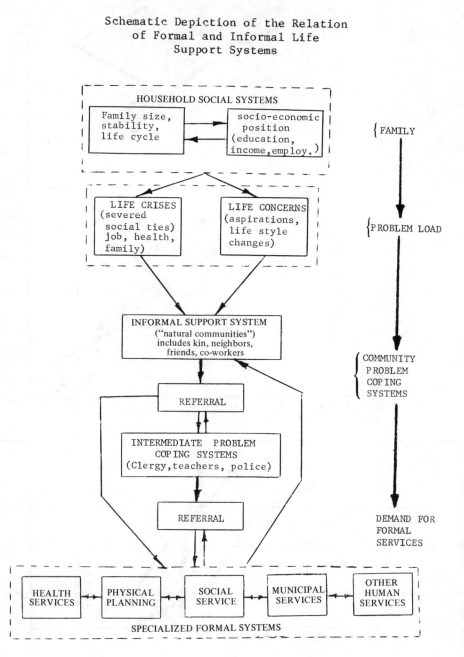

The degree to which the various problem areas defined
in Chart VII-4 are linked is also an important feature of the
analysis model. Efforts to increase interagency coordination, the sharing of information, and referral of clients and
consumers are important features which determine demand
within formal subsystems and the total service demand.

A major feature of the schematic model presented in
Chart VII-4 is that arrows directing family outreach may
include direct and indirect linkages between 1) informal, 2)
intermediate, and 3) professional systems. Thus, individuals
may go through several systems before using a formal agency
or may be forced directly into a formal system because of
weak, absent, or poorly integrated referral patterns within
informal and intermediate systems of problem-coping.

Overall the model implies a set of varying levels of
integration between problem-coping systems of a community.
The degree of that integration as well as the total capacity
of each system is clearly a function of the resources available through local and nonlocal revenues, the socio-economic
level of the municipality or its regional administrative or
political jurisdiction, and the overall economic conditions
of the population and society at the time of the measurement.
Clearly Chart VII-4 defines a conceptual model derived from
a specific data set. It does not seek to include the full
range of variables that might be included in a more comprehensive predictive system of variables to be used in
predicting the utilization of formal services or demand at a
given time or over an extended period. As such, the research
design is aimed at the refinement and elaboration of the
specific empirical findings in one data set as it may inform
a subsequent more complete conceptualization.

THE CONTEMPORARY CONTEXT OF HUMAN SERVICE PROGRAMS

One of the most critical policy issues facing highly
industrialized societies is the demand for public services at
the local community level. Given the increased cost of such
services coupled with a social movement of tax revolt, many
assumptions about public policy and social programs which
have prevailed in the recent past must now be reconsidered.

Until now twentieth-century human service programs have
been premised on the growth in service demand--the "revolution" of rising quality of life expectations. With a present
or anticipated slowing of economic growth in most Western
democracies until the end of the century, a gap is opening up
in urban communities. There is an almost geometric increase
in constituency needs (interest group multiplication) which
must vie with relatively smaller--perhaps arithmetic growth--

in formal service capacity. In turn, this discrepancy places
greater strain on values of equity, access, and fairness in
the delivery of a variety of social and municipal services.

     Zald (1977) has focused his analysis on economic
aspects of social processes. His more specialized conclusion
on the broad trend is congruent with what we have expressed.
Says Zald:

> A moderate prediction would be that until the end of
> the century (economic) growth rates will be substan-
> tially lower than they have been for the past quarter
> century, unemployment will be higher than it has been
> for the past quarter-century . . . . Thus, we are
> unlikely to see an expanded welfare state fueled out of
> a burgeoning economy . . . the welfare state in
> Western industrial countries will be in low gear
> (1977:120).

     In a climate of austerity local communities have two
broad options. The first is to react with passive resigna-
tion, accepting new hard conditions fatalistically. Another
is to respond in a determined self-actualizing way, applying
indigenous energies to maximize whatever potentialities exist
in the local situation.

     The concept of professionalism is based on the
following assumptions: professionals, by virtue of their
training, possess superior knowledge about a certain aspect
of human life that sets them apart from the rest of the
population. In the field of mental health, that means that
professionals are supposed to know more about what people
need to be mentally healthy or to overcome mental illness
than do their clients. Because of this superior knowledge,
professionals deserve to have more power and authority in
determining what services they should offer than their
clients or the political system. Professionals should be
primarily accountable to their profession, and only
secondarily to society at large or to the organization which
may employ them. It is assumed that primary accountability
to the profession is identical with accountability to the
client. It often is not.

     The irony of the concept of professionalism is that
while individual achievement through hard work and self-
sufficiency is believed to lead one to the realm of professionalism, the perpetuation of professional power depends
on the faith and acquiescence of the service user. Karno and
Schwartz compare the role of client in any human service
system to that of a child, with the professional acting as
parent. They state, "even more we believe that the failure
to recognize the existence of the parent-child model as the

principal one in all service systems is itself an impediment
to the development of the rehabilitative stance." They
emphasize, furthermore, that "clients and professionals alike
appear to be comfortable with the client in the less
autonomous role of the child-adult than they are when he is
asked to assume more autonomous roles in the process."

This uneven balance of power does not exist only in the
one-to-one relationship between client and professional. It
carries over to the relationship between professional service
delivery systems and the general society. McKnight points
out that our population as a whole is becoming more and more
dependent on a service economy, and thus we are becoming a
nation of clients, who in the aggregate tend to be more
valuable in terms of the GNP for our disabilities, not for
our individual self-sufficiency. He offers a disturbing case
in point:

> Consider your own value in a serving economy should you
> die of cancer next year. If you have a long, fully
> treated "quality-care" death, its value could appear
> within next year's Gross National Product as $250,000.
> There are very few people who can be that productive in
> one year, or several years (McKnight, 1977:37).

As a society we have turned more and more to the culture of
professionalism and faith in technology to meet human service
concerns. Historians, sociologists and other analytic inter-
preters of the past offer various theories to account for
these trends. But the fact remains that with the disintegration of small, family-oriented communities and the growth of
social fragmentation, it is the formal specialist who has
been called on to provide the coping knowledge.

There is a growing recognition of our increasing
dependence on professionals to solve every problem and meet
every human need. And from within the ranks of professionals
themselves have come some of the most searching critiques of
overreliance on formal experts. The self-help health movement is one of the most significant of such responses.

POPULISM AND THE "COMMUNITY AS EXPERT"

To round out the picture it is necessary to recognize
another tendency accompanying the economic trends we have
identified. This is a populist revolt by "middle America"
against what it perceives as governmental interferences and
lavish public spending (see Warren, The Radical Center,
1976). This is interrelated with what Glazer terms the
"limits" of problem-solving capacity by professionals.

Because professionals have lost credibility as experts, local communities have begun to make claims for sharing in decision-making affecting indigenous situations. The argument is heard that localities themselves hold some of the expertise required to cope with contemporary problems. This is an element of the movement toward local self-help.

Formal public and private agencies have essentially two strategies for dealing with the problem we have identified: 1) limit services using highly standardized and uniform definitions of problems and administrative procedures for allocating resources and assessing need, or 2) develop linkages with informal helpers and social networks.

The emergence of a variety of self-help and mutual-aid organizations in urban communities can be viewed as a significant social movement which can either increase or reduce reliance on professional helping systems. One of the sources of such organizations is the sense of disenchantment with professional hegemony over the treatment of social problems, i.e., the perceived imbalance between indigenous, informal sources of helping and mutual aid and the professional helping system.

Explanations for the rise of self-help strategies are as varied as the phenomenon itself. Among the most intriguing of the theories or speculations is the view that the social scale of society and the bureaucratization of service delivery are alienative and associated with a sense of powerlessness. Berger and Neuhaus (1977) have recently called for the strengthening of "mediating institutions" such as the church, family, voluntary associations, and the neighborhood. These institutions are viewed as "the principal expressions of the real values and the real needs of people in our society." Berger and Neuhaus go on to argue that such "people-sized" social institutions should be "empowered" by public policies that recognize and give respect to these rather than to continue to increase society's, and particularly the less affluent group's, reliance on "alleged child experts," special interests, and "utopian planners."

Christopher Lasch in The Family Besieged echoes a similar theme to that of Berger and Neuhaus. He argues that since the beginning of the century the family has been the victim of the "helping professions:"

> The proliferating flock of teachers, doctors, psychologists, counselors, social workers, and juvenile court officers--who claiming expertism assumed the family's main function: raising children.

He goes on to suggest that:

Once you define parents as consumers of advice you've
already defined a dependent relationship so it doesn't
do much good to tell parents, in effect, to become more
knowledgeable in their consumption.

Lasch sees only one solution: to persuade people they are
able to solve their own problems. He encourages parents to
organize with others:

It never occurs to them that since every family is confronted with the same problems that maybe they could
solve them if they got together . . . . The achievement of individualism . . . requires cooperation with
others . . .

Dangers in the self-help, self-care movement have been cited
by several commentators who express worry over whether health
care will deteriorate. George Silver of Yale University in a
paper delivered to the National Center for Health Statistics
suggests that self-care projects can become a cheap alternative of providing first-class medical care to the poor and
those living in rural areas. Lowell Levin notes that most
initial medical treatment follows some appropriate action by
the patient before seeking professional help. Lawrence Green
of Johns Hopkins indicates that despite initial concern by
physicians many self-help health efforts have now gained
greater acceptance among professionals.
    The loss or breakdown of community has been seen as a
major source of reliance on specialized professional helping
as a substitute system of problem-coping. Recent public
policy directions as well as "consumer control" grass-roots
pressures have reinforced the view that natural, small-scale,
and indigenous systems of helping are systematically being
eroded in urban life. Reinforcing this view are the
increasing cost of professional services and the resistance
of the public to support professional care for specific
social groups and categories of high-risk populations such as
minorities, low income, youth, and the elderly.
    In light of the combination of social forces within
contemporary urban life which tend to de-emphasize professional helping and stress informal helping, it becomes
critical to understand the types of "informal social ties"
that serve to increase referrals and those which insulate
individuals from utilization of formal helpers.

AN OVERVIEW: BALANCED HELPING SYSTEMS

A key goal of this chapter has been to define and
describe the use of professional helping services as a series
of key decision points that result in a pathway of help-
seeking and utilization which is often socially bounded and
impermeable. This "style of coping" concept then implies
that informal social bonds are themselves shaped and in turn
determine the resources used by the individual. Especially
if there is no objective standard of performance or treatment, the various systems of helping are competitive rather
than monopolistic in terms of expertise and problem-solving
success levels.

The widely recognized interdependence of professionals
and natural helping systems inevitably prompts concern about
potential conflicts between them. Conflict may arise if the
parties are reluctant to respect those fundamental
differences in values, social goals, and modes of influence
which are characteristic of primary groups and professional
experts.[6] Reports of professionals who have successfully
established working relationships with informal helpers contain strong cautions against grafting professional styles of
influence onto these natural systems.[7] Second, there is some
danger of a competitive relationship evolving between professional service providers and the more organized forms of
support systems in which each not only attempts to limit the
other's sphere of influence in the human services, but
competes with the other for resources such as clients,
political sanction, funding, volunteers, and media exposure.
In theory these related conflicts can be minimized if each
party is encouraged first to recognize the unique and legitimate functions of the other, and then to plan new human
services which capitalize upon complementary helping roles.

A core principle developed in the work of Roland Warren
is a definition of the community as a set of vertical as well
as horizontal systems of helping and services. Research
indicates that horizontal relationships, specifically those
which treat local neighborhoods as distinct social systems,
involve a variety of individual roles and organizations which
are often unrelated to formal service delivery systems. At
the same time, in the vertical structure of a community the
formal agencies are often operating without any effective
knowledge of the local helping systems and resources for
problem-solving that are utilized or potentially available to
persons that an agency is mandated to serve.

We must see the local community as a partnership
involving three critical dimensions: 1) direct clinical and
group therapy provided by fully trained and licensed professionals, 2) utilization of formal, intermediate

community-based helpers, such as clergy, teachers, police, and others who are often asked to intervene in or provide referral and problem-coping aids for health problems, and 3) informal helpers such as kin, neighbors, co-workers, friends, and others. The latter groups' referral knowledge and skills often spell the difference between a need for using professional help or institutionalization and taking the first step toward improvement in one's life or reducing social isolation. There is a potential linkage among these layers or systems of helping as they naturally occur in a community.

Often components of a community social-support system are separate and may even be working at cross purposes. Social services and support are available through both formal and informal systems. However, both the informal and formal systems have limitations and lack experience at working together to provide services. This program is designed to assist social science agencies to develop or improve methods of tapping into natural helping networks in positive, productive ways.

The formal social-service delivery system operates under a number of constraints, the first of which is financial. Despite growing federal, state, and local budgets, human services programs do not now nor will they ever have the financial or personnel resources to effectively address the range of social problems. The problems are too widespread and entrenched to be solved by the formal helping system alone. The current tax revolt symbolized by Proposition 13 in California signals that development of alternative methods of providing services is a particularly timely phenomenon.

In many cases the informal system may not be fully aware of the formal services or how to use them appropriately. On the other hand, natural helpers face the danger of being co-opted by the formal system and losing effectiveness, either by becoming professionalized or becoming convinced that only professionals have the knowledge to help others. Professionals may also have problems in dealing with natural networks as new forms of networks emerge which are novel to professionals more familiar with the old forms based on kinship, ethnicity, or neighborhood. It is the view of this author that in the period ahead, increased reliance will be placed by our society on concepts such as local initiative, self-help, local community capacity and grass-roots participation. Ever tightening economic constrictions will make this a dominant social development and policy option.

Informal helping networks sometimes become organized into collective-action structures which are formalized. In other cases, mutual problem-coping and mutual aid remain at a

more individualistic level not including community action or
association. In those instances a measure of a healthy
community may be the development of appropriate linkages
between informal helping networks and the formal agencies
mandated to deliver human services.

THE JURISDICTION OVER PROBLEMS IS FLUID

The idea of the community as expert in extreme form
implies that communities can solve problems without professional help. This is more appropriately conceived of as a
continuum of invoked expertise. Thus, for some problems, we
might agree there exists a technology that is very effective.
If individuals can gain access to that technology, in some
sense they are cured or helped with their problem. Let us
locate that at one end of the continuum and call it high
invoked expertise. This could entail diagnosing sickle cell
anemia, or designing a neighborhood traffic pattern.
On the other end of the continuum there are bubbling up
from normal life a whole range of concerns that people may
have, but for which there may not even be a common definition
or label. For example, in all our research on helping networks we asked about depression. The term that people use is
highly variable; feeling low, having the blues, being lonely,
etc. When we asked people about "feeling blue" we find there
are different ways that they cope often using a natural
helping system. This is a typical instance of low invoked
expertise, in the sense that, when depressed a person simply
talks to someone else about it. Other individuals following
norms of their social milieu will call a doctor or other
professional.
Where a problem has this very diffuse character it
represents a typical instance of low invoked expertise--let
us call this grass-roots expertise. No professional group
can claim full technical jurisdiction over it.
There is also a middle point in this where there is a
competitive market between professionals and grass-roots
people. Drug abuse programs, alcoholism, obesity, smoking,
and child discipline all fit into a kind of medium invoked
expertise situation. Multiple strategies here exist
involving informal groups and organizations which can help
with that problem, and the individual has a choice as to how
to take action.
There is a hint from our research that the grass-roots
problem may move into the medium area when self-help
organizations emerge. Thus, the problem formulation continuum is subject to community organization. Problems can
shift in their meaning, but the nature of community is

constantly creating new grass-roots expertise problems. It
would be impossible to train people and to start developing
programs to address all of these types of problems. Therefore, this kind of very creative problem-solving that goes on
is very critical in preventing a series of problems from
getting dumped into the professional system or into the
"competitive market" problem arena.

        In recent years we seem to be accepting a philosophy
that has the following implications: 1) It appears that the
development of professional specialization has increased the
likelihood that we designate a specialized group to deal with
formerly treated, informal helpers--kin, neighbors, and
friends. Death and dying is one of the most recent examples.
A large literature is emerging in sociology and other
disciplines on teaching people how to die or how to help kin
go through the experience of terminal illness. 2) It implies
a public policy in which an entire range of problems can be
shifted or addressed by professionals or by some combinations
of professionals working with community.

        In a sense the jurisdiction of the professionals has
expanded greatly to include a wide range of grass-roots
expertise problems. Presumably the dangers of that are: 1)
that the professionals themselves find that their training
often becomes rapidly obsolete, 2) their ability to define
and serve a given clientele and screen out clients whom they
do not wish to serve, or feel incapable of serving, is
reduced, and 3) the match of professional training to demand
for services often may become inconsistent.

A FINAL NOTE

        Clearly we have posed the problem too simply and have
implied a determinism which may not be demonstrated by
empirical fact. What is implicit and what we seek to make
explicit are the tensions and dynamics for establishing
either an equilibrium point or some optimal level of service
delivery.

        We see a problem that is not simply one of technologi-
cal capacity or demonstrated success, but of normative constraints and, in particular, trade-offs between informal
(natural helping systems) and formal systems of problem-
coping utilized by urban populations.

        If natural helping networks are left behind in a
faddish overreliance on professional specialization and
problem-solving "overdesign," or if agencies ignore the way
they can work with these networks, both the economic and
social costs of services and the quality of life suffers.

Government agencies cannot create natural helping networks, but they can destroy them through ignorance or
policies which act to erode their social environmental base.
There are many examples of overcentralization of professional
training in medical and social service fields where training
is geared to staffing inaccessible bureaucratic systems which
have unit-cost efficiencies but suffer in terms of underutilization by many individuals who need help. Many action
service programs generate duplication of effort and treatment
since they are carried out in a vacuum outside of the life
context of the individual. All too often these simply
increase the separation between professional services and
other anchors of human community.

CHAPTER VIII

VARIETIES OF URBAN SOCIAL TIES:
A NEW FRAMEWORK FOR UNDERSTANDING COMMUNITY

Symbiosis is the biological process which makes complex
life possible. This long recognized principle of animal and
plant ecosystems can apply as well to the health of vitality
of human communities.[1] Essential to that process is the
coexistence of unlike elements in the same local environment.
In just this manner we can define a set of very different
social structures and processes which provide the basis of
problem-coping and helping systems. This "social symbiosis"
has already been hinted at in much of the analysis we have
presented thus far. We now need to draw it into a full and
coherent perspective.

     In this chapter we shall draw upon the common themes
that have been developed in our discussion of neighborhoods,
communities, and the dynamic process of informal and formal
helping patterns. We use the term "organic" to refer to the
coordination of different elements within and between systems
of helping. In contrast to a simple notion of a highly
coordinated and explicitly organized set of services and
helping, the reality of urban community life is one of
pluralism and differentiation. Often this complexity leads
to terrible isolation. On occasion, all of the different
pieces fit together in a remarkable way to form very healthy
communities and neighborhoods. More typical, however, the
reality is one of incomplete and underutilized links between
one kind of helping system and another. To describe an ideal
symbiotic system is to consider what distance lies between
theory and practice.

PROBLEM-ANCHORED HELPING NETWORKS

     The research conducted in the Detroit metropolitan area
has provided (beyond its original intent) a basis for
defining a distinct network in which the linkage between

159

friends, neighbors, relatives, co-workers, and professional
agency helpers is defined by the reported "talking about a
recent concern or problem." Specifically we have distinguished as Problem-Anchored Helping Networks (PAHNs):

> *Social contacts that an individual makes with any
> number of other persons (not necessarily intimates or
> status equals) with the result that a particular
> problem or concern or crisis is discussed and advice or
> help provided.*

Problem anchored helping networks are heterogeneous in
composition and can readily expand in a chain fashion outward
to other networks. The individual thus belongs to several
networks simultaneously; these networks are knitted only in
terms of the common link of that one ego and are not cohesive
in any other way.

It is exactly such a process that we have described in
the preceeding chapters. These patterns of helper usage for
recent concerns (and life crises) have been differentiated by
neighborhood and community, by race, and in regard to other
social patterns. Taken as a whole, however, there are overall patterns of "extrusion" of problems from one helper to
another. In Chart VIII-1 we show how many times one particular helper tends to form a pathway to another. The
patterns noted place the neighbor in a frequently used
"linkage" position: there are six other helpers with whom he
or she is tied. Friend, clergy, and teacher each have five
helping pathways; doctor has four, co-workers and police
three. By contrast, the spouse-relative pairing is frequently an exclusive base for problem-coping.

Taking into account the ten varieties of helpers from
spouse to social worker or psychiatrist, some clear pathways
can be discerned. Of the total of 45 paired links of one
helper to another for coping with recent concerns, eleven are
statistically significant (see Appendix Table VIII-1). When
the follow-up interviews are analyzed this clustering has
expanded to 32 out of a possible 45 pairings. The spouse-
relative connection is the strongest; friend-neighbor is next
in order of prevalence; co-worker-friend follows. Several
pairs link formal to informal helpers: physician-friend,
police-neighbor, clergy-neighbor, and physician-neighbor (see
Appendix Table VIII-2).

In addition to a number of paired links among different
kinds of helpers, there are several triangles of helping
which emerge from the data of the helping network study.
These include: neighbor with co-worker and friend; physician
with friend and neighbor; clergy with teacher and neighbor;
counselor (social worker or mental health professional) with

CHART VIII - 1

Linkages Between Different Helpers

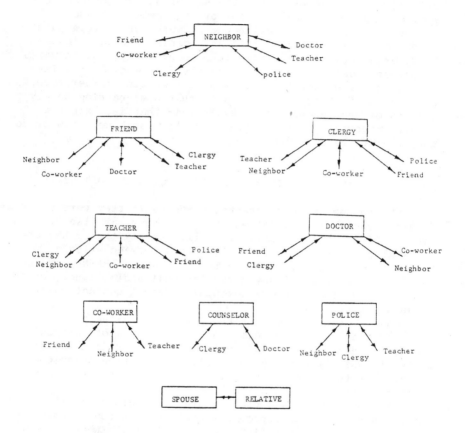

physician and clergy; and finally police with teacher and neighbor. For each of these five clusters the use of one helper usually means also seeking help from the others (see Appendix Table VIII-3).

In terms of an institutional setting or a structural notion, helping networks are always there even if a given individual does not utilize them. To this degree problem-defined helping networks are the set of helpers sought out by a given individual, and the sum or aggregation of such choices can be used to define the networks of a given population such as a working unit of an organization, a neighborhood, or a voluntary organization. Conversely, the networks of helpers used may be defined by the frequency of utilization by a given individual in a social setting. Therefore, the access of other individuals in that same setting to key helpers can be independently evaluated—that is, "are newcomers, minorities, etc., able to utilize such networks or do they tend to be excluded?"

THE FUNCTION OF PAHNs WITHIN ONGOING SOCIAL SUPPORT SYSTEMS

Up to now, we have treated PAHNs as if they were a separate social structural entity. Yet they may also be seen from a different perspective as well: namely that PAHNs are a social process that occurs within and between existing ties. In this specific view helping networks (PAHNs) are an intrinsic component of any given informal social bond. Often they serve as the boundary defining external contact points of such structures.

Social contact implies the potential for helping behaviors defined by the existence of a matrix of informal social contacts. These informal networks provide a social milieu in which proximity and social interaction suggest a probability that social support and helping activities may be available from these relationships.

Social support and problem-specific helping in this context are viewed as separate social network functions. They provide distinct activities to individuals who experience recent concerns or crises. Thus, social support activities are concerned with social-emotional feedback, reinforcement, providing for the release of negative effects, and enhancing social integration. Problem-specific helping activities, on the other hand, are based on specific actions taken on the part of informal helpers to provide individuals with problem-coping mechanisms.

A typology of functional relationships within the small group context was posited by Parsons and Bales (1955) and illustrates the balance between interpersonal ties. The "task specialist" is concerned primarily with "instrumental" operations within the group—how to reach a specific goal— while the "socio-emotional specialist" concentrates on the "expressive" interactions keeping the group together and undertaking motivation to participate (1955:151). Thus, within any group (or network) there are those who provide predominantly instrumental resources oriented toward achieving the goals or purposes of the group, and those who offer primarily expressive support.

We submit that within any given social network there will be a balance between expressive and instrumental activities provided by all of the members in the network. The important issue is that the nature of the interpersonal ties will determine to a large extent the predominance of expressive versus instrumental network activities. We would expect that social networks characterized as loose-knit are more likely to feature a predominance of instrumental activities oriented toward problem-solving tasks. Close-knit social networks, on the other hand, are more likely to provide expressive support to members of the social network oriented toward sociability, network integration, and coping efforts. In order to achieve effective problem-solving capabilities, however, both expressive and instrumental skills must be present in the social network. The helping behaviors of "referring" and "taking action" are good examples of instrumental helping versus the more expressive "listening" or "asking questions."

While the various functions of informal social networks are viewed as separate activities, they are interdependent. Thus, it is unlikely that problem-specific (instrumental) helping will occur within informal social networks where some degree of social interaction and expressive support does not already exist. An exception might be in an emergency situation. Moreover, it is impossible for either social support or helping activities to occur if individuals do not come into contact with one another initially and share at least some degree of social interaction.

Closeness versus Helping

The findings we have discussed in earlier chapters support the view that social intimacy and helping are separable activities.

Thus, in the 1975 survey we find that people who report they have no close friends in the neighborhood—about one out of three persons in the overall sample—use neighbors as PAHN helpers 20 percent of the time. For relatives who are not close, the percentage is nearly one out of two. Individuals who report having no close friends among co-workers

nevertheless use co-workers for helping 25 percent of the
time.

　　Self-conscious helping may be antithetical to the
sociability, expressive support, and reinforcement provided
by close friendship. That is, intimate social ties which
become dominantly excessive requests for problem-specific
helping may undermine these social bonds. By the same token,
helping behaviors which introduce individuals to other
informal social contacts (i.e., through referral) may lead to
the establishment of new or expanded intimate networks. Yet
in a given "intimate network" help and sociability are in an
adversarial relationship. Thus, as the instrumental helping
process increases, the expressive aspects of a social network
or primary group may be weakened. A duality is present which
may often be maintained in coexistence by a rough balancing.

　　The persistence or duration of a PAHN is a function of
the type of instrumental help provided. If it is able to
generate referral, new knowledge, or treatment for a problem,
then it is likely to be used again—either for the same or a
new problem. Any friendship dominated by helping tends to
corrode, overspecialize, and render the relationship exploi-
tive.

　　Basic to our argument is the assumption that people
turn to intimates for help because they are socially proximal
and not because of their helping expertise.

Social Cohesion and Helping Patterns

　　The term "social integration" refers to the ties
between parts of a group—what holds it together in the face
of pressures and challenges, both external and internal.
Applied at the community level, sociologists from Durkheim to
Parsons have seen the chief mechanisms for integration as
political parties, interest groups, and particularly the
juridical system. But this usage of the term is applied at a
highly formal level of analysis. Community integration can
be examined at a more informal level. The concept as
commonly applied refers to stresses related to serious
social, societal, and personal problems and extreme circumstances.

　　Laws and courts do not hold society together on a day-
to-day basis. People are related and bound to each other and
society by more subtle and less specified patterns of
personal relationships, settings, interactions, and sentiments. The courts and other mechanisms of formal systems are
to that type of societal integration as the emergency wards
and crisis clinics are to the level of interpersonal and
community integration operationalized in the social support
system of a local population. They are both invoked in

extreme circumstances. They represent the mechanisms that intervene when there is a breakdown, or an exceeding of the capacity, of the settings and relationships which govern people's coping with every day events, stresses, and inter-personal relationships.

The low invoked (grass-roots) expertise problems used to elicit the coping and helping experiences of people in the Detroit area study represent the day-to-day ups and downs and stresses with which people must cope. The helping relation-ships in which people are imbedded are the glue that helps hold them and society together.[2] These patterns of social integration as one author states "refer to the ways in which individuals relate to one another and to the community as well as to the ways in which resources are coordinated for the common good" (Klein, 1968: 106). Such dynamics of integration encompass how ". . . individuals become related to one another through informal associations and formal organizations; individuals, groups, and organizations interact in order to deal with recurring problems and meet new challenges, and (how) the community copes with growing demands from the world outside . . ." Leighton and his colleagues extensively explored this linkage between individual and "collective" health in their longitudinal studies of small towns in rural Nova Scotia:

> What we have, then, are pictures of two aspects of the same phenomenon: on the one hand, the relative absence of a patterned and stable network of interaction and reciprocity among a group of people and, on the other, reflections of the meaning which this lack of a group system has for the individual (Hughes, et al., 1960: 400).

The sociologist Robert Angell (1951) distinguishes between two kinds of community integration. The first he calls "moral integration" which is solidarity based on shared values, mutual respect, and feelings of common purpose. Operationally, this type of integration is measured by a community's support of public charities and welfare. The second he calls "social integration." This is the equivalent to the "friendliness" of the whole community.[3] The relation-ship between the two is neither strong nor direct.

THE DIVERSE NATURE OF URBAN SOCIAL TIES: A SYMBIOTIC PATTERN

In his classical definition of primary groups, Cooley (1933:208-12) identified several essential properties: 1) face to face contact, 2) unspecialized interaction, 3)

"sympathy and natural expression," 4) relative permanence, and 5) small size. Cooley's definition is an ideal type, the elements of which contrast in most respects with properties of secondary or formal groups.

Much of urban community research suggests neighbors are not likely to be close friends, relatives, or co-workers. Rather, within the contemporary urban neighborhood, neighboring relationships have become characterized largely by low-intensity nodding acquaintanceships, limited superficial visiting, and occasional mutual aid.[4]

In attempts to rediscover territorial cohesiveness and solidarity sentiments within the context of modern community structure, early urban scholars confused the diffuse nature of informal social ties with their absence. For a long time many urban scholars contended that primary relationships in the modern city had given way to weak, disorganized social ties bound up only in formal, bureaucratically oriented relationships. Such relationships were often viewed as "impersonal, transitory, and segmental" (Wirth, 1938:12).

In reaction to the so-called demise of primary group solidarity in modern urban community, many urban scholars now contend that "intense, intimate" social relationships still exist within community-based social networks.

Tight-knit or close-knit social networks are formed by the intimate relationships established among friends, relatives, neighbors, and sometimes co-workers. These informal social ties provide critical support to individuals and often serve as resources for helping. The nature of close-knit social networks is described by Elizabeth Bott:

> I use the word "close-knit" to describe a network in which there are many relationships among the component units. When many of the people a person knows interact with one another, that is when the person's network is close-knit, the members of his network tend to reach consensus on norms and they exert consistent informal pressure on one another to conform to the norms, to keep in touch with one another, and, if need be, to help one another (1957:59-60).

Loose-knit social networks, on the other hand, represent a heterogeneous set of individuals lacking both a self-perceived common bond and a shared social status. Loose-knit social networks are often temporary alliances consisting largely of superficial interactions and nonintimate relationships. Yet, if such relationships are prolonged in duration, they may serve as nascent staging grounds for significant social structures similar to that of the traditional primary group.

WHAT ACCOUNTS FOR CHANGE IN SOCIAL TIES?

The neglect and erosion of traditional social ties is a
theme linked to social alienation, isolation, and the
burgeoning case loads of public agencies. We view the issue
of the strength and character of social networks within the
context of several major social trends. Our approach is
hypothetical rather than definitive.

We shall suggest five kinds of social dynamics
affecting the balance and distribution of social network
forms.

The first of these is the absolute size of population
groups--growth in population aggregations seen both geographically and in terms of institutional or social differentiation. Simply put: as groups increase in size and
complexity of roles and strata, the jurisdiction of a given
informal social system becomes narrowed either as to content
or to behavior setting. In sum, the traditional primary
group is superseded by social ties which are setting-
specific, problem-specific, or both. As a consequence of
multiplication of such social nodules, the individual's
commitment to and span of participation in any given setting
is attenuated. Total friendship ties are not thereby reduced
by urbanization or size of community, but the options of
participation are increased and the competition for immersion
in a given setting reduced.[5]

A second mechanism which shifts both the distribution
of informal social ties and increases their diversification
in a given population is the degree of social and geographic
mobility which occurs. When individuals shift jobs they also
tend to shift job- and nonjob-related social ties.[6] In some
cases this is mediated by the role of technology such as
long-distance telephone contact or by the availability of
efficient transportation systems.[7] In still other instances,
the fact of social mobility--first noted by Durkheim then by
Sorokin and others--implies a severing of social ties.
Again, technology may attenuate the effects somewhat, but the
cost of communication across newly increased social distances
may more than surpass the ready access to telephone and jet-
liner.

A third mechanism affecting the change and differentiation of forms of social ties is that of formal education. As
the average urban dweller comes to be specialized in occupational training and as the public school system no longer
focuses on its homogenizing function, individuals develop
greater social contacts which are expressive of specific
identities--whether these are work-related, or are rooted in
ethnicity or in newly emergent leisure/hobby communities and
subcultures.

Thus, a dual impetus has been given to the proliferation of nontraditional forms of informal social ties: alienation from the common setting of the workplace (and the escape to new social ties) or the elaboration of social ties in the work organization itself. Bureaucratization of work has tended to also imply the professionalization of work-- especially that aspect of the professional's lifestyle.

Institutions which elaborate loose-knit ties include annual or more frequent meetings and conventions, the presentation of scholarly or pseudo-scholarly reports and papers, and union meetings and conventions for non- professional white- and blue-collar workers. Moonlighting and other sources of periodicity in the location of work provide elaboration of loose social ties with co-workers and others in both higher- and lower-status job settings.

A fourth important source for the emergence of new and more varied kinds of informal social ties are the cultural and historic events of the past several decades--especially since the 1960's--in which individual expression of the frontier tradition of American culture has turned inward to the psychic plane of exploration of the self. In the course of this expedition, individuals seek out new values and lifestyles--such as therapeutic communities and other new group expriences. Occasionally this search to break out of confining status and social class identities goes beyond terrestrial limits.[8] The composite of these social trends offers a veritable cafeteria of social contacts out of which varied social linkages, interactions, and group identities emerge.

A FUNCTIONAL BALANCE THEORY OF URBAN SOCIAL TIES

Let us now draw upon a theoretical construct developed in the work of the 19th-century French sociologist Emile Durkheim: urban social ties can be dichotomized into bases of mechanical and organic solidarity.[9] Those involving direct (mechanical) social bonds include: 1) traditional primary groups, 2) task groups such as in a work setting or voluntary organization, and 3) close-knit social networks. Each shares small size, intimacy of relationships, and common values of the individuals involved. There are three forms of organic solidarity: 1) problem-anchored helping networks, 2) loose-knit social networks, and 3) weak ties. Each of these has in common the lack of dependence of face-to-face communi- cation, infrequent interaction, specialized spheres of expertise or jurisdiction (or problem-solving capacity), and diverse social composition.

The essential argument is that a mixture of both types of social patterns--mechanically and organically based--provides the most effective and salutary forms of community life in a contemporary society. The nature of human community is problem-coping--particularly as it is organized in terms of organic solidarity. Neither social networks nor primary groups provide the basis of organic community. Each is a necessary but not sufficient component of organic community. Loose-knit ties are largely problem-centered and seldom serve as bases for expressive needs. The reverse is also true: tight-knit ties are not effective for utilitarian goals. This basic division of labor means that loose-knit ties are more volatile and multiplicative: they emerge at the periphery of the more enduring central group forms devoted to integrative functions. Having both kinds of group ties is therefore an optimal pattern for the individual and also insures the well-being of a community through the balance of tight- and loose-knit ties (see Warren Dunham, 1977).

THE BRIDGING ROLES OF PROBLEM-ANCHORED HELPING NETWORKS

A wide variety of social ties may exist in the behavior settings of the neighborhood, the workplace, and the voluntary association. It is possible to characterize the mix of forms for a whole community or population or for a given individual within a specific locale.

We have posited a functional balance theory of loose- and tight-knit ties. A pivotal role in the linkage between these varieties of informal social ties is played by problem-anchored helping networks: they overlap both the traditional, close-knit and the dispersed, loose-knit patterns of a given population group or individual.

There are at least three major ways in which problem-anchored helping networks act in a bridging or brokerage role between an individual's loose- and tight-knit ties by creating or strengthening one or the other type. First, by the fact of keeping alive (as a loose tie) some aspect of a relationship with former members of close-knit social groups. Rather than geographic movement or social mobility totally severing contact with a former work group, neighborhood, or organization, occasional help-seeking can maintain knowledge about the activities and whereabouts of a former intimate. Even though none of the present members of a problem-anchored network may have been part of that earlier close-knit group, there is a greater than random-chance probability of a present neighbor knowing a former neighbor, a present work mate knowing a prior one, or the people now active in a local

chapter of a civic organization knowing a former member. All
of these links enhance the opportunity of present social contact with those who are no longer one's intimates.

        Secondly, problem-anchored helping networks serve as
potential spawning grounds for the creation of new close-knit
ties by virtue of the shared problems and crises that
occasionally emerge. These infrequent events intensify the
social ties that are otherwise relatively specific in focus
and bring together members of the network so that they come
to know one another. Such instances may include the severe
winter (not just a bad snow storm) that requires neighbors to
help each other in larger numbers or over a longer problem
sequence than for such helping as watching a home when a
neighbor is on vacation or keeping an eye on children playing
in the street.

        A threat of school bussing, urban renewal clearance, or
traffic hazards may bring neighbors together in ways that
were previously lacking in collective dimensions and enduring
social action. These potential problem incidents can be
found in the work setting and the voluntary association context as well. Such events are idiosyncratic and are not the
normal basis of helping. Moreover, they generally do not
spill over into linkages with other groups or individuals.
But individuals rooted in a single setting may begin to call
upon helpers outside that milieu and thereby mobilize a network of helping ties which may bring together in a face-
to-face and intimate sense as a "social web" individuals who
were previously linked solely by their having been referrals
from one person in a proximity-based social setting.

        The third way in which problem-anchored social networks
bridge or strengthen other social ties is by creating a base
of reciprocity in terms of past favors or help. While there
are no requirements for such reciprocity they are relationships in which the norm of reciprocity is implied even if it
is not immediately satisfied. It is this future contingency
of a social tie that provides continuity to loose-knit
relationships and may require the cashing in of favors
precisely in one of the problem or crisis situations where
close-knit ties are likely to be built.

PAHNs ARE ONE EXPRESSION OF ORGANIC SOLIDARITY

        In contrast to other informal social ties, PAHNs do not
require that a named intimate provide the basis of networking. Thus, the Detroit research deals with links between
social arenas such as neighborhood, workplace, and formal
agencies, and not specific persons located in these settings.
From one time to another the problem-experiencing individual

may use a different neighbor or the same one--the key point
is that the social arena of the neighborhood is utilized.

In Chart VIII-2 we have depicted the indirect networking which is the PAHN social process. For any given
behavior arena, one can visualize a pool of potential helpers
whose capacity to form a network is based on the single
individual who seeks aid in that setting. These otherwise
disparate spheres are tied together to the degree that the
same person also goes to other arenas for problem-coping.
This process is one of very indirect versus direct social
integration. Neither the seeker of help nor the giver of aid
need be in a close social relationship for linkage to occur.

Specifically we have argued that: Community and
individual health or well-being (or effectiveness in problem-
coping) is a function of the range of informal social ties
utilized by members and the diversity of pattern
characterizing a population; a pivotal role in the linkage

CHART VIII-2

The "PAHN" Process as a Form of Community Organic
Solidarity

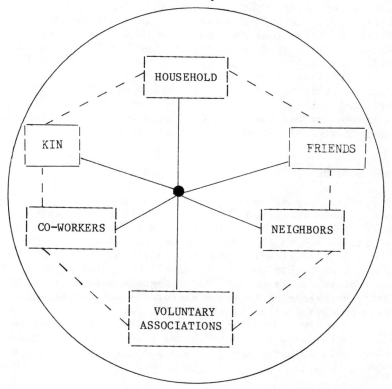

between varieties of informal social ties is played by
problem-anchored helping networks: they tie in with both
loose- and tight-knit patterns of a given population group or
individual; and the major dynamic of change or shift in the
balance of loose- or tight-knit ties is to be located in the
role of problem-anchored helping networks.

All of the brokerage roles we have ascribed to problem-
anchored helping networks may be viewed as sources of
strength in regard to a given community or individual. Thus,
it may be argued that it is not simply the variety of loose-
and tight-knit ties alone (that is, the volume and diversity
of social ties which makes for a healthy community), but the
fact that they can be interlinked through the pivotal role of
one type of social tie--the problem-anchored helping network.
Without this knitting or bridging form of social network the
depersonalizing and transient character of loose-knit ties
might indeed produce the negative effects on individual well-
being and community strength that have been ascribed to them.
The essential point is this: loose-knit ties in the context
of the availability of problem-anchored helping networks have
a potential for being qualitatively more significant than if
loose ties are treated in isolation. Moreover, helping networks alone are not the basis of community. Instead, PAHNs
are the bridging mechanism that ties primary groups and
social networks (all considered as informal social ties) to
formal organizations and generally to all secondary groups in
society. This process is depicted by the diagram of Chart
VIII-3).

If PAHNs are viewed as emergent in the normal communication within all forms of informal social bonds, the
critical interaction is not between conscious, instrumental
help-seeking but the potential for help to be realized out of
the dynamics of social interaction per se.

ARE NETWORK TIES THE NEW FORM OF URBAN COMMUNITY?

Our discussion has revealed the complexity of the
social network concept and the variability with which it has
been employed by researchers. We have distinguished each in
a sixfold schema that has been offered both as a synthesis
and as a clarification and elaboration of the term "network."
Thus, when focused at the level of the individual, the concept offers a measure of the strength and supportive role of
different kinds of social ties for the well-being and
problem-coping capacity of a single person.

One new therapy program using "small world groups"
claims that as a response "to the alienation, isolation, and
loneliness in our culture" . . . support groups are a safe

CHART VIII-3

Problem-Coping Systems Used by the Individual

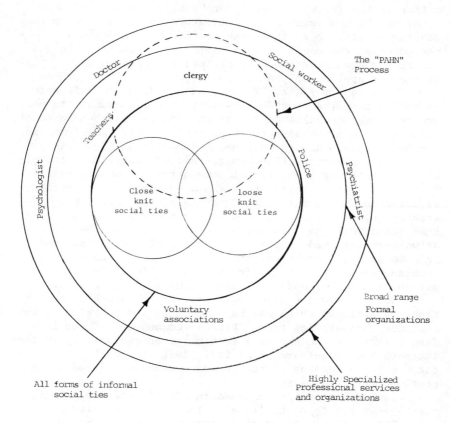

place for seven to ten people to gather once a week for the purpose of growth, friendship, and *community*" (emphasis added). This example suggests that the importance of wider group ties is seen to be in decline in favor of a focus on smaller group activity and assistance.

There is a kind of ironic paradox here: that as small-scale helping networks succeed we can discern a concept of society that suggests a withdrawal from what used to be the notion of the larger community or "public" person. In considering the new psychiatric literature about narcissism in modern society, there is a link to the inward-looking character of the social network approach--especially in the way it has been operationally defined in research and frequently applied in practice.

Thus, one may ask, "To what extent does the existence of social networks provide a capacity for a community to meet new problems or challenges?" To what degree is the "sense of belonging" to a social network psychologically satisfying in the same way as knowing that one belongs to an identified, recognized, geographically demarcated, or socially observable ethnic, class, or occupational community? To what degree is the sociability of social networks a substitute for participation in the larger community--the nation state, the greater culture, etc.? Some of the network studies suggest that the traditional cosmopolitan is the same as the social networker--informed, powerful by virtue of connections and able to flexibly adapt and anticipate the next change or problem to be confronted. Traditional solidarities of parochial neighborhoods or closed primary groups cannot.

Social networks often describe very parochial, insular kinds of patterns which may be helpful to the individual, but that may be isolating from a broader community. There is a danger that, to the extent a person relies exclusively on the intimate social network, that individual is less likely to take an active coping stance toward a number of broad social problems this view asserts.

If one is totally immersed in social networks, one may not have energy to participate in the wider community.

The helping network study suggests that social support is not what people want when they face daily problems, or even life crises. Instead, often what is sought is a different way of looking at the world, some specific resources: "While I'm thinking about going back to school it's nice that you are telling me that it is a good idea, but can you show me how I can actually apply?" And if I have some kids to take care of: "What kind of schedule can I work out?" "Is there a day-care service somewhere around that I can use in connection with that?" "As a good friend you tell me I ought to go back to school; but how am I going to do it?"

Being part of a helping network can direct an individual's attention to the needs of others in a community. Yet the helping that is indigenous to a community is not self-conscious or necessarily instrumental--it grows out of sociability; it becomes an expression of a potential, unspoken reciprocity.

That we all may become referral agents in problem-helping is one indicator of community health. From one perspective a problem-anchored helping network is based on entering into the larger community through a series of steps or pathways (combinations of resources) that are not based on an intimacy but simply on the sharing of the same problem with another individual.

Helping networks are characterized by people moving across different social arenas--out of their neighborhood, out of their work setting, out of the PTA group, or whatever organization they belong to that might be the basis of close social bonds--now linked to a range of other arenas outside these intimate circles. To the extent that such structures provide information about how to get a different job they may provide information that is new to the individual. Or they may intervene in such a way that the individual's view of the problem is changed. Helping network relationships may be somewhat more impersonal since they are not based on friendship. They may sometimes be accidental and non-recurring. The "bottom line" of such relationships is that they are critical to the society as an organic structure compared to a circle of homogeneous peers.

It is perhaps most fruitful to consider social networks less as the cement of community than as the transmission lines over which messages about the health or sickness of community may be carried. Networks may be a means to community; but they cannot be postulated as synonymous with it.

Our perspective rejects the concept of community as simply the sum or product of often unintended or accidental meetings. Instead, community is a resultant of shared behaviors and communications. It is not coterminous with the lines of communication themselves. Networks are best viewed as emanations of community.

The potential for new forms of human communities is multiplying due to technology and media resources. Yet they are also competing with one another. It is a dynamic process that social network analysis helps to illuminate rather than define.

If we treat networks as the vestigial remains of what
was once community, then the value question posed is one of
assessing their capacity to do what was presumably once done
by other social ties.

If, as we suggest, intimate social networks say little
about the state of community, they nevertheless provide a
basis for asking better questions about what community is or
is not. For it would appear to be premature to redefine the
basis of community by reducing it to the informal exchange of
intimacy. Rather, social/helping network analysis yields yet
another form which permits community to emerge out of a
variety of informal social ties--particularly under conditions of rapid social change. When helping networks and
informal social bonds interact, their relative dominance
shapes the form and strength of community.

Problem-anchored helping networks are so variable in
structure that they can be creative forms of new community
identity. Considered in terms of a continuum, PAHNs may be
generative of either self-help organizations at one extreme
(which replaces or supplants reliance of formal agencies or
organizations), or at the opposite pole PAHNs may be
stepping-stones to the use of formal services. For instance,
a person may become locked-in as a client based on a friend's
recommendation.

Where one has communities of identity separate from
one's helping networks--where the two do not overlap--the
best of both forms of social integration may result: one
maintains the social support of believing in a community of
residence or ethnic group without having to put that strength
of belonging and set of resources to the test.

Where problem load goes up, the overlap of potential
community and helping network is likely to increase. Thus,
even one failure can weaken both the sense of community and
the instrumental value of the kind of help needed to solve or
cope with a problem: a double loss. This is less likely
where the two systems are relatively autonomous. For this
reason, social distance serves many positive functions within
intimate social networks or even within larger communities.
So long as friendship remains untested one can draw psychic
strength from the knowledge that one has good friends. When
they fail to come through, the results may be psychologically
devastating.

COMMUNITY AS HELPING POTENTIAL

The distinction between actual and perceived community
is not simply a measurement issue in research, it is conceptual. Such lack of clarity has led many social observers to

find either stronger or weaker community than they had anticipated--among a low-income group, an ethnic minority, or those living in a given geographic locale. Thus, "sense of community" refers to the perceptions individuals hold about the potential for active problem-coping resources to be available from "significant others." Therefore, a critical element in the construct of community is the expectation or the perceived probability of receiving help--not necessarily proffered as help but available in terms of the attributes of the referent of community, such as neighborhood, family, ethnic group, etc. Thus, help potentially available is a critical dimension of community outside of the actual existence and utilization of helping networks.

The bridging role of helping networks is not simply a structural one in the sense that such a pattern of sometimes temporary, nonintimate links to others in several social arenas leads to the formation of a concrete group, but in a special sense that the process of community emerges within such helping networks. Without a problem there is no helping, but various informal social ties may bind individuals into small-scale components of community or may serve as community itself. To this degree, individuals may find more important social meaning in the potential for helping than in its actual utilization.

By confronting a problem and attempting to seek help or use resources, the individual may come to a different awareness of the capacity of one's community. We hypothesize that there is a likelihood that such a testing will reduce its perceived value.

THE EMERGENT FUNCTIONS OF HELP-SEEKING

When the capacity of a social network to provide both expressive and instrumental helping is high, then allegiance to that group may be retained, even if outside referral contacts of the type defined by helping networks occur from time to time.

What is critical to the concept of emergent community is that smaller-scale social ties are likely to fail the test of adequacy at some point. There is a critical mass idea at work here. If one retreats to small-scale intimate primary groups and finds that the kinds of problems one faces (or that are introduced from the outside) cannot be solved by the intimate network, then its role as a self-sufficient community will diminish.

What if the circle is drawn tighter, and the group is unable to absorb the symptoms of stress that the individual may manifest? For example, what if one person in the network dumps all of his or her problems into that setting? At this point the prescribed norms of problem-sharing or the etiquette of ego submergence in the network may come into conflict with the problem load of the individual. Then community begins to expand so as to include a variety of helpers and types of social ties to obtain effective help.

The enlargement of community may indeed be associated with the weakening of ties to a single arena such as neighborhood. The degree of intimacy of social (such as neighboring) ties should not be confused with the instrumental role of neighborhood. If neighbors fail to help as one had expected, this may indeed trigger a reaction that community within the neighborhood has broken down. But if there is an alternative arena of community which is not tested by the same problem, the result may not be detrimental to the mental health of the individual. We would argue that it is only when a general testing of all of one's communities occurs and finds help inadequate that the results will be detrimental to individual well-being.

Thus, the essential basis of modern community is that social integration depends not on primary groups or helping networks alone, but rather on the dynamic linkages between the two. These relationships cannot be understood by using social structural constructs alone; problem content must be specified as well--not just what are the traffic patterns, but what is being transported. Friends are believed to be friends until a public test of commitment fails; friends may be used for helping so long as the interaction is not recognized or defined publicly as help.

The point we want to stress is to recognize two separate functions of community: one hypothetical and potential; the other actualized and finite through the role of PAHNs. Both are essential for individual well-being; the first may be most valuable when not fully put to the test.

A SUMMARY PERSPECTIVE

We began this chapter with a specific idea in mind: that the helping process of an individual must be placed in a larger context: that of the social cohesion of the contemporary urban community. After exploring the ideas of theorists who have attempted to define what is the basis of that solidarity, we presented information from the core study to illustrate the interrelated patterns of helping--how one level meshes with another in different neighborhoods and municipalities. We then went on to depict the process of problem-coping as a built-in function of community life. We further specified the nature of problem-anchored helping networks (PAHNs) as a separable basis of organic linkages within a given population or geographic locale. In addition, several propositions—more accurately hypotheses—were generated to identify the meaning of helping symbiotic ties between individuals.

Our original point of departure, the coexistence of unlike elements, now emerges in more specific form. In fact, it has three facets: 1) a balance of helping systems from informal to formal, 2) a balance of helping content—social support and instrumental aid, and 3) problem-anchored helping as a bridge between close-knit social groups and very free-floating, occasional social contacts. Each of these and all of them express the variety of organic diversification found in urban life. They are expressions of social cohesion but often in very indirect ways.

The helping network study has provided a basis for exploring and testing out new concepts as to how a community fits together. Many of the concepts discussed in this chapter represent hypotheses and propositions about which additional data must be gathered to render them definitive and of practical utility. To address what we have learned we must now review a range of earlier findings and summarize them before pursuing their potential for application.

CHAPTER IX

FINDINGS AND IMPLICATIONS OF THE HELPING NETWORK
STUDY: AN OVERVIEW

       In earlier chapters we have described discrete elements
of the research. At this point we seek to pull the various
threads of analysis together and present a review of what has
been learned in the helping network project. Moreover, we
wish to reach beyond the data patterns to indicate more of
the potential significance of our findings. This process
will be developed in the remaining two chapters. In the
first of these, the emphasis is on summary and synthesis. We
shall subsequently discuss social policy and program examples
of this and other related network projects, and then indicate
the future directions of this area of social science theory
and practice. Finally, we shall take a glimpse at the future
possibilities and human service issues for which network
analysis is most pertinent.
       In this first step we shall focus on what we have noted
in detail in earlier parts of this book.

NEIGHBORHOOD CONTEXT AND HELPING: A SUMMARY

       Utilization of a sevenfold typology of neighborhoods
indicates statistically significant differences in the types
of helpers individuals may call upon for dealing with both
recent concerns and life crises. There is some significant
difference associated with types of neighborhoods in regard
to the probability of seeking any help for recent concerns.
       Help from either neighborhood or co-worker is pivotal
in terms of coordinate use of other informal or formal
helpers. Neighbors are significant brokers in the patterns
of helping utilized. This occurs in three ways: 1) in over
one out of four of all helping transactions neighbors are
used directly as helpers, 2) neighbors refer individuals to
other helpers--formal and informal, and 3) the neighborhood

context influences the volume and persistence of problems experienced by the individual.

For blacks the direct helping role of neighbor is significantly greater than for whites.

In general, the higher the satisfaction with the help given by neighbors the lower the risk to well-being scores for individuals residing in each neighborhood type. In particular, referral and action helping by neighbors is negatively related to the risk to well-being score of neighborhoods. "Listening" help, while at first limiting risk to well-being in problem-coping, does not continue to play this positive role.

Both the anomic neighborhood and the transitory type appear to influence individual well-being in a negative direction apart from the role of problem-coping. In the other neighborhood settings, however, the nature of helping utilized by the individual is more critical to well-being than the intrinsic fact of residence in each environment.

PERCEIVED NEIGHBORHOOD TYPE

Apart from the summed data on individuals used to type a neighborhood, the description of the neighborhood drawn from each person's own view has a slightly predictive role in terms of 1) the risk to well-being score of the individual and 2) the type of help-seeking the person engages in for recent concerns. Persons who perceived themselves in parochial neighborhoods report fewer recent concerns and also have a lower risk to well-being score for each number of recent concerns than persons in other perceived neighborhood contexts. Persons perceiving themselves in anomic neighborhood contexts show an opposite pattern.

The perceived neighborhood context explains more of the variance in the well-being score for individuals than does the objective neighborhood type.

When the perceived and actual neighborhood are combined, a fourfold pattern emerges in which use of neighbor and the risk to well-being are determined by being in a strong neighborhood or perceiving it as a strong context rather than perceiving it to be weak whether it is or not. Consistency between perception and actuality of neighborhood contexts leads to under- or overuse depending on the particular type of locale involved.

MUNICIPALITY-COMMUNITY CONTEXT

Sampling in eight different cities ranging in population from 15,000 to 200,000 suggests that the prevailing social status of residents plays a major role in the pattern of helping networks found in each locale. *To a greater extent than either real or perceived neighborhood context, the larger community setting influences the probability that an individual will seek any help from others for dealing with recent concerns.* The particular combinations of helpers are also importantly influenced by community. There are predominantly blue-collar and predominantly white-collar communities whose helping patterns match each other in spite of the general class-linked community differences.

The healthier communities, with patterns involving a high incidence of recent concerns coupled with a large variety of helpers utilized for problem-coping, manifest lower risk to well-being scores over time than do communities with a less healthy pattern--that is, few recent problems and few helpers per problem.

Community context appears to influence individual well-being via the helping process and the sustaining or non-sustaining of recent concerns more than the differences of the social class attributes of such settings.

The character of community helping may be utilized as an index of the social integration of a population in terms of direct linkages among helpers utilized versus indirect ties based on modal combinations of different kinds of helpers. Both the number of helpers used per problem and the number of different helping behaviors used per problem can be employed as basic measures of the strength or resilience of community social life.

In terms of the total predictive power in regard to measures of simple depression and risk to individual well-being, the combination of perceived and actual neighborhood coupled with municipality of residence appears to be as powerful a measure as individual family income, a person's education, age, and work status.

Municipality accounts for significant variance in the probability that a neighbor will be used for helping. At the same time, given types of neighborhoods found within a community provide a functional substitute for the restricted variety of helpers and types of helping behaviors which generally prevail in the total community.

THE ROLE OF NEIGHBORHOOD AS THE GATEKEEPER

The various neighborhood environments differentiated in this study do not seem to play a major role in the extent to which an individual will have a problem. There is no significant difference in the average number of problems between different neighborhood types. The differences between these neighborhood settings turns out to be how their inhabitants go about getting help.

Neighborhood affects the combination of helpers used or sustained. That is, an individual with a problem may or may not find that he or she is able to use the neighborhood resources proferred; or a person may use them only at the beginning of a problem and then break away at some later time. Neighborhood influences the accessibility to various kinds of helpers, particularly to the professional system. The probability than an individual will call upon a professional varies importantly with the neighborhood context. Therefore, the neighborhood is a critical filtering mechanism for help, more than it is a helping resource per se.

The neighborhood context—the geographical location—is not the center of resources in problem-solving. Rather, it tends to function as an arena in which an individual can gain access to various kinds of resources through the social network of other neighbors. The extent to which a neighbor knows someone who can be helpful is critical to whether or not a person will eventually get help from a professional—a psychiatrist, for example. We looked at the frequency of using the community mental health clinics or private psychiatrists. In some neighborhoods it is directly a function of whether you have a friend who works in a mental health clinic or is a private psychiatrist; in other neighborhoods, the two things are unrelated.

The referral system within a neighborhood is extremely important. Whether a person will know about a resource is not simply a question of if there is someone in the neighborhood who knows about it, but whether you are linked to your neighborhood in a way that you are liable to draw upon your neighbor's knowledge of that resource. Therefore, the two critical factors in successful referral are 1) the extent to which individuals in a neighborhood have linkages, and 2) the extent to which the neighborhood itself has resources or knowledge of resources.

DESCRIPTIVE COMMENTS: BLACK VERSUS WHITE NEIGHBORHOODS

A variety of findings from the helping network study suggest that black neighborhoods play a more important role

in the help-seeking behavior of individuals than do white
neighborhoods. The effectiveness of neighborhood social
organization, therefore, becomes a more salient contextual
variable in the black community than in the white community.
Prevalent types of neighborhood, such as the stepping-stone
in the case of the black sample and the diffuse in the
instance of the white sample, reflect bases for accounting
for differential effects of neighborhood. Another source of
race-linked neighborhood patterns is the higher proportion of
black neighborhoods which are characterized by social status
diversity.[1]

Some Observations on the Black Church and Black Neighborhood Linkages

        The black church can be viewed in terms of its multiple
functions and as a basic therapeutic dimension of the black
neighborhood and community. The role of the church would
make it possible for individuals to remain tied to neighborhoods of previous residence. The relationship between one's
current neighborhood and affiliation with the rest of the
black community is enhanced by the fact that many individuals
can return to a church that is located in a neighborhood in
which they resided previously. In this situation blacks
really have multiple neighborhoods from which to choose. If
the current neighborhood is unsatisfactory, one can retain a
tie with another neighborhood or actually establish a link
with a church located in a very different neighborhood from
that of current residency.
        The major implication is that blacks are tied to
neighborhoods in terms of church affiliations, so that movement between neighborhoods is a significant basis for
retaining the black community's spatial compression. As
blacks move out from neighborhoods, church institutions might
move to accommodate a predominant or large-scale movement of
blacks but would be relatively inelastic in a geographic
sense compared to several other social groups in the urban
community.
        Our line of analysis further emphasizes the role of the
socially homogeneous black neighborhood. This is the setting
which has the greatest capacity to tie people together in
some important ways, and in which the church plays a key
role. One neighborhood observer used the phrase "all the
children belong to the neighborhood" or "I was a child of the
neighborhood." This suggests the important sharing and
communal value system that can emerge in a homogeneous black
neighborhood, in sharp contrast to the pattern of isolated
nuclear families that tends to be the predominant life
pattern of the white suburbanite.

The question is not, "Can black churches be an
effective basis for organizing group therapy?" but, "Can the
concept of group therapy as developed in white middle-class
cultural patterns really be adapted or be appropriate within
the black church setting?" In this instance we can talk
about the role of the charismatic leader who permits collective, public expression of grief, of tension, of anxiety, and
the whole gamut of human emotions. In that sense the group
therapy which occurs is not so much the specific catharsis of
telling your own individual problems to others--a common
pattern in various kinds of encounter groups. Rather, the
emotions themselves are let out--apart from any problem-
solving advice or insight.

Such a style is consistent with the kinds of goals that
group therapy seeks, which are to permit people to feel their
emotions. One of the important aspects of such therapy is to
allow individuals to return and experience once again those
hurts and problems which they had covered over or in other
ways had restricted within their inner psychic world,
creating a burden of restricted scars, unresolved grievances,
and other kinds of experimental traumas due to which they
cannot function adequately or fully as individuals.

In the black-church therapy model, individuals need not
bare their souls as individuals in a public forum, but rather
are able to express in important ways the emotional links
with the "whole self" which might otherwise be detached or
segmented in terms of the multiple social roles which
characterize the white urban sophisticate.

The Socially Diverse Black Neighborhood

Here we are dealing with the fact that the church
institution may provide therapeutic functions for only a segment of its neighborhood. Increasingly there are pressures
for maintaining a congregational grouping that provides for
the increased needs felt in many black neighborhoods. Staff
field observers in the helping network study described the
growing church membership during a time of economic retrench-
ment (1974-75) that many blacks and whites in Detroit were
experiencing. How might such churches then accommodate this?
In times of economic stress there was no displaced commitment
to the church financially; rather, they were able to provide
the membership fee because of their firm attachment to the
church and its increasing significance under conditions of
economic distress.

The greater demand for the functions that the black
church can provide may help to accelerate the movement out of
a particular local neighborhood in which the physical
attributes could not allow for expansion or for the desired

status attainments and desired environments for the church
structure.

Are there different well-being consequences of upward
mobility in the black community in contrast to that occurring
in the white community?

Our study suggests a situation where the secularization
process does not serve to create any of the prevalent
institutions that the black church has generated. Thus, the
stepping-stone, transitory, or diffuse neighborhoods in the
white community provide merely a set of superficial, informal
support systems which have none of the depth or richness of
traditional parochial neighborhoods or the effective linkage
to service agencies of the integral neighborhood. In this
sense, of course, the local school and those kinds of
neighborhood organizations which may emerge can readily be
seen as the basis for building the kind of social support
that would serve as functional substitutes for the other
informal supports. It is important to consider how such
institutions take up the slack.

By contrast, the black neighborhood which is highly
heterogeneous or which lacks readily accessible church structures or which is reflective of a highly mobile, striving
sort of group would be expected to have some difficulty in
providing social support of the black homogeneous neighborhood.

Implications for Racially Changing Neighborhoods

In light of this analysis, the integrated neighborhood
is a form of double bind for both white and blacks. Whites
begin to see the cooperative norms of the black neighborhood
when it is a strong one. The emphasis on communal organization betokens the increasing domination of the blacks in
their racially changing area. At the same time, blacks newly
moved into a neighborhood would be extremely isolated and
would not have the institutional supports of the traditional
black neighborhood.

In other words, black individuals who are not living in
a black neighborhood might find it important to retain their
tie to the church, while those living in highly integrated
neighborhoods would perhaps suffer particularly from the
absence of that church in their own immediate area.

The racially integrated neighborhood is most likely to
be a multiproblem area. Blacks are able to draw upon only
limited networks in such a setting and whites no longer can
rely on the natural homogeneity of that neighborhood.
Residents of such areas may find that their social contacts
outside of that neighborhood become more restricted as
friends and relatives put informal pressures upon the

individual to return to the fold and join them in their more
homogeneous social environments.

In racially changing neighborhood contexts the perceptions of both blacks and whites may be heightened sources of
individual stress. Even the slightest problem may become
exaggerated. Where there are indeed significant problems of
crime or a decline in the services provided in these
neighborhoods, the effect is both to heighten the sense of
threat and lower the well-being of individuals of both races.
Such behavior patterns are seen from the perspective of the
helping network study to be a product of the weak informal
support systems that exist for the black as well as for the
white residents under conditions of rapid neighborhood
succession.

SOME GENERAL GUIDELINES FOR NEIGHBORHOOD INTERVENTION

We have found that neighborhood contexts are definable
and measurable, and that the differences can be observed.
They suggest that neighborhood is not usually the primary
base of helping. We must recognize the strengths of
neighborhood--even those neighborhoods that look very weak
since people do not seem to interact very much or fail to
identify with the neighborhood--that all of these peculiar
patterns that do not fit our idea of what a neighborhood
should be, are, in fact, the dominant patterns of urban
neighborhoods. The type of neighborhood--not simply the
degree to which there are neighborhood context factors of
significance--must be considered.

Our research suggests that there is often a dissonant
perspective held by the individual regarding what kind of
help is available (the capacity of a perceived neighborhood).
Even the objectively strong neighborhood contexts, such as
the integral and parochial, may contain many individuals who
will not use the available resources simply because their
perceptual definition suggests there is little out there to
draw upon in time of trouble or help-seeking. This pattern
is especially prevalent in the middle-strength neighborhoods
--diffuse, transitory and stepping-stone--where substantial
resources are available but are underutilized. In such
settings the identification of key helpers and the
strengthening of information flow between neighbors could be
the most effective strategy to reduce isolation and give
choices in helping and problem-coping to those who may have
lost faith in the professional system. Moreover, we have
found a great deal of evidence that people in many locales
start out using professionals earlier and more frequently
than people in other neighborhood contexts. In later stages

of problem-coping they tend to withdraw from such contacts
and instead of finding other quasi-formal or lay helping
resources, they tend to become socially isolated or to turn
to the family for help. Strengthening of such moderately
well-organized neighborhood contexts could be a valuable
alternative of help. While the same basic problem exists in
the strong neighborhoods, the natural resiliency and initiative of helpers in these settings suggest that little stimu-
lation is needed, certainly less than in the moderately
strong neighborhoods.

Strengthening Weak Neighborhoods

In the case of a weak neighborhood, we find that those
individuals who see it in more positive terms than the facts
warrant may continue to draw upon neighbors for help despite
its relative ineffectiveness. Two implications follow from
this: there is a need in anomic, transitory, and diffuse
neighborhoods 1) to re-educate people about what are other
helping resources and 2) to try to reach those helpers who
are heavily used by neighbors to give them information on how
to be more effective in their role. The meager resources of
weak neighborhoods are often overtaxed by those few residents
with positive expectations about their neighborhood and who
during times of crisis may overtax whatever helping resources
they find.

It would indeed be a very poor strategy to view weak
neighborhoods as suffering mainly from a loss of community.
If these areas tend to be lower-income and minority
neighborhoods--which our data somewhat supports--then the
crime rate or general alienation to be found in such locales
will not be reduced by improving people's sense of community.
In fact it may serve only to further alienate them and dis-
courage their use of outside resources.

The reliance of low-income families on neighborhood is
often a necessity and not a genuine choice. At the same
time, reducing social distance between neighbors in moderate-
income neighborhoods may be less important in the
strengthening of sense of community than protecting the
economic values within the local area. In still other situations in which economic values are treated as central and no
attention is paid to improving the sense of community,
working to reduce social distance may prove equally futile.
In such a situation all that may be accomplished is to permit
individuals to sell out and move to a more desirable
neighborhood. To reach problems of alienation via improving
the perceived sense of local community is a dangerous policy
direction to follow and a misreading of the implications of
our findings.

The strategy of first improving the level of perceived neighborhood quality is highly desirable when there are in fact useful and well-developed helping resources in the actual neighborhood. Increasing the individual's willingness to relate to and draw upon such resources can serve two functions: first, it gives that individual another arena in which to become linked to a helping network or to have a valuable helper; secondly, it can strengthen the neighborhood as a whole in terms of meeting a wide range of common problems and identifying ways to resolve such problems since more individuals participate in and are available for neighborhood mobilization.

Neighborhood Changes by Means of Observable Behaviors

Clearly the strengthening of actual neighborhood helping resources is not simply a re-education or attitude-change task, but involves the behavior and information about problems and resources which is diffused through the resident population. Starting at that side of the equation seems most warranted when there is already a highly develoepd sense of local community but actual resources are overtaxed. It is likely to show immediate benefits and results. In the case where both sense of neighborhood and actual resources are limited, the problem may involve reaching out and generating more helping resources in that neighborhood context, and then increasing the use of such resources once they are enhanced. Perhaps this is best done when a highly specific type of help is identified as missing in a neighborhood and when the "need" level appears to be climbing. Supervision of children playing in the streets, for example, as part of a special summer effort where neighbors are asked to help, or the case of house sitting, generate capacity for helping where people begin to actually use help and then may become more positive about the potential of the neighborhood to serve as a resource for various problems.

It is important to recognize that the varieties of neighborhood contexts described may each have specialized capacities for helping: one being more expressive and socially supportive, another more task oriented. Thus, one goal may be not necessarily to increase the amount of help or the probability of seeking help, but change what the helper does when called upon.

Attacking Social Isolation in Neighborhoods

While the lack of any helpers for problem-coping is more highly related to the larger municipality in which an individual lives than to their local neighborhood--perceived or actual--not using outside helpers or overlooking an available proximal helper is affected critically by the local context. The sense of isolation in particular may be as significantly if not more significantly affected by what one perceives and experiences in the immediate residential setting--especially for the elderly, for women who are largely involved with child rearing or not in the job market, or for people without income or education. Consequently, the banishment of loneliness and the ability of a person to cope with problems depend very largly, we would argue, on what the actual and perceived resources available in the neighborhood context are.

Basic to the findings of the helping network study is the proposition that a lack of sense of neighborhood as community is one of several major causes of individual social isolation and risk to well-being. However, it should be clearly understood that such a social problem occurs because of the structural implications of local community weakness and not simply because of the abstract value of "small is beautiful." *The psychological stress resulting from restricted access to helping networks during the time of problem coping is the critical and the central implication derived from our research.*

Should We Build Neighborhood Self-Sufficiency?

Most individuals, regardless of social class or ethnic group, do not reside in settings which maximize a protected and self-contained, self-reliant neighborhood context. Some have suggested that our only hope as a nation (and particularly in the rehabilitation of older urban areas) is to create such social worlds. Indeed, this is often what is common in the yearnings of a wide variety of groups--social critics, blacks in ghettoized neighborhoods, white ethnics who feel that their values and traditions have been submerged in an assimilationist mobile lifestyle, and to a new generation of young adults who see a simpler and more valid existence in the intimacy of small community life.

But the reality is that most urbanites live in neighborhoods which fail to provide that kind of womb-like security. We often may have arenas of such communality in organizations, work, family, or leisure-avocational "cults." While much of our research has implications for understanding how neighborhood relates to the more fundamental problem of individual alienation or sense of belonging, we cannot claim that strengthening neighborhood of residence is the primary or even the most cost-effective way to reach that goal. It is nevertheless important to understand how neighborhoods

function and when their strengths and weaknesses may
influence the larger issues to which we have alluded.

It would be a great disservice both to those interested
in the neighborhood revitalization movement and to those who
wish to reduce the cost of industrial society's disruptions
and discontinuities to view the research findings as
suggesting any slackening of their efforts. But a number of
significant cautions and clues as to how to act most
effectively are to be found in our results. Primarily, these
are findings about what neighborhood is for many urban area
dwellers, and what it is not.

We should not put our economic or service system
investment into neighborhoods without at first assessing the
risks and likely short- and long-term benefits. These differ
markedly, as we have noted, and the setting of differential
program goals for each situation is viewed as a critical
caveat. At the same time, certain broad trends and implications that affect all neighborhood contexts are to be found.
These include the fact that, regardless of how strong or weak
the actual resources of a neighborhood are, it is a critical
part of the individual's capacity to meet many of life's
crises and a vehicle for achieving individual improvement in
family, job, and other spheres. This is especially true for
lower-income, minority, and suburban residents.

Most neighborhoods are limited to their helping
resources and could benefit from efforts which provide
information, lay training, and selective location of professional helping resources targeted to a given type of
population or geographical locale. Many individuals are
socially isolated in the neighborhoods in which they reside,
and social programs that designate slum or deteriorating
neighborhoods in a physical sense as those most in need of
governmental aid overlook and ignore many critical needs of
neighborhoods in moderate and even fairly affluent locales.
Such efforts need not involve the generation of a continuous
service effort or require a shift from the priority on low-
income multiproblem neighborhoods and population groups.

There is a hidden cost to our society in the neglect of
neighborhood in other than its purely economic viability and
character. The quality of life of the neighborhood is
correlated with social class, and we should recognize that
link. But the relationship is only a moderate one, and in
the absence of a policy of improving the quality of neighborhood in general, our society as a whole suffers.

MIDDLE-AMERICAN HELPING NETWORKS

Our study has shown a majority (72 percent of urban populations) enter and leave helping pathways and resources at frequent intervals. Most of this group experiences the same problems over a one-year span. There are many individuals who experience these same concerns only once, so that problem turn-over is very high. This suggests that the flexibility of helping systems and the ability of these resources to expand fairly quickly for short times and then contract at others and to give individuals choices and alternative resources for help is of utmost importance. The barriers between the professional system on the one hand, and the lay system on the other, need to be reduced. Individuals should not have to feel that going to a professional precludes his or her returning to informal networks or that using a friend or a neighbor as a helper will preclude his calling upon a professional. The goal is to maximize the choices of the individual and the capacity and equality of the alternative systems of helping.

Most mental health programs have been directed at life crises and the breaking of relationships due to marital separation, divorce, death, and so forth. But our findings show that recent concerns have an equal, if not greater, impact on the mental outlook of many other persons in our society. This points to another system of problem-coping that must be taken into account whenever we try to understand the mental health of an individual or community beyond life crises in the Holmes and Rahe sense.

The direct administrative implication seems to be that many of these individuals move quickly into and out of high- or moderate-risk situations; and, therefore, there are a very large number of people who, at any given time, might fall into a risk population group. This may be due to job or economic disruptions. It may be due to unrealized aspirations. It may be due to crime in the neighborhood. The fact is that we do not have social service delivery systems that respond very effectively to these individuals and these particular kinds of concerns.

At the same time, it is precisely these middle-income individuals with a moderate to high problem load who are most resistant to social policies directed to low-income families. There are at least two issues here. One is how we deal with a kind of moderate-risk, large-scope population in terms of giving people quick, effective responses to their problems. Also, how can they be brought into a professional system considering that that system is generally utilized and reserved for more serious, chronic problems? There is a third, political issue: the tendency of this middle-income

group to feel that governmental services seem to be directed
mainly at the disadvantaged and those in a highly identifiable minority group.

TO SUM UP

     The role of helping networks has been shown to be an
important one in terms of the pathways to helping which
individuals follow in regard to recent concerns and life
crises. The data on entrance into a help-seeking sequence
suggests that factors other than neighborhood or social network ties are central. Once the initial contact is made,
however, the volume, content, and variety of help given and
sought is importantly shaped by the social context. In our
investigation of the character and impact of these patterns,
the process which emerges can be described in the following
way: help-seeking is conditioned by the access to helpers in
the sense of those who are socially close and those who are
accessible directly or by networking in the behavior setting
of the local neighborhood. In particular, the neighbor can
seek a key intermediary in the referral to other helpers and
types of problem-coping behaviors and resources.
     The role of professional helpers is, in part, related
to the probability that such help will be sought early or
late in the problem-coping sequence. The social context of
community and neighborhood appears to influence the timing
and effectiveness of such help-seeking more than the probability that such help will be sought.
     Seeking help from informal helpers is highly variable
in terms of what kind of behaviors will be provided and, in
turn, how such helping is perceived by the recipient.
     The matching of needed help to the help-seeker is a
critical dimension of effectiveness. Thus, anomic, transitory, and stepping-stone settings appear to be less able to
provide such matching in comparison to integral, parochial,
and diffuse settings. In the mosaic setting, the intense use
of a few helpers--whether neighbor, friend, or co-
worker--tends to be a basic way social support systems are
effective for residents of such milieux. Help-seeking which
is initially too widely scattered or eventually too reliant
on formal or professional helpers appears less effective in
reducing the stress associated with having several recent
concerns or life crisis.
     The ability to open a series of alternative helping
pathways and to permit variability in that mix is associated
with reducing risk to individual well-being. While the
number of behaviors is not always a good guide to an effective helping system, it is true that those neighborhood

contexts where a wide scope of helping is provided show lower
risk to well-being when such help is sought.

The simple notion of a modal pathway to helping does
not, however, provide a useful description of how such networks of helping function. For example, it is clear that in
every neighborhood context some individuals do not enter any
helping network, while others rely on one or two helpers over
a period of time, and still others appear to shop around or
shift with time and the type of problem. All of this makes a
description of an average or modal pattern difficult to
apply. It is possible, however, to identify more frequently
employed helpers in one social context compared to another--
for a person of a given age, sex, or social context.

In a broader sense, however, it is the richness and
flexibility of helping systems which provide the difference.
Effective neighborhood contexts are those which either
maximize choice and entry points or provide a consistent and
secure cluster of helpers and well-tread pathways. Contexts
which fluctuate too quickly or widely or which are under-
developed in scope do not insure that problem-coping will be
least disruptive to individual well-being. Effective
neighborhood contexts are those which permit the largest
number of persons to enter a system of helping and to pursue
life-changing and life-developing problem-coping.

Where systems of helping are bypassed and individuals
withdraw from seeking life change and improvement, such contexts are as ineffective as when the person seeks help for a
problem and cannot find it. Where help-seeking for problems
is responsive to needs, the effects of such encounters need
not be detrimental to the balance and well-being of the
individual.

While the absence of life crises and recent concerns
may reduce the risk to well-being of the individual, such
insulation is not the normal course of urban life.

Social isolation and withdrawal from help-seeking is
not itself a test of the quality of life of a local environment. But the capacity of any social setting to generate
problem-coping resources may serve as a more realistic and
useful basis for assessing an individual's "life chances."

Nowhere is the duality of the modern, compart-
mentalized urbanite more typically described than in his or
her neighborhood ties. The helping network study suggests
the following perspective: Individuals carry with them a
"cognitive" map of two kinds of social ties: friendship and
helping. Those social bonds are often overlapping and in the
research literature have frequently been confused with one
another. Nowhere is this distinction more evident than in
the neighborhood context. Here the two worlds of close

social ties and the emergency or utilitarian need for help
co-exist.

We find that individuals have more close friends who
are neighbors in stronger neighborhoods than in weaker
neighborhoods. Yet we also find that the bulk of close ties
for urbanites—friends—are not to be found in the neighborhood.

Thus, the local residential area is a bilateral system
of weak and strong ties—the latter found in even the most
anomic of neighborhoods, and the former more pronounced in
the integral and parochial neighborhood types.

We cannot readily dismiss either the potential of
neighborhoods for helping or their often transient and highly
circumscribed social integration.

We dare not evaluate the helping of a close friend as
the basis of maintaining that relationship. This would
indeed undermine the very moral and sociological character of
that tie. But we certainly can distinguish when a neighbor
is a valuable friend, an occasional problem-helper, or can
only be turned to for the most immediate and sudden
emergencies.

Amid the complexity of urban life neighboring is a
varied and often emphemeral tie. Our research indicates that
neighborhood is not so much an alternative to formal agency
helping or links to kin and "significant others" as it is an
arena within which the individual is integrated or isolated
from a larger world of helping resources, information, and
social support. For it is in this way that the term "context" takes on a very special meaning derived from our
findings: that neighborhood is not so much a place where
social closeness flourishes, as it is a hypothetical
community whose actual resources may be hidden from our view
by barriers of personal time investment and social distance.

To call upon a neighbor is less an act of affirmation
of "sense of community" than it is a testing of "what is out
there." Our data show that individuals, regardless of their
objective neighborhood, are quite often testing or in need of
using the resources of help and social support that neighbors
can provide. What occurs once that system has been tried out
differs markedly from one type of neighborhood to another.

It would indeed be valid to conclude that no objective
reality of neighborhood life can fully describe the idea of
neighborhood that people may carry in their heads. Of
course, this is true of many social institutions and structures. But in the case of neighborhood we have a
particularly indicative reflection of the contemporary
changes in society that do not fit our traditional images and
stereotypes.

We all bemoan the passing of the traditional close-knit neighborhood, but few care to invest in its restoration. For most urbanites with a moderate level of economic choice (and released from the bonds of racial or ethnic discrimination) the freedom from the neighborhood is as important to well-being as the need to reside in a safe, sanitary, and economically viable locale to which they may retreat and restore their sense of self and stability. I would argue that it is this very conservative or preservative value in a psychological and sociological sense that parallels our concern with the physical dimensions of neighborhood.

If the hypotheses and evaluative judgments we have developed vis-a-vis the linkages of community and individual well-being are to merit the attention of either human service professionals or those concerned with the urban condition, such insights must be placed in a context of potential applications and comparative research. To these considerations of practitioners and policy makers we now turn.

CHAPTER X

PROGRAMMATIC USES OF HELPING/SOCIAL NETWORK ANALYSIS

The thesis of this chapter is that a new perspective has emerged regarding the basis of social intervention and public policy in terms of human service programs. Simply stated, the concept of social networks has become a topical byword for describing strategies of problem prevention and treatment, a lay basis for health and social service outreach efforts. Essential to this new orientation is a view that social programs involving initiatives from professional experts, formal agency bureaucrats, and hierarchical planning have either failed to produce significant success outcomes (largely efforts dating from the 1960s) or have only added to the weight of citizen alienation from government in general.

We have already hinted at the wider horizon of programs and social-policy issues relating to social/helping networks. Some of these have a clear research basis—most do not. They are exploratory and grow out of often pragmatic concerns of a specific agency or local group. Still others go beyond one specific project and relate to broad social forces in American society.

With the rise of the "community as expert" movement in and out of government we find many new public initiatives for which funds are being made available to try out and perfect partnerships between informal and formal helpers that address many human problems of urban life.[1] "Social Networks" to some is the new organizing principle which replaces the "Great Society" with the "Small is Beautiful" perspective.

Where once patient, client, or target population goals existed, one now finds community support strategies defined by increased citizen participation acting in concert with indigenous or natural helpers who are able to supplement or even to supplant experts. Thus, a dichotomy of formal

versus grass-roots expertise has arisen in which the proper
boundary or optimal mix and balance between the two has yet
to be defined. Although a number of human service agencies
are now experimenting with such strategies, as yet no
detailed evaluation studies of how specific programs can
successfully build such partnerships have been undertaken.[2]
    We cannot explore in this single chapter the full
panoply of policy issues raised by network analysis. We
shall however, focus on several questions regarding the
design of social intervention projects aimed at improving
human services and problem resources of individuals:

1. Can natural networks be built by professionals?
2. What is the range of strategies for linking
    networks of informal/communal helping with
    professional service programs?
3. How effective are social/helping networks?
4. Does the helping network approach offer a
    substitute for, a complement to, or a supplement to
    professional helping?
5. Can or should natural networks be built by public
    agencies?

As researchers and practitioners learn more about the
positive functions of informal social support systems in
helping people cope with stress and a variety of life
concerns, the importance of assuring that public and private
agencies offering services are not destroying or discouraging
the natural support systems becomes clear. Some of the
functions which have been performed by formal services may
devolve back onto the informal systems due to rising costs.
Hospital stays, for example, are growing shorter, placing a
greater burden on the informal systems to provide
convalescent care. Thirty years ago women commonly spent ten
days in the hospital after having a baby. Now they are
routinely discharged after two or three days. The community
is also being asked to care for chronically disabled persons
who were previously institutionalized.
    A rather classic argument about an alternative to
professionalization of problem solving is that of Nathan
Glazer's "Limits of Social Policy" article:

    But aside from these problems of cost, of
    professionalization, and of knowledge, there is the
    simple reality that every piece of social policy
    substitutes for some traditional arrangement, whether
    good or bad, a new arrangement in which public
    authorities take over, at least in part, the role of
    the family, of the ethnic and neighborhood group, or of

the voluntary association. In doing so, social policy
weakens the position of these traditional agents and
encourages needy people to depend on the government
rather than on the traditional structure for help
(Glazer, 1971:54).

And that,

> Ultimately, we are not kept healthy, I believe, by
> new scientific knowledge, or more effective cures, or
> even better organized medical-care services. We are
> kept healthy by certain patterns of life. These, it is
> true, are modified for the better by increased scien-
> tific knowledge, but this knowledge is itself com-
> municated through such functioning traditional organi-
> zations as the school, the voluntary organization, the
> family. We are kept healthy by having access to tra-
> ditional means of support in distress and illness,
> through the family, the neighborhood, the informal
> social organizations (Glazer, 1971:57).

Schon, while aware of the problems of overprofessionalization, also points out some perils of "network
related intervention" by government:

> When government intervenes in such a way as to
> mobilize or enhance informal networks, there is a risk
> both to government and to the networks. The risk to
> government comes from certain principles and values
> which informal networks are likely to abrogate. The
> risk to the networks comes from the actions governments
> may take in order to protect their espoused
> values. . . .
> Suppose, for example, that government espouses a
> commitment to allocation of services on the basis of
> need, merit, and equity, whereas informal networks
> provide access to services partly on the basis of need,
> partly on the basis of merit (as measured by the
> ability and willingness to offer other services in
> exchange), but also on the basis of kinship,
> friendship, or political allegiance. Or suppose,
> again, that government espouses commitment to certain
> principles such as freedom from racial or sexual
> prejudice, and that particular informal networks are
> based on race or on sex. Government then finds itself
> in a dilemma. How can it honor both its wish to
> support informal networks and its commitment to its
> espoused principles? Moreover, the likelihood that
> such issues will arise is far from negligible; for it

is entirely characteristic of informal networks that
they are preferentially structured around considerations of kinship, friendship, political
allegiance, race, and sex (Schon, 1977:67).

The very definition of social networks as informal and
natural often means that the conventional concept of
"organizing networks" as one would organize in a neighborhood
does not seem feasible. By their very nature a self-help
group must emerge out of community dynamics. By trying to
help neighborhoods all we often do is bureaucratize them. We
draw in another leadership group from the outside. When the
agency cannot find the right kind of leadership they bring in
their own or identify what is thought to be the right kind of
leader.
Although the helping network study treats a series of
questions about networks and public policy of a more
restricted nature than those raised by Glazer or Schon, its
relevance is to assess traditional means of support and to
seek to deal with them in an operational way.

SOME PRINCIPLES OF EFFECTIVE HELPING

The pattern of problem load and increased stress is
mitigated importantly by the use of helpers when that contact
involves more than a person serving as a good listener.
Individuals who remain isolated from others in the experiencing of life crises or recent concerns show a clear pattern
of increased risk to well-being as the number of problems
increase.
The single problem level of stress may be such that it
is too evanescent a concern or too vague a discontent to
warrant an answer, advice, or even passive emotional support
of the "good listener." The problem may be worsened by
hearing a wide variety of opinions on the matter. Moreover,
it may even be less stressful to "keep it in" if that is the
initial personality style of the individual.
Problems may not be harmful for mental health if they
are linked to effective coping and social integration. That
is, the problem and its solution may give rise to new social
ties and to a sense of belonging which in the absence of the
stress or problem would not occur. Lack of problems may be a
function of social withdrawal--the sense that it is no use
trying something new or responding to a change, merely accept
it or ignore the effects. The result is poor mental health.
Problems which occur without seeking help may be detrimental
for mental health if it is assumed by the individual that no
one will be effective as a helper or even that no one cares,

or that various potential helpers are simply not within reach. Use of helpers particularly in anomic neighborhood settings is less a matter of selection than of having no options in help-seeking.

As problem load goes up, so does the demand for help under normal mental health conditions. The issue is how much can the various systems of help expand so that once the problem load is reduced it will no longer be mandatory to use the helper. This is an especially critical problem for professional help givers who must often choose among which clients to serve and must decide when treatment is advanced enough or successful enough to warrant reducing attention to that client.

If informal systems can take over the situation after some initial help by the professional, then this denotes a kind of rapid response or short term role for professionals, perhaps at an early point in problem-coping--a sort of efficient and universally available helping system whose goals and procedures are impartial and yet provide perspective and help on a problem even before it is possible to consider its related crisis dimensions. This kind of early-bird counseling can be very helpful. It may then provide the individual with a willingness to talk to others, having bridged the barrier and with a sense of not being unique, deviant, isolated, or sick.

The adaptive capacity of an environment is the ability of such a setting to facilitate the individual's getting help from several kinds of helpers. This means not being locked into just one system--whether it is lay or professional.

That there is a range of applications and ways to implement clinical and "at risk" assessments of individuals is implied by the patterns that have been reviewed in this chapter.

To fully employ the principles or premises of the helping networks to which we have alluded requires very specific information about the group or individual that is the target of help or is a client or patient. Within the scope of this review and analysis we cannot fully address such diagnostic and practical utilization possibilities of our findings. At best we can hint at the possibilities whereby agencies and helpers--professional and lay--can improve their effectiveness.

GENERAL INTERVENTION STRATEGIES WHICH USE INFORMAL NETWORKS

There are a number of programs scattered throughout the U.S.A. in the health, social service, planning, crime control, and neighborhood redevelopment spheres which have

attempted to identify and link up with natural/informal
helpers. Some programs have developed their own terminology
(e.g., "capacity building"), while others use very general
terms that are likely to cover a variety of activities (e.g.,
"outreach"). Three major approaches can be identified:

   1. Focusing on the individual case: Here networks and
natural helpers are seen as providing resources for actual or
potential clients of a formal agency. An elderly person, for
example, may be having trouble caring for himself in his own
home but would not have to be institutionalized if some
informal supports can be developed. At least three subtypes
of agency interventions can be delineated: a) agency staff
identify members of the client's family, friendship, or
neighborhood network and help them on the client's behalf, b)
agency staff identify specific services which the informal
network cannot supply to the client and provide these
services without usurping the other functions of the natural
network, and c) agency staff refer isolated individuals to
ongoing informal networks in their neighborhood or other
social arenas such as work or leisure groups.

   The work of Speck and Attneuve (1973) in regard to
convening all members of one's social support network is an
example of the first approach. The efforts of the North
Shore Child Guidance Center in New York include efforts under
the second category. This provision focuses on providing
help to single-parent families by establishing a Family Life
Center where survey data showed that natural helpers could
not cope with the need of this segment of the population to
have problems of adolescents effectively addressed. Under
the third category is the work done in Chicago's RSVP program
conducted by ACTION through the Hull House affiliate
program--Senior Centers of Metropolitan Chicago--largely
aimed at reducing social isolation of the elderly. This
program includes volunteers who make regular telephone or
personal social calls and seek to provide routine shopping,
errands, or other small-scale helping services.

   2. Increase the capacity of the informal system as a
whole: In this approach the formal agency does not identify
specific clients or "at risk" groups but instead attempts to
strengthen the community network for the benefit of all
members. This may mean reducing residential mobility or
supporting family life by modifying work schedules or the
like. Many of these efforts may involve the identification
of "key figures" or natural helpers who have influence over
others in the network:

   a) Some programs provide key figures with information
      to disseminate to other members of the network.
      For example, information about health problems and

available services is provided to key figures in a
network of mothers who are not prone to seek
preventative medical services for their children.

b) Mental health consultation--(focusing on specific
problems faced by natural helpers as they attempt
to help members of their networks) has been
provided by professionals. NIMH has supported
training of bartenders and beauty operators to deal
with depression and aid in a referral process.

c) Several projects have offered training to natural
helpers in communication skills, crisis
intervention techniques, and use of formal service,
including highly technical ones such as home
improvement loans.

Toward these ends partnerships of various kinds have
been established with natural helpers and persons who are
veterans of the problem or life predicament, and with
community institutions such as churches, synagogues, social
clubs etc. Examples of how this was done are illustrated by
Collins's work with neighbors who provide neighborhood
day-care services for children (1973); by the work of Smith
who identified central figures who provided services within
their neighborhood to the elderly (1975); by Pancoast (1970)
who discovered and worked with a natural network of boarding
homes for discharged mental patients in an urban poverty
area; by Silverman (1970) who catalyzed the development of an
outreach program to the newly bereaved, the Widow-to-Widow
Program; by Ellis (1972) who initiated a program to help
needy groups, isolated elderly and "latch key" children, by
working with the elderly to develop after-school programs
staffed by elders; by Patterson and Twente (1971) in
developing mental health services in a rural area where no
professional helping resources existed, using natural
helpers and local counselors, such as ministers, lawyers,
bankers, and county extension agents; and by G. Caplan (1967)
who organized support systems in a time of war and developed
a framework for professional involvement, "supporting the
supporters."

Vallance and his colleagues at Pennsylvania State
University College of Human Development, in collaboration
with the Geisinger Mental Health Center in Danville, are
developing an experimental model to identify and train
natural caregivers in order to extend preventive mental
health manpower and to reduce costs of service delivery. In
the first instance, professional educators will teach
trainers to train direct-service providers; then these
trainers in turn will train a group of formal and informal
helpers in basic helping skills, crisis intervention skills,

and life development skills; finally, these natural helpers
will enhance the development of life skills in others in
their communities. The goal is to establish an
administrative structure within a mental health system that
can sustain and expand community helping networks.
    3. Focus on the community or neighborhood. Sometimes
agencies are less interested in particular individuals,
whether they are clients or members of networks, than they
are in the general livability of a geographical area. They
may use an approach based on natural helpers to deal with
issues such as neighborhood deterioration or racial tensions.
Two different approaches have been identified:

    a)   agency staff encourage neighbors to identify common
        concerns, such as inadequate formal services, and
        to organize and bring pressure on institutions to
        improve their services. (indirect linkage)
    b)   agency staff help natural helper/neighbors to
        identify underutilized resources within the
        informal system and to develop ways to make better
        use of them. (direct linkage)

    The first approach is based on the concept of indirect
capacity building, or "empowerment." Here an effort is made
to consciously mobilize an indigenous population so that it
can shape services to meet neighborhood needs. One such
capacity-building program is the Neighborhood and Family
Services Project of the Washington Public Affairs Center of
the University of Southern California. The focus of this
project is to examine needs and resources from a neighborhood
perspective in two ethnic communities in Baltimore and
Milwaukee in order to determine ways of linking professional
services to the natural helping networks in the neighborhood
(churches, ethnic, fraternal, and social organizations, and
natural helpers or gatekeepers).
    In each city, the project is designed to work through a
local commumnity organization that is representative of, and
controlled by, the residents of the community, thus giving
neighborhood people more control over human service programs
in their communities. Its objective is consultation and
education as determined by this population's identification
of needs, gaps, and lacks in their neighborhood's formal and
informal support systems for women who were single parents.
The Center's currently projected next step, in addition to
its ongoing direct treatment services, will be to develop a
new project, a Family Life Center, utilizing professional
resources in collaboration with neighborhood volunteers to
service natural helping networks in all seven communities in

ways that will strengthen their ongoing ability to be
responsive to the needs of families in stressful situations.

These new projects using local informal networks are
part of a broader pattern of neighborhood participation and
voluntary association activity. There has been a sustained
level of grass-roots activity of this type. Citizen participation has come to be associated with the decade of the 60s,
but precursors existed before and other developments have
followed into the mid and late 70s. The frenetic 60s dis-
played a vivid mosaic of organization activities: civil
rights, black power, A.I.M., La Raza, O.E.O., community
action, Alinsky, the student movement, the peace movement,
Model Cities, welfare rights, feminism, gay liberation,
environmental protection, consumer rights, white ethnic
activism, and political reform. Grass-roots civic action is
often likened to a falling star, reaching its apex in the 60s
and plummeting to earth, burned out and dissipated with the
transition into the 70s. A closer look revealed that the
legacy of the 60s has been carried forward, not in a spec-
tacular way, but nevertheless in a wide set of programs.

One element of this is the inclusion of provision for
citizen involvement in governmental programs of all sorts. A
kind of participation revolution has been carried out
somewhat imperceptibly, but at least at the level of formal
requirements.[5]

HOW EFFECTIVE ARE INFORMAL SOCIAL NETWORKS?

One of the implications of the discussion by Schon is
the dangers of direct funding by government to strengthen
helping networks. There are two reasons. The first is the
limited knowledge base. This is the same problem with OEO,
Model Cities, and some of the other efforts of the 60s. We
do not understand (so runs this argument) the complexity of
neighborhoods and communities well enough so that, even if it
were thought philosophically correct to try to organize
another group's neighborhood, there is a high risk that
consistent success cannot be achieved.

The multifaceted interest in strategies using the
rubric of support networks, helping networks, and natural
helpers represents a stimulating field of new community
action. At the same time, the documentation of successes and
failures has yet to be undertaken. In the President's
Commission on Mental Health report released in April, 1978,
the Task Force on Community Support included a recommendation
"to initiate research to increase our knowledge of informal
and formal community support systems and networks." (p. 15)

This task force indicated additionally that mental health
research activity should include:

> . . . exchanges of information among lay community
> groups and mental health professionals about model,
> ongoing community support programs;
> . . . development, through grants and contracts of
> demonstration programs with an evaluation component
> that can identify effective ways to establish linkages
> between community mental health services and community
> support systems, and
> development of research initiatives on the efficacy of
> social networks as adjuncts to mental health service
> delivery systems, and on the effects of informal and
> formal community support systems on the utilization of
> health and mental health services (President's
> Commission on Mental Health, Volume I, 1978:61).

At the time of this writing, a significant project of
evaluation of natural helping network projects has been
undertaken by Diane Pancoast and her colleagues at the
Regional Research Institute of Portland State University.
Results from this effort and the growing number of related
individual studies, such as the Health and Social Support
studies by Kahn, French, and others at the Survey Research
Institute at the University of Michigan, will undoubtedly
help other researchers provide a basis for the design and
implementation of effective social/helping network programs.
There are problems of dealing with natural helpers and
informal support networks. Such systems may be too selective
and not include many who could benefit and contribute. There
are undoubtedly many urban neighborhoods in which people do
not know each other and cannot rely on a neighborhood-based
helping system.
In the meantime there remain limits of public policy
regarding use of informal community systems in intervention
efforts. In the same way that such caveats have emerged for
formal systems, cautions about informal networks need to be
considered. Among the important one Schon raises are these:

> 1) In spite of the disposition on the part of
> some observers to believe that informal networks are
> superior in quality and equity to formal services, the
> quality of service provided through informal networks
> is apt to be highly variable and the distribution of
> services is apt to be inequitable.
> 2) The effort by government to support, enhance,
> and control informal networks tends to conflict with
> certain espoused principles of government and to

interfere with certain informal network processes; as a
result, governmental intervention is likely to fail,
or if successful, to convert informal networks to
formal systems.
        3) The very success of informal networks may put
excessive demand upon network capacity (Schon,
1977:62).

We would agree with the "state of the art" description of
network intervention by Schon:

        The superiority of informal networks to formal
    institutions is a proposition to be explored and tested
    in each instance of its assertion. The myth of the
    formal professional service ethos has its counterpart
    in the romantic myth of the superiority of informal
    networks. There is little evidence, at least in the
    context of the social programs of the sixties, that
    formal professional services are broadly effective in
    achieveing their espoused objectives and values. And
    there is little evidence that informal social networks
    are broadly superior in responsiveness, quality and
    equity to the offerings of formal service systems
    (Schon, 1977:66).

WHAT ROLE FOR HELPING NETWORKS AND PUBLIC POLICY?

        The neglect and erosion of natural helping networks is
a major source of social alienation, isolation, and the
burgeoning public agency problem-solving load.
        There are many causes for this trend. Increased social
mobility, geographic mobility, family dissolution, the
generation gap, loss of trust in neighbors, overspecialization in professional training, and community segregation by
race, social class, age, and social attitudes.
        One consequence of the decline of city life is the
weakening of social integration due to a lack of shared
experiences between different segments of our society.
        Given a society of mobile people in search of a better
life, the vitality of natural helping networks can no longer
be based exclusively on local ties. Helping networks reach
out via long distance telephone and rapid travel.
Understanding these crisscrossing patterns and how they
function to provide individual well-being is a vital task of
governmental service agencies or programs funded to give
professional help.
        In our view formal agencies cannot create natural
helping networks, but they can destroy them through ignorance

or policies which act to erode their social environmental
base. This implies that federal agencies and subsidized
programs need to use natural helping networks as allies in
the fight against disease, poverty, discrimination, and
threats to the well-being of the individual and the family
unit. This is particularly true in urban areas. Helping
networks can often facilitate the most efficient and
effective delivery of professional services by screening out
persons who, if given advice, social support, or a referral
from a friend, neighbor, or co-worker to another helper will
not monopolize professional personnel time for mild (albeit
real) symptoms and problems.
      There is a need for a national policy of balanced
helping systems between informal and formal community
resources. This critical equation can be calculated and
evaluations made as to cost and benefits:

> Professional service agencies can disseminate
> information about their programs via key neighborhood
> and other natural helpers.
>   Agencies can monitor and target resources more
> effectively by diagnosing the strength and distinctive
> patterns of the natural helping systems utilized by
> client anmd target populations in specific
> neighborhoods they are mandated to serve.
>   The term "needs assessment" should connote an
> obligation of public agencies to carry out
> environmental impact analyses to determine the role of
> their service programs in complementing, supplementing,
> or supplanting natural helping networks.

We suggest that there are at least three ways in which
human service programs can draw upon network analysis:
      In prevention: Identifying and mapping the density,
distribution, and vitality of natural helping networks can
aid in program planning and evaluation by directing attention
to where professional services should be increased, maintained, or can be reduced to avoid duplication, and where a
local informal solution is just as successful.[7]
      In treatment: Most professionals see a patient who has
first been in touch with many natural helpers. Patients
often go as a last resort or because they trust the advice of
the person who sent them to the professional; they are
otherwise fearful and misinformed about formal helpers and
what they can do.
      In ninety percent of the cases so-called self-referral
really involves a person who has talked with at least one
natural helper first--a spouse, friend, neighbor, co-worker,
or friend--before he or she goes to an agency for help. The

pathway to the professional is either blocked or facilitated
by the role of natural helpers.

In the vast majority of instances the therapy or
treatment process itself relies for ultimate success on the
role of informal helpers--family, friends, co-workers. The
professional is always in an invisible partnership with a
host of colleagues in the natural environment of the patient.
The absence or subversion of the natural helpers is a major
obstacle to treatment and often to diagnosis itself.

After-care: Here the case for natural helpers is
especially strong. Many kinds of illness and social service
help require the cooperation of natural helpers in the
environment of the patient or client. Monitoring of
symptoms, therapeutic interventions, and medical regimens
such as dieting or other behavior controls cannot be mainly
dependent on professional visitations and contact. All of
the patterns of patient behavior and treatment that are out
of the hands of the professional depend on natural helping
systems.

Many programs of community placement--returning the
person to the community--depend for their success on the
strength and role of informal helping networks. Agencies
that use and understand these dynamics can make maximum use
of their staffs and insure the highest level of success in
de-institutionalization and general out-patient care. Often
natural helping networks are used as an intuitive insight by
administrators. But we need to have all health and social
welfare agencies using natural helping networks by locating
and seeking to build relationships with key members of such
networks.

It is a basic premise of community mental health[8] that
social interventions (programs) which are most likely to be
successful are those which build upon natural, already
existing relationships and social structures in a geographic
setting. There is a need for further theoretical development
and empirical testing of such assumptions before it is clear
what the full implications of such a premise are or what its
operational limits might be.

A SUMMARY: CONCEPTS TO BEAR IN MIND

The applied approach we have taken to social/helping
networks has attempted to reveal and grapple with the complex
and often diffuse attributes of what some see as a broad
social movement in American society. This movement
symbolizes a reaction to the overprofessionalization and high
cost of services and at the same time a search for better
ways to provide such services. In this concluding section we

should like to crystalize some premises underlying the
approaches that we have advanced.

1. There are "limits to social policy" intervention
    styles, as Glazer has articulated. The use of
    government, professionals, and formal procedures is
    a finite strategy for coping with social ills.
2. Voluntary grass-roots involvement is a key to
    maximizing community action and local
    problem-solving. Such actions can be conducted
    independently or in some reciprocal relationship
    with specialized and formalized human service
    agencies and institutions.
3. Recognizing that local skills and resources can
    constribute to problem-coping, and that some of the
    social bonds at the local level have been weakened,
    there is a need for empowerment of small-scale,
    locality-based interest groups in society. Micro
    units such as families, social networks, and
    neighborhoods should be acknowledged and come to
    see themselves as significant entities capable of
    contributing to their own well-being.

The first of these premises assumes that communities,
regardless of size, may have different agendas and value
systems (Roland Warren, 1977), and that in a pluralistic
society it is not reasonable to design social interventions
that are based on the establishment of models which are not
grounded in differential consumer needs and interests.
Without such grounding, policy formulations may miss the mark
of their intentions by considerable margins.

There is a variety of opinion among different actors
and interests concerning what constitutes a problem or
symptom; hence, highly standarized and predetermined formulae
concerning ideal solutions should be avoided. The notions of
locality, variability, and strategy flexibility have been
widely recognized. Moreover, the right to reject proffered
expertise and service delivery modalities rejuvenates local
democracy and fosters community viability.

The second premise takes note of the potential of local
voluntary effort. In a national study funded by the Mott and
Kettering Foundations in 1977, the Gallup organization
reported numerous examples of underutilization of citizen
voluntary effort and yet notes its strength in the
neighborhood context. McBride (1978) in reporting findings
of this study states that:

Perhaps the most striking finding of the survey is the
willingness of urban residents to become involved at

the local level--contrary to the apparent apathy
reflected in dismally low voter turnouts in local
elections. According to the survey, 89 percent of the
neighborhood residents would be willing to volunteer,
and more than half (52 percent) have engaged in some
sort of community activity in the last five years
(Stewart Dill McBride, "Gallup Urban Poll--Residents
View Their Cities," Nation's Cities, Volume 16, Number
11, November 1978: 42-43).

A wide variety of formal programs are now tapping the
volunteer market. Evidence suggests that the effectiveness
of many agency programs rests on an appropriate pattern of
referral and linkages with informal helping networks. Much
of what is considered our national economy, in fact, rests on
a myriad of unpaid and underpaid services that are not
calculated in the GNP statistics. This informal economy is a
basic element of the locality strategies we have reviewed.
  Our third premise deals with the emergent social-
psychological properties of small social networks. The very
act of communicating a need or concern to others--whether
professional helpers or informal peers--encompasses the
potential for common purpose and a shared sense of justice or
injustice.
  There is much overlap and interplay between individual
problems and community problems. Service delivery programs
can instill a sense of self-confidence among clients that can
lead to new and more far-reaching demands for service. The
consciousness-raising tactics of many social networks are, of
course, widely recognized. Therefore, any applied work on
networks and community systems may generate a new meaning of
community and form a basis of social action that goes beyond
the initial personalistic goals or motivations of the
participants in a small-scale helping network.
  General economic conditions of the present epoch and
the immediate future effectively curb the past excesses of
professional helping strategies. Now the primary task is to
identify the right kind of partnership linkages between
formal and informal helpers and to be clear about the "limits
of public policy" which suggest we can create community where
it is lacking.
  The practical dilemmas we have noted in regard to the
role of helping networks in program interventions and public
policies are cautionary, not categorical. I strongly advocate that we develop this new direction of social intervention with a parallel investment in evaluation and comparative research. Service practitioners, policymakers,
planners, and students of urban life will undoubtedly find

many new directions emerging as we learn more from various
studies now underway.

NOTES

CHAPTER II

    1. Traditional approaches to social support have
developed from social behavior studies of animals and humans.
There has been a continuing trend to view social support in
terms of some combination of interpersonal ties and helping
behaviors that allows individuals to cope with problems and
to maintain a state of functional homeostasis. More
recently, with a growing emphasis regarding the influence of
social stress on health and well-being, some investigators
have broadened their scope of study to include the role
social support plays in mitigating the effects of stress (cf.
Cassel, 1974; Cobb, 1976; Kaplan, Cassel, and Gore, 1977).
    This new direction, however, has not been systemati-
cally developed as pointed out in a recent report to the
President's Commission of Mental Health.

> Unfortunately, [social support] studies contain certain
> conceptual and methodological weaknesses that limit
> their usefulness with regard to a precise explanation
> of support systems in disease etiology. Principle
> among these weaknesses has been a failure of most
> researchers to relate one set of psychosocial factors
> (e.g., support systems) to others that have also been
> shown to influence health, such as stress (1978:180).

    Gore (1978) investigated the effects of social support
on health as a result of unemployment in a two-year longitudinal study of the physical and mental health consequences
of involuntary job loss. Social support was operationally
defined as 1) the perception of support from spouse, friends,
and relatives; 2) frequency of contact with these informal
social network participants; and 3) individual's "perceived
opportunity for social activities which provide expressive
feelings of well-being and a milieu for discussing problems"
(Gore, 1978:160). Her findings indicate that "levels of

215

social support seem to modify the severity of psychological
and health-related responses to unemployment" (1978:163).
These levels of social support are identified as "tangible"
and "psychological" dimensions of social support which can be
interpreted as providing some degree of helping behaviors as
well as social-emotional or "expressive" support. Consistent
with previous research findings, she concludes that "social
support increases coping ability, which is the etiological
gate to health and well-being" (1978:157).

Numerous studies and research reviews over the past
decade have concluded that social supports provided by the
primary groups of most importance to the individual function
as protective factors buffering or cushioning the individual
from the physiologic or psychologic consequences of exposure
to stress situations. Moss (1973) views social support as a
"general social therapy" factor which provides relief from
information incongruities. The lack of social support not
only enhances one's susceptability to illness, but also
directly affects one's feelings of belongingness and well-
being. Moss (1973:237) describes the implications of this
lack of social support:

> People who do not receive support or who are unable to
> establish such relationships because they do not know
> how to go about establishing or maintaining them may
> have to resort to instrumental accomplishments of
> various approved goals of communication networks for
> their feelings of worth, belonging, and self-esteem.

Cassel (1970:195) notes that individuals deprived of
"meaningful human contact or group membership" are higher
risks for schizophrenia, accidents, suicide, hypertension,
and respiratory diseases. In a later review of the literature, Cassel (1974) pointed out that many investigations of
social support have restricted themselves to relating the
absence of social support to some stressful situation or
disease.

Cassell suggests that efforts should be directed at
improving and strengthening the social supports rather than
attempting to prevent the stress situation (1974:479). We
agree with this notion and further submit that exposure to
stressful situations may lead to building helping networks
within informal social networks. We suggest that encounters
with recent problems or life crises will lead to changes
within informal support systems. Such changes may expand and
strengthen social support efforts, help to maintain existing
social supports, or weaken the support network depending on
the nature of support (or lack of support) relationships
within the social network. The dissertation by Forrest W.
Graves, Jr., (1979) develops this theory in an empirical
fashion from data in the Detroit study.

2. For a discussion of this pathways approach see Friedson, 1961; Lefton and Rosengren, 1966; and McKinley, 1973.

3. The work is best summarized in the following references: Litwak and Meyer, 1966; 1967; Litwak, 1968; Litwak and Meyer, 1974.

CHAPTER III

1. In the pre-tests of two alternative formats of an instrument prior to synthesizing the final questionnaire, both closed and open-ended approaches were tried. The fixed list of ten helpers plus "someone else" was decided upon when it was found that the open-ended unstructured responses yielded more detail of how a particular person affected a person's life but not as good a response in terms of who people talked to about the problem. This may be due, in part, to the fact that in the more open-ended format the problems mentioned by the respondents tended to be much more global and vague (e.g., "money problems" or "illness") than the more tightly stated problem list ultimately used.

The second objective of the interview was to gather data on the content of these "helping transactions" to answer the question, "What happened when the respondent talked to this other person about a particular problem?" This measurement of the "media of exchange" in the helping transaction provided a much wider range of choice and, thus, a more difficult decision than the determination of the range and combination of helpers talked to. The fact that all elements of exchange can be classified as material (matter), action (energy), or information provided only the roughest guidelines.

2. Adolph Meyer invented an analytical tool for organizing medical data as a dynamic biography which he called the "life chart." This device resulted in the classification of many events which were considered to have an effect on life style. Such events classified by Meyer included:

> . . . changes of habitat, of social entrance, gradua-
> tions, or changes or failures; the various jobs; the
> dates of possibly important births and deaths in the
> family, and other fundamentally important environmental
> influences (Lief, 1948:420).

Development of the life chart and similar analytical tools for measuring environmental influences on illness susceptibility has generated much research. Using Meyer's life chart, Rahe and others studied the number and type of life events that were empirically observed to cluster during

the onset of disease. A random sample of six hospitals in
the Seattle area consisted of seven patient samples,
representing five distinct medical conditions, and two control groups. A self-administered questionnaire, the
"Schedule of Recent Experiences," was given to the total
sample (N = 292). This instrument documented information
concerning "residence, occupation, social, and marital
status, personal and economic factors, and health status."
The instrument also identified major social readjustments by
year of occurrence over a ten-year period. Their findings
suggested that the time of disease onset coincided with
significant environmental alterations requiring adaptive or
coping behavior on the part of the individual. In addition,
their study indicated that sustained adaptive or coping
behavior, evoked by naturally occurring or experimentally
induced life situations, also evoked significant alterations
in the functions of bodily tissues, organs, and systems.
These alterations, they argued, often enhance the body's
vulnerability or susceptibility to disease. While these
changes or alterations have relevance to the etiology and
epidemiology of disease, Rahe cautions that such changes
become a necessary, but not sufficient, cause of disease.

Ruch and Holmes (1971) replicated the original study on
two American samples. They compared the original sample with
a college population (average age, 18) and found a significant correlation of consensus regarding magnitude estimations
of life change events.

Similarly, Pasley (1969) used the SRRS to study the
intercorrelations between seventh-grade students, college
freshman, and Holmes and Rahe's original adult sample. In
addition to finding a significant correlation about consensus
of magnitude estimations of life change events, his study
indicated that consensus about life change events seems well
established by the beginning of adolescence.

Rahe (1968) used the SRRS to measure life change and
illness of naval personnel. He sampled approximately 2,500
officers and enlisted men aboard three U.S. Navy cruisers and
gathered health-change data after six months at sea. He
divided the sample into high-risk and low-risk groups in
terms of life-change scores reported on the SRRS. The upper
30 percent of the life change units provided subjects for the
high-risk group while the lower 30 percent of the subjects
comprised the low-risk group. Rahe discovered in the first
month of the cruise that the high-risk group had nearly 90
percent more first illnesses than the low-risk group.
Further, the high-risk group consistently reported more
illnesses each month for the six-month period.

3. Langer and Michael (1963:6) use the terms stress
and strain to signify the various causes and effects of

environmental forces on the individual. They emphasize that the use of these terms for social scientific purposes must be given clear, distinct meanings rather than used as synonyms for terms associated with the natural sciences.

Efforts to provide an adequate, operational definition of stress have not been successful despite its wide usage as a key variable in social research. Selye (1974:17) noted that "since the term 'stress' is often used quite loosely, many confusing and contradictory definitions of it have been formulated." According to Selye, the major source of this confusion emanates from a generally accepted perspective that views stress as negative and something to be avoided. He argues that stress is associated with both pleasant and unpleasant activities. Thus, stress is not only part of all human experience, it is, in fact, necessary for a healthy life. Selye refers to unpleasant or damaging stress as "distress" which he points out is the negative aspect of stress. Discussing both the benefits and the problems associated with stress, Selye (1974:83) contends: "Stress is the spice of life. Since stress is associated with all types of activity, we could avoid most of it only by never doing anything."

Kiritz and Moos (1974) conclude that current evidence supports the view that social environmental factors have pronounced effects on human physiological processes. They write: "Social stimuli associated with the relationship dimensions of *support, cohesion, and affiliation* [emphasis theirs] generally have positive effects--enhancing normal development and reducing recovery time from illness" (1974: 29). Addressing the problem of expressing their findings in terms of the generic concept of stress, they point out:

> One might argue that most of these physiological changes could be subsumed under the rubric of "stress" and that the evidence merely indicates that too little support and clarity or too much responsibility and change lead to stress responses. . . . Rather than label the process by means of the global term *stress*, however, we feel that it is more fruitful to investigate the specific physiological effects of distinct social environmental dimensions (1974:29--emphasis theirs).

4. In the first instance--"begin" was only twelve percent of the total, while spouse "stopped work" was eight percent of the total.

5. In our original conceptualization of the role of recent concerns, we had intended to consider the total range of problems listed as a single stimulus to helping that would be "class free." Moreover, the high average number of recent concerns for moderate income whites has importance for those

examining the problems of Middle Americans and their alienation and sense of exclusion from formal social service agencies and relative deprivation in terms of government programs and policies (see D. I. Warren, The Radical Center, 1976). Thus, we have identified a set of concerns of problems as occurring more among middle-income groups, among black than white respondents. This suggests a somewhat different kind of stress index than those conventionally employed in social research.

When both life crises and recent concerns are utilized simultaneously they may reduce the social class bias of various sources of risk to mental health and stress which has been such a major arena of scholarly and program design controversy. The counterbalancing of life crises predominating among lower-status groups and recent concerns among higher-status individuals thus serves as a useful and universal basis for comparing the capacity of different environments both to provide coping resources and to generate, in an etiological sense, risk to individual well-being.

6. The first involves two indicators of personality aspects that could affect help-seeking. A second is the direct expression of attitudes about helping. In the former case two variables measuring personality style were employed: "extrovertic personality" and "action personality." Each is a simple additive scale employing a set of dichotomous responses. The items used for the first variable are as follows:

"I usually take the initiative in making new friends"
"I would be unhappy if I weren't around a lot of people"
"I think of myself as a lively individual"

To create the "action personality" score the following items were employed:

"I prefer action to making plans"
"I am usually sure and quick in the actions I take"

Scores for each of the two indices were then dichotomized using categories which divided the sample at the point closest to a 50 percent division. Individuals above each cutting point are designated as respectively "extrovertic" and "action" personalities.

7. Each of these helping behaviors could be indicated one or more times for each problem mentioned since more than one helper might have been contacted. The behaviors themselves are initial descriptions of a variety of formal and informal therapeutic behaviors, and fit categories of supportive, referral, and active helping modalities. An elaborate matrix of helping behaviors is thus created for each respondent with a recent concern. We have found it useful for this analysis to employ the nine recent concerns as a

set of feelings or events that can elicit a set of interactions with others in one's informal and formal web of
available helping resources. Thus, for this analysis we will
not compare responses to specific concerns but consolidate
them and compare instead responses to a set of stimuli.

The format adopted raises two points which are
important to bear in mind. First, the questions ask about
experiences or problems the respondent has had (in the last
month or so) and people he/she has actually talked to about
the problem. Second, the format is essentially "closed," as
it presents the person with a fixed list of choices. The
data being collected refer to things that have happened to
the respondent in the very recent past (thus maximizing
accurate recall and adding more of a sense of immediacy and
reality to the responses). This way the interview avoided
dealing in hypothetical situations and preferences for
helping which would not meet the goal of describing the
existence, structure, and use of actual operating systems of
help, support, and resources.

8. By a helping "transaction" we refer to the talking
of the individual with a recent concern to one helper. In
effect, a person can have many transactions dealing with a
single problem, and several transactions of contacting one
helper for a multiple number of recent concerns. Given a
total of nine recent concerns and ten different kinds of
helpers, it would have been theoretically possible for a
person in the helping network study to have had ninety total
helping transactions.

9. The first subscale "Depressed Mental Outlook" (DMO)
includes the following responses cumulated:
"Felt so 'blue' or 'low' it ruined your whole day.
Felt it's no use trying to do things because so many
things go wrong.
Have there ever been times when you couldn't take care
of things because you just couldn't get going?"
The first two items--which are contained as part of the
list of nine recent concerns while the third item is contained in a list of symptoms elsewhere in the interview.
Depending on the frequency of reported occurrence of these
feelings, a scale was constructed by adding the values of
all items to form a score ranging from 0 to 22. For the
total population interviewed in 1974, the mean score for DMO
is 5.882 with a standard deviation of 5.381.

A second scale focuses on psychosomatic complaints.
The items used to construct this score are as follows:
"People often have tension headaches or similar
complaints. Have you ever felt tension in this way?
Do you ever have any trouble getting to sleep or
staying asleep?

Have you ever been bothered by nervousness, feeling
fidgety, and tense?
Have you ever had spells of dizziness?"
These items--derived and modified--have been utilized
in a number of studies including the Gurin-Veroff study of
1960 "How Americans View Their Mental Health." Using the
reported frequency of these symptoms, a score ranging from 0
to 20 was constructed. The mean score for the sample is
5.073 with a standard deviation of 4.495.

The third index constructed as a dependent-variable
measure of helping is "perceived ill health." It consists
simply of two items linked in an additive fashion. These are
the following:

"Now we have a few questions about your overall health.
How has your health been over the last year or so?
Would you say you've been in poor health, fair health,
good health, or excellent health?
Has any ill health affected the amount of work you do?"
Scoring of the values for these items provides a score
range from 0 to 20 with a sample mean occurrence of 4.609 and
a standard deviation of 4.821.

An additional overall measure of the well-being of the
individual is derived by adding the scores of each of the
three indices to form an index of "Risk to well-being" which
we shall refer to subsequently in the analysis as simply
"RISK." The score could range from 0 to 62. On this
measure, the sample population has a mean score of 15.587 and
a standard deviation of 10.335 (N = 2429).

10.   In reviewing the trends and patterns in regard to
the major variables of the study, we have drawn largely upon
the baseline interview findings. These are the most reliable
and least subject to the bias of the reinterview and the
problem of socio-demographic and other self-selection
factors. Apart from the fact that those individuals who fell
out of the sample tended to be more socially isolated and
less likely to report recent concerns when they were interviewed in 1974, several trends emerge from the second-wave
interviews which show direct rather than spurious changes in
problem load and help-seeking.

11.   The implication of the pattern of life-crisis
volume from 1974 to 1975 is that items from the Holmes and
Rahe scale of life events are a "constant." In effect, at
any given time interval, an individual has about the same
probability of experiencing one of these events as another
individual. At the same time, some of the data from our
present analysis suggest that such probabilities are subject
to socioeconomic change. Lower status individuals may have a
higher risk but such variations are not of a large magnitude

relatd to time--at least this one interval in which our comparison is conducted.

    12. The follow-up 1975 survey provided an added dimen-
sion not contained in the preliminary interviews: the
contrast between how help occurs for both crises and recent
concerns. The follow-up interviews show that the same population of people use each type of helper differentially and
that what those helpers do is also a function of what type of
problem is involved. For crises, people rely on the physician far more than for recent concerns due largely but not
exclusively to the major role of illness as the frequent
crisis (see Chapter II, Table 2). Thus, a doctor is a helper
51 percent of the time for crises compared to only twelve
percent for recent concerns. Clergy are used more than three
times as often for crises versus concerns; co-workers are
used nearly half of the time for recent concerns in 1975 but
only 37 percent of the time for crises. Overall, life-crisis
helping tends to involve a formal helper to a greater extent
than is the case for recent concerns. Thus, in the first
instance 69 percent of the time a formal helper is utilized
(mainly a physician) while in the latter case such helpers
are implicated in helping only thirteen percent of the time.

    Life-crisis helping is different from recent-concern
helping in still a second major way: The kind of help
provided. While "just listening" and "asking questions" are
the first and second most frequently provided helping
behaviors for both crises and recent concerns, the other
kinds of behaviors differ significantly. "Referral" helping
is more than twice as prevalent for crises--53 percent versus
25 percent for recent concerns; taking action occurs for half
of all life crises but only one out of three recent concerns
in 1975. By contrast, "showing a new way to look at a
problem" is more typical of recent concerns than crises--43
versus 36 percent.

    An initial judgment that life crises call for different
helpers than recent concerns is clearly borne out in the
follow-up survey. Although about the same number of helpers
are utilized for each type of problem (3.0 for recent concerns and 2.8 for crises), who is sought out and what they do
varies: social supportive behavior for concerns and more
action and referring for crises. In fact, even the same type
of helper varies his or her helping depending on whether the
issue is a life crises or a recent concern. Relatives give
referral and action helping for crises, but are "listeners"
more for recent concerns; neighbors do more "showing a new
way to look" at crises than they do for recent concerns;
clergy take action for crises, while focusing more on "asking
questions" and referring fo recent concerns; doctors are more

likely to give passive and active social support for recent
concerns, but referrals and concrete action for crises.

    13. Recent concerns differ in a basic way from life
crises by their very nature: they are emergent and developmental, they are experienced as sought life change rather
than imposed single events. If life crises have a regular
rate of occurrence, do the recent concerns ebb and flow in
the period of a single year? To pursue this issue requires
not merely comparing the number of recent concerns in 1974
versus 1975, but the recurrence of each particular
experience. This varies as we shall observe. Thus, several
recent concerns have high rates of persistence--for example,
"thinking about retirement"--here three out of four people
who experience that problem in 1974 "within the last month"
of their interview also do so in 1975. "Feeling blue" and
"thinking about going back to school" show similar recurrence
levels. By contrast, dividing up family activities between
spouses recurs in only one out of three instances. The
remaining list of recent concerns shows relatively high
recurrence rates. For seven of the nine problems, once they
have emerged in 1974 they tend to persist for about half of
the people who reported them initially (see Appendix Table
III-10).

    What factors contribute to the recurrence of recent
concerns? Clearly, this is a highly complex issue that the
present research cannot adequately explore. One factor does
stand out: that of having sought help for the problem
initially. In all nine instances, problem recurrence
increases if a helper had been talked to in 1974 about this
same problem. The largest effects of helper contact are for
dividing up family responsibilities and concern over
suspicious people in the neighborhood. Desire for job
change, blowing up in the job setting, and feeling blue show
the smallest differential in recurrence in 1975 as a function
of helper contact in 1974 (see Appendix Table III-11).

    In the findings reviewed the persistence of recent con-
cerns depends on reinforcement from social networks. This
is germaine to the theory and conceptual role of social
support systems as discussed by Moss (1973) and others.
Perceptual factors as well as "labeling" are involved in
problem persistence. We have seen from our data evidence
that social contact enhances the probability that a problem
experienced initially will recur with help seeking.

    We cannot in this particular analysis unravel the
causal nexus as to whether, for example, help-seeking implies
a greater motivation to deal with a problem or whether such
motivation derives from contact about the problem. The
evidence of some fits with theory problem-coping literature
which sees the emergence as well as the solution of problems

emerging in a reciprocal from social interaction. Basic to
our discussion of the emergence and persistence of recent
concerns is the interpretation of these problems as efforts
to master or improve one's life, not simply to restore a
broken social tie or overcome loneliness.

Our basic view is that recent concerns in comparison
with life crises are derived from and are often strengthened
in their importance by social reinforcement. This is an
important implication for the functions of helping and
support networks. Such contacts may have a "typhoid Mary"
effect: even negative experiences are reinforced. Therefore, how life satisfaction is generated must take into
account help-seeking and the feed-back it elicits. Problems
which are negative in and of themselves may be shared social
experiences. Dissatisfaction and a desire to improve one's
life are inextricably intertwined in networks of helping.

If the concept of social reinforcement is valid (the
absence of help-seeking tends to lower the probability of a
recent concern persisting) then such a relationship can help
explain the decline in the number of such concerns between
1974 and 1975. Over time, the persistence of such problems
requires social interaction. If the individual does not find
that kind of contact accessible, or if helpers do not
reinforce either a positive life change or "consciousness
raising" about a negative element in one's life, then the
problem may well recede or totally disappear.

CHAPTER IV

1. Ethnographic Report, June 18, 1975; Helping Network
Study. In this chapter a number of quotations and excerpts
from neighborhood ethnographic reports will be utilized.
These are drawn either from written reports or transcripts of
"de-briefing" discussions held as part of the field observation design of the study. These statements will be noted in
the text and not specifically footnoted.

2. There is more than semantics underlying the confusing definitions of "community" versus "non-community."
Any urban neighborhood is in some ways merely a geographical
plot which has no meaning apart from the larger urban context. However, in some other ways the neighborhood does
possess unique, identifiable features which distinguish it
from other neighborhoods. These unique attributes simply
reflect the social fact that urban neighborhoods and the
social interactions of the people who live there are not
randomly distributed.

The distinction between "neighborhood" and "community"
should not be made on the basis of the size or closeness of

social relations. For if we now see many communities we
belong to as "impersonal"--i.e., large and abstract--the
neighborhood may be no different. Indeed, one study of a
low-income area makes this point: "It is important to keep
distinct the ideas of intimacy and common order. A person
cannot be intimate with an entire neighborhood. . . .
Neighborhood involvement can never be based on intimacy."
     The seeming lack of interest in grappling with the dis-
tinctions between community and neighborhood may be a
methodological artifact resulting from a lack of consensus
regarding the definition of community. Attempts to identify,
sort out, and define communities are well documented in the
literature (Davis, 1948; Gans, 1951; Hillery, 1955; Nisbet,
1960; Minar and Greer, 1969). Yet, the impact of research
which points to differences between community and neighborhood in terms of structure and dynamics remains to be
demonstrated empirically. We submit that substantial
differences exist between these two concepts which warrant
separate consideration and application.
     3. See Warren, 1969, 1971, 1975, and Warren and
Warren, 1977, and Warren, 1978.
     4. In the present investigation the anomic type of
neighborhood (which lacks a positive reference group orientation, extensive formal or informal interaction or linkages of
residents to the outside community) is further subdivided
according to whether or not residents use their immediate
neighbors--those across the street or next door--as the basis
of neighborhood or whether they use a larger unit. In the
first instance we have labeled this a "mosaic neighborhood"
to denote the isolation into small clusters which
characterize the district in which such a pattern occurs.
The "ordinary" anomic neighborhood is one that lacks this
small unit preference. In other respects the types of
neighborhoods remain as described in previous studies.
     Respondents in the present study were grouped into each
of the seven types of neighborhoods for the purpose of comparing the helping patterns found for each context. Spearman
rank-order correlations are used in the analysis as the means
to statistically evaluate differences among them.
     5. When compared by race in terms of responses to the
question: "How often do you get together with neighbors for
visits at your house or theirs?" 21 percent of whites visit
at least once or twice a week; for blacks only 15 percent
have this frequent contact. Each racial group has the same
proportion of respondents in the sample who report no contact
with neighbors during the year.
     Does the somewhat lower social contact between blacks
and their neighbors imply less neighbor helping with
problems? We find that, despite the slightly lower

"sociability quotient" for blacks, helping for recent concerns is more frequent for blacks compared to whites--27
versus 18 percent.

For blacks this greater use of neighbors as helpers is
consistent with the basic argument of the earlier study of
the black ghetto: geographical compression of blacks leads
to a greater reliance on the neighborhood, even if it is not
the most effectively organized unit to carry the additional
burden which exclusion from other social resources imposes.

Thus blacks use neighbors as a less voluntaristic
helping system than do whites.

6. By dichotomizing responses in each case at the
"many" and "a few" versus "don't know" and "hardly any"
categories, an operationalization comparable to the one based
on aggregated data forms the three typology dimensions of
identity, interaction, and outside linkages. We tested the
responses to the item on perceived neighbor interaction
against the report of the respondent's own visiting of
neighbors. The perception of one's neighbors' social contact
is not simply a projection of the individual's own interaction pattern: it is a relatively independent judgment.

CHAPTER V

1. The communities were not selected on the basis of
any characteristics of helping but instead in terms of their
proximity to Detroit and to provide a geographic spread in
terms of the borders of the central city. To this extent it
would be appropriate to describe the sample of communities as
"purposive" in regard to spatial dispersion.

2. Clifford develops a very useful typology of the
sampled communities using measures of "extensivity,"
"intensivity" and problem load. This formulation is similar
to but differs in several respects from that employed in this
chapter. The results of using each approach provide somewhat
different findings. Also, different dependent variables are
employed in the two analyses. See Clifford (1975).

3. The sample of households is based on the Bresser's
Index and is an address listing rather than an area probability sample. The resulting sample is closer to a random
residential address type than any other form.

4. For a further discussion and tabular presentation
of the multivariate analyses conducted on the survey data the
reader is referred to the companion volume to the present
one.

5. This finding is consistent with a study conducted
by the United Automobile Workers which focused on the

underutilization of mental health services provided in their labor contract. For a review of this study see Brown (1976).

CHAPTER VI

    1. For an excellent review of the literature on this rather consistent sex differential in reported mental health symptomotology see Lois Verbrugge (1977).

CHAPTER VII

    1. See for example, David Landy (1960); Phillips (1963) and Gurin et al. (1960); Hollingshead and Redlich (1958); Gardner and Babigan (1966); Schaefer and Myers (1954); Philips and Segal (1969); and Rosenblatt and Suchman (1964).
    2. See for example, Rosengren (1970); Zola (1966); Srole (1962); Kadushin (1966) and (1962); Rosenblatt and Suchman (1964); Smith et al. (1963); Richart and Miller (1969); and Hall et al. (1970).
    3. See Hollingshead and Redlich (1958); Hall et al. (1970); and Meyers and Bean (1968).
    4. See for example Leighton (1959); Hughes (1960); and Blackman and Goldstein (1968).
    5. This is the same study refered to in Chapter V in which the data was gathered in Pontiac, Michigan (see Brown, 1976).
    6. See for example Glidewell (1972); Litwak and Meyer (1966); and Litwak, Shiroi et al. (1970).
    7. See for example the President's Commission on Mental Health, "Community Support" Chapter 1, (1978); Gerlad Caplan (1974); and Pattison and Twente (1971).

CHAPTER VIII

    1. The work of Amos Hawley is of particular note and is among the leading contributions to the "human ecology" tradition in sociology. See Hawley (1950).
    2. This theme is developed in the doctoral dissertations by Clifford (1975) and by Graves (1979).
    3. The idea that "warmth" or "sociability" or "friendliness" are coterminus with other functions of community is not supported in empirical studies. Thus Waren and Warren (1977) describe a "sociability quotient" which is based on the frequency and size of neighbor contacts. This is but one of six functions of a neighborhood that are

identified. Their intercorrelations are only moderate. See
also Warren (1975).

4. See for example Jacobs (1961); Keller (1968); and
Warren (1975).

5. This theme is very fully explored and well defined
in the work of the sociologist Claude Fischer (1973, 1976).

6. See Granovetter (1973, 1974). There are of course
a number of mechanisms by which people can keep track of the
"old gang" in the school or work or neighborhood setting.
Such things as yearbooks and reunion gatherings are some of
these. What such social institutions do is to help integrate
newcomers and to also provide an ever widening set of loose-
knit social ties. However, close-knit links are generally
impacted in a negative way by geographic movement.

7. The work of Barry Wellman and his colleagues at the
University of Toronto explores this theme very fully and
significantly. See Craven and Wellman (1973); and Wellman
(1976).

8. Such a phenomenon is described in terms of the UFO
craze in which persons of inconsistent social-status rankings
are found to be more susceptible to sighting and believing in
the possibility of extraterrestrial landings. All of this is
interpreted as a means for individuals to "break out of"
their status confines or to discount their present status
discrepancies. See Warren, 1970.

9. The work of Durkheim is of course basic to much of
present-day sociological theory about community and social
organization. His major work on this topic, which focuses on
the dichotomy of "mechanical" versus "organic" social
cohesion, is the Division of Labor in Society. See Durkheim
(1964).

CHAPTER IX

1. This theme of neighborhood "status diversity" is
developed in Warren, Black Neighborhoods, 1975. The essential argument is that the spatial compression of the ghetto
results in a greater probability that a small-scale neighborhood will have a wide range of household income, occupation,
and education attributes in comparison to other areas. In
the research each neighborhood was classified in terms of
whether a "modal" income, occupation, or education range was
present or not in the sampled respondent head of household
group. In the first study in 1969 it was found that eleven
of sixteen black and only six of twelve white neighborhoods
were status heterogeneous. In the present sample we find
that twelve of the 17 black neighborhoods were high on status
heterogeneity and 19 of the 39 all-white neighborhoods. This

is a statistically significant difference in the direction of
a greater probability of black areas being status diverse.

CHAPTER X

    1. The National Institute of Mental Health is now
engaged in training bartenders and beauty parlor operators to
be therapists and referral agents. The National Institute of
Education is seeking ways that social networks apply in the
following situations.
        When individuals confront a problem, need to obtain
        information, and seek material resources . . . they
        often rely on informal contacts with others . . . .
        Such voluntary relationships cut across formal roles
        and organizational ties . . . . A school principal
        considering adoption of an innovation such as modular
        scheduling will seek information from other principals
        who have already adopted it; parents with a grievance
        bring pressure on the school their children attend and
        will ally with other parents to bring pressure on the
        school's administration . . . . Research on Social
        Networks in Education, NIE., May 23, 1978.
Recently the President's Commission on Mental Health placed
the concept of "community support systems" number one on the
agenda for future directions of mental health prevention:
        Throughout America . . . there are personal and social
        networks of families, neighbors, and community
        organizations to which people naturally turn as they
        cope with their problems . . . . These supports are
        important adjuncts to more formal mental health
        services and can be especially valuable to individuals
        with chronic mental illness (Report to the President,
        Volume I, p. 14).
Still another example of the public policy directed as
social networks is the following RFP solicitation from the
Justice Department:
        Informal social control processes may be affected by
        acquaintanceship and friendship networks within the
        controlled area . . . actual group processes by which
        these informal social control processes and networks
        may operate . . . have not been adequately described or
        analyzed (Law Enforcement Assistance Administration
        Program Announcement, March 30, 1978).
    2. A valuable study is now under way directed by Diane
Pancoast of Portland State University. She and her
colleagues are sampling several national programs which have
been structured in terms of the principle of using "natural
helping networks" in providing human services.

REFERENCES

Abrahams, Ruby B. "Mutual Helping Styles of Caregiving in a Mutual Aid Programm--The Widowed Service Line." In Kaplan and Killiam (1976):245-259.

Adams, Bert. Kinship in an Urban Setting. Chicago: Markham Publishing Company, 1968.

Angell, Robert. "The Moral Integration of American Cities." American Journal of Sociology 57 (July 1951):1-140.

Appleyard, D.; Lynch, K.; and Meyer, J. R. The View from the Road. Cambridge, Mass.: MIT Press, 1964.

Arno, M., and Schwartz, D. Community Mental Health: Reflections and Explorations. Flushing, N. Y.: Spectrum Publications, 1974.

Arrow, Kenneth J. The Limits of Organization. New York: W. W. Norton, 1974.

Austin, David M. "Influence of Community Setting on Neighborhood Action." In John B. Turner (ed.) Neighborhood Organization for Community Action. National Association of Social Work (1968):76-105.

Axelrod, Morris. "Urban Structure and Social Participation." American Sociological Review 21 (February 1956):14-18.

Bell, Wendell, and Boat, Marion. "Urban Neighborhoods and Informal Social Relations." American Journal of Sociology 62 (January 1952):391-398.

Berger, Peter L., and Neuhaus, Richard J. To Empower People: The Role of Mediating Structures in Public Policy. Washington, D.C.: American Enterprise Institute, 1977.

Blackman, Sheldon and Goldstein, Kenneth. "Some Aspects of a Theory of Community Mental Health." Community Mental Health Journal 4 (February 1968).

Blau, Peter M. and Scott, Richard W. Formal Organizations: A Comparative Approach. San Francisco: Chandler Publishing Company, 1962.

Blaut, J. M., and Stea, D. "Place Learning." Place
    Perception Research Reports. Worcester, Mass.: Clark
    University, No. 4, 1969.
Blum, Alan. "Social Structure, Social Class and
    Participation in Primary Relationshiops." In Arthur
    Shostak and William Gomberg (eds.) Blue Collar World.
    Englewood Cliffs, N. J.: Prentice Hall, 1964:145-207.
Bott, Elizabeth. Family and Social Network: Roles, Norms
    and External Relationships in Ordinary Urban Families.
    London: Tavistock Publications, 1957.
Brieger, Robert L. "Career Attributes and Network Structure:
    A Blockmodel Study of Biomedical Research Specialty."
    American Sociological Review 41 (February 1976):
    117-135.
Briggs, R. "Urban Cognative Distances," unpublished doctoral
    dissertation, Ohio State University, 1971.
Broskowski, Anthony and Baker, Frank. "Professional,
    Organizational, and Social Barriers to Primary
    Prevention." American Journal of Orthopsychiatry 44
    (October 1974):707-719.
Brown, Bertram S. "Obstacles to Treatment for Blue-Collar
    Workers," New Dimensions in Mental Health, Report from
    the Director, National Institute of Mental Health,
    Public Health Service, June 1976.
Bryan, James and Test, Mary. "Models and Helping:
    Naturalistic Studies in Aiding Behavior." Journal of
    Personality and Social Psychology 6 (August 1967):
    400-407.
Budman, S. H. "A Strategy for Preventive Mental Health
    Intervention." Professional Psychology 6 (1975):
    394-398.
Caplan, Gerald. Principles of Preventive Psychiatry. New
    York: Basic Books, 1964.
Caplan, Gerald. "Support Systems." Keynote address to
    conference of Psychiatry, Rutgers Medical School and
    New Jersey Mental Health Association on June 8, 1972,
    at Newark, N. J.
_____. "Support Systems." In Support Systems and Community
    Mental Health, pp. 1-40. Edited by Gerald Caplan.
    New York: Behavioral Publications, 1974.
Caplan, Natie Killilen. Support Systems and Mutual Help.
    New York: Grune and Stratten, 1976.
Caplow, Theodore and Forman, Robert. "Neighborhood
    Interaction in the Homogeneous Community." American
    Sociological Review 15 (June 1950):357-366.
Cassel, J. C. "Psychosocial Processes and 'Stress':
    Theoretical Formulation." International Journal of
    Health Services 4(3) 1974:471-482.

Clark, Terry. "Community or Communities." In Community Structure and Decision Making: Comparative Analyses, pp. 83-90. Edited by Terry Clark. San Francisco: Chandler Publishing Company, 1968.

Clifford, David L. A Comparative Study of Helping Patterns in Eight Urban Communities, University of Michigan Doctoral Dissertation, 1976.

Collins, A. H. "Natural Delivery Systems: Accessible Sources of Power for Mental Health." American Journal of Orthopsychiatry, 43 (1973):46-52.

Collins, Alice H., and Pancoast, Diane. Natural Helping Networks: A Strategy for Prevention. New York: National Association of Social Workers, 1974.

Collins, Alice H. and Pancoast, Diane. Natural Helping Network, A Strategy for Prevention. Washington, D.C.: National Association of Social Workers, 1976.

Cooley, Charles Horton; Angell, Robert C.; and Carr, L. J. Introductory Sociology. New York: Schribners, 1933.

Cooley, Charles Horton. Social Organization. New York: Scribners, 1966.

Craik, K. H. "Environmental Psychology." In Craik, K. H., et al., eds., New Directions in Psychology. New York: Holt Publishers, 1970.

Craven, Paul and Wellman, Barry. "Informal Interpersonal Relations and Social Networks." Sociological Inquiry 43(3 and 4) (1973):57-88.

Croog, Sydney; Lipson, Alberta; and Levine, Sol. "Help Patterns in Severe Illness: Non-Family Resources, and Institutions." Journal of Marriage and the Family 34 (February 1973):32-41.

Crump, Barry N. "The Portability of Urban Ties." (Unpublished paper), Centre for Urban and Community Studies, University of Toronto, 1977.

Cumming, Elaine. Systems of Social Regulation. New York: Atherton Press, 1968.

Davis, James; Spaeth, Joe; and Huson, Carolyn. "A Technique for Analyzing the Effects of Group Composition." American Sociological Review 26 (April 1961):215-225.

Davis, Kingsley. Human Society. New York: The Macmillan Company, 1948.

DeJonge, D. "Images of Urban Areas." Journal of the American Institute of Planners 28:266-276.

Denzin, Norman. "Participant Observation: Varieties and Strategies of the Field Method." In McCall, G. and Simmons, J. Issues in Participant Observation, 1969: 186-218.

Department of Health, Education, and Welfare, Volume I: Americans of Spanish Origin, a Study of Selected

Socioeconomic Characteristics of Ethnic Minorities Based on the 1970 Census. Washington, D.C., HEW Publication no. (OS) (1974):75-120.

Diaz, M. "Ethnicity, Hispanic Communities and Issues in Mental Health: A Commentary." Proceedings of the Puerto Rican Conferences on Human Services, National Coalition of Spanish-speaking Mental Health Organizations, (1975):31-36.

Dinitz, Simon M.; Angnst, Lefton S.; and Pasamarick, B. "Psychiatric and Social Attributes as Predictors of Case Outcome in Mental Hospitalization." In Thomas Scheff (ed.) Mental Illness and Social Process. New York: Harper and Row, 1967.

Downs, R. M., and Stea, D. Cognative Mapping: Images of Spatial Environment. Chicago: Aldine Books, 1971.
_____. Image and Environment: Cognative Mapping and Spatial Behavior. Chicago: Aldine Books, 1973:22.

Duff, Raymond W. and Liu, William T. "The Strength in Weak Ties." Public Opinion Quarterly, 36 (Fall 1972): 361-366.

Dunham, H. Warren. "Community As Process: Maintaining a Delicate Balance." American Journal of Community Psychology (3) 1977:257-268.

Durkheim, Emile. The Division of Labor in Society. New York: The Free Press, 1933.

Ellis, J. B. "Love to Share: A Community Project Tailored by Oldsters for 'Latch-Key' Children." Paper presented at the meeting of the American Orthopsychiatric Association, Detroit, 1972.

Emlen, Arthur. Child Care by Kith. Portland, Oregon: DCE Books, 1971.

Erickson, J. D. "The Concept of Personal Network in Clinical Practice." Family Process 14 (4):487-498.

Etzioni, Amitai. "The Ghetto--A Re-evaluation." Social Forces 37 (March 1959):255-263.

Faris, R. and Dunham, H. Mental Disorders in Urban Areas. Chicago: University of Chicago Press, 1939.

Farley, Reynolds. "The Changing Distribution of Negroes within Metropolitan Areas: The Emergence of Black Suburbs." American Journal of Sociology 75(4) Part 1 (January):512-529.

Fava, Sylvia. "Beyond Suburbia." Annals of the American Association of Political and Social Science, 422 (November):10-24.

Feinstein, O. "Why Ethnicity?" In Hartman, D. (ed.) Immigrants and Migrants: The Detroit Ethnic Experience. Detroit Center for Urban Studies, Wayne State University, 1974.

Fellin, Phillip, and Litwak, Eugene. "Neighborhood Cohesion Under Conditions of Mobility." American Sociological Review 28 (June 1963):364-376.

Festinger, L., Schachter, S., and Back, K. Social Pressures in Informal Groups. New York: Harper and Bros., 1950.

Fischer, Claude S. "On Urban Alienation and Anomie: Powerlessness and Social Isolation." American Sociological Review 38 (June 1973):311-326.

Fischer, Claude and Jackson, Robert M. "Suburbs, Networks, and Attitudes." In Barry Schwartz (ed.,) The Changing Face of the Suburbs. Chicago: The University of Chicago Press, 1976.

Fischer, Claude. Networks and Places: Social Relations in the Urban Setting. New York: Free Press, 1977.

Form, William H., and Sigmund, Nosow. Community in Disaster. New York: Harper and Row, 1958.

Fox, J. R. "Therapeutic Rituals and Social Structure in Cohiti Pueblo." Human Relations 13(4) (November 1960):291-303.

Fried, Marc. "Grieving for a Lost Home." In L. J. Duhl (ed.) The Urban Condition. New York: Basic Books, 1963.

Fried, Marc, and Gleicher, Peggy. "Some Sources of Residential Satisfaction in an Urban Slum." Journal of the American Institute of Planners 27 (November 1961): 305-315.

Friedson, Elliot. "Client Control and Medical Practice." American Journal of Sociology 65 (January 1960): 374-382.

_____. Patients' Views of Mental Practice. New York: Russell Sage, 1961.

_____. Profession of Medicine. New York: Dodd-Mead, 1970.

Gans, Herbert. "Urbanism and Suburbanism as Ways of Life: A Reevaluation of Definitions." In Human Behavior and Social Process, Edited by Rose Arnold. Boston: Houghton Mifflin Company, 1962a:625-648.

_____. The Levittowners: Ways of Life and Politics in a New Suburban Community. New York: Vintage Books, 1969.

_____. The Urban Villagers: Group and Class in the Life of Italian Americans. New York: The Free Press, 1962.

Gardner, Elmer and Babigan, Harontun. "The Longitudinal Comparison of Psychiatric Service." American Journal of Orthopsychiatry 36 (October 1966):818-828.

Gartner, Alan and Rlessman, Frank. "Self-Help Models and
    Consumer Intensive Health Practice." American Journal
    of Public Health, 66(8) August 1976:783-786.
Glazer, Nathan. "The Limits of Social Policy." Commentary
    52(3) (September 1971), pp. 51-58.
Goffman. Asylums, New York: Anchor Press, 1961.
_____. Stigma, Englewood, Cal.: Prentice Hall, 1963.
Gore, Susan. The Influence of Social Support and Related
    Variables in Ameliorating the Consequences of Job Loss.
    Doctoral dissertation, University of Pennsylvania,
    1973.
Gottlieb, B. H. "The Contribution of Natural Support Systems
    to Primary Prevention among Four Social Subgroups of
    Adolescent Males." Adolescence 10 (1975):207-220.
_____. "Lay Influences on the Utilization and Provision
    Health Services: A Review." Canadian Psychological
    Review 17(2) (1976):126-136.
Gottlieb, Benjamin H. and Schroter, Candice. "Resource
    Exchanges Between Professional and Natural Support
    Systems." Professional Psychologist 9(4) (November
    1978):614-622.
Granovetter, Mark. "The Strength of Weak Ties." American
    Journal of Sociology 78 (May 1973):1360-1380.
Granovetter, Mark S. "Granovetter Replies to Gans."
    American Journal of Sociology 80 (January 1975):
    527-529.
Graves, Forrest W. "Psychosomatic Symptoms Associated with
    Vital-Life Crises: An Exploratory Analysis of Self-
    Perceived Neighborhood Contexts." Unpublished Master's
    Thesis, Eastern Michigan University, 1975.
Graves, Forrest W., "Social Support Versus Problem-Specific
    Helping: An Analysis of a Large-Scale Urban Sample."
    Doctoral Dissertation, Department of Sociology, Wayne
    State University, Detroit, Michigan, June, 1979.
Glidewell, J. C. "A Social Psychology of Mental Health." In
    S. E. Golann & C. Eisdorfer (eds.) Handbook of
    Community Mental Health. New York: Appleton-Century-
    Crofts, 1972.
Goering, John and Coe, Rodeny. "Cultural Versus Situational
    Explanations of the Medical Behavior of the Poor."
    Social Science Quarterly 51(2) (September 1970):
    309-319.
Grove, Walter, and Howell, Patrick "Individual Resources and
    Mental Hospitalization: A Comparison and Evaluation of
    the Societal Reaction and Psychiatric Perspectives."
    American Sociological Review 39(1) (February 1974):
    96-100.
Gurin, Gerald; Veroff, Joseph; and Feld, Sheila. Americans
    View Their Mental Health, Monograph 4. Joint

Commission on Mental Illness and Health. New York.
Basic Books, 1960.

Hall, James; Smith, K.; and Bradley, A. "Delivering Mental
Health Services to the Urban Poor." Social Work 15
(April 1970):108-115.

Hall, A. L., and Bourne, P. G. "Indigenous Therapists in a
Southern Black Community." Archives of General
Psychiatry 28 (1973):137-142.

Hanley, Amos. Human Ecology, Boston: Beacon Press, 1950.

Hillery, George A., Jr. "Definitions of Community: Areas of
Agreement." Rural Sociology 20 (June 1955):118.

Hochschild, Arlie Russell. The Unexpected Community.
Berkeley: University of California, 1973.

Hollinghead, August and Redlich, Fredrick. Social Class and
Mental Illness: A Community Study. New York: John
Wiley and Sons, 1958.

Holmes, T. Stevenson and Holmes, Thomas H. "Short-Term
Instrusions Into the Life Style Routine." Journal of
Psychosomatic Research 14 (September 1969):121-132.

Holmes, Thomas H., and Rahe, Richard H. "The Social
Readjustment Rating Scale." Journal of Psychosomatic
Research 11 (June 1967):213-218.

Homans, George C. The Human Group. New York: Harcourt,
Brace, 1950.

Hughes, Charles; Tremblay, Marc; Rapoport, Robert; and
Leighton, Alexander. People of Cove and Woodlot:
Communities From the Viewpoint of Social Psychiatry.
The Stirling County Studies, vol. 11. New York: Basic
Books, 1960.

Hyman, M. D. "Social Isolation and Performance in Rehabilitation." Journal of Chronic Disease 25, (1972):85-97.

Ittelson, W. H. "Environment Perception and Contemporary
Perceptual Theory." In W. H. Ittelson (ed.)
Environment and Cognition. New York: Seminar Press,
1972, p. 1.

Ittelson, W. H.; Proshansky, H.; Rivlin, K.; Winkel, G. An
Introduction to Environmental Psychology. New York:
Holt, Rinehart and Winston, 1974:114.

Jaco, E. G. "Mental Health of the Spanish-American in
Texas." In Opler, M. E. (ed.) Culture and Mental
Health. New York: Macmillan Co., 1959.
_____. The Social Epidemiology of Mental Disorder; A
Psychiatric Survey of Texas. New York: Russell Sage
Foundation, 1960.

Jahoda, Marie. Current Concepts of Positive Mental Health.
New York: Basic Books, 1958.

Jenkins, C. David. "Social and Epidemiologic Factors in
Psychosomatic Disease." Psychiatric Annals, 11
(August 1972):8-21.

Kadushin, Charles. "Social Distance Between Client and
     Professional." American Journal of Sociology 67 (March
     1962):517-531.
          . The Friends and Supporters of Psychotherapy: On
     Social Circles in Urban Life." American Sociological
     Review 31 (December 1966):786-802.
          . Why People Go to Psychiatrists. New York:
     Atherton Press, 1969.
Kahn, Robert L. "Mental Health, Social Support and
     Metropolitan Problems." Unpublished proposal,
     Institute for Social Research, University of Michigan,
     1976.
Kapferer, Bruce. "Norms and Manipulation of Relationships in
     a Work Context," in T. Clyde Mitchell (ed.) Social
     Networks in Urban Situations. Manchester: Manchester
     University Press, 1969.
Kaplan, B., Reed, R.; and Richardson, W. "A Comparison of
     the Incidence of Hospitalized and Non-Hospitalized
     Cases of Psychosis in Two Communities." American
     Sociological Review 21(4) (August 1956):472-479.
Katz, A. H. and Bender, E. I. The Strength in Us: Self-Help
     Groups in the Modern World. New York: New Viewpoints,
     Franklin Watts, 1979.
Katz, Daniel; Gutek, B.; Kahn, R.; Barton, E. Bureaucratic
     Encounters: A Pilot Study in the Evaluation of
     Government Services. University of Michigan, Ann
     Arbor, Institute for Social Research, 1975.
Keller, Suzanne. The Urban Neighborhood: A Sociological
     Perspective. New York: Random House, 1968.
Kent, James A. Death of Colonialism in Health Programs for
     the Urban Poor. Denver: Foundation for Urban and
     Neighborhood Development, 1978.
Killilea, Maria. "Mutual Help Organizations:
     Interpretations in the Literature." In Support Systems
     and Mutual Help Multidisciplinary Explorations. New
     York: Gryne and Stratton, 1976.
Klein, Donald. Community Dynamics and Mental Health. New
     York: John Wiley and Sons, 1968.
Kreps, Juanita M. "Intergenerational Transfers and the
     Bureaucracy." In Ethel Shanas and Marvin B. Sussman,
     Family, Bureaucracy and the Elderly. Durham, N. C.:
     Duke University Press, 1977.
Lazarsfeld, Paul F., and Stanton, Frank. "The Analysis of
     Deviant Cases in Communication Research."
     Communications Research 11 (1948-49):152-157.
Landy, David. "Problems of the Person Seeking Help in our
     Culture" in Social Welfare Reform. New York:
     Columbia University Press, 1960:127-145.

Landecker, Werner. "Types of Integration and Their
    Measurement." American Journal of Sociology 56
    (January 1951):332-346.
Lasch, Christopher. The Family Besieged: Haven in a
    Heartless New York. New York: Basic Books, 1977.
Laumann, Edward O. Prestige and Association in the Urban
    Community. Indianapolis: Bobbs-Merrill, 1966.
_____. Bonds of Pluralism. New York: Wiley
    Interscience Publications, 1973.
Lee, Terence. "Urban Neighborhood as a Socio-spatial
    Schema." Human Relations 21:241-267.
_____. "The Psychology of Spatial Orientation."
    Architectural Association Quarterly 1 (1969):11-15.
_____. "Perceived Distance as a Function of Direction
    in the City," Environment and Behavior 2 (1970):40-51.
Leighton, Alexander. My Name is Legion. The Stirling County
    Studies, vol. 1. New York: Basic Books, 1959.
Levy, Leo and Visotsky, Harold. "The Quality of Urban Life:
    An Analysis From the Perspective of Mental Health," in
    Henry Schmandt and Warner Bloomberg (eds.) The Quality
    of Urban Life. Urban Affairs Annual Reviews, vol.3,
    Beverly Hills, California, Sage Publications, 1969:
    255-268.
Levy, Leo H. "Self-Help Groups: Types and Psychological
    Processes." The Journal of Applied Behavioral Science
    12 (1976):310-322.
Liebow, Elliot. Tally's Corner. Boston: Little, Brown and
    Company, 1967.
Lief, Alfred. The Commonsense Psychiatry of Dr. Adolf Meyer.
    (New York: McGraw-Hill, 1948):433.
Liem, J. H. and Leim, R. "Life Events Social Supports and
    Physical and Psychological Well Being." Unpublished
    paper presented at the 84th Annual Meeting of the
    American Psychological Association, 1976.
Litwak, Eugene. "Occupational Mobility and Extended Family
    Cohesion." American Sociological Review 25 (February
    1960s):9-21.
_____. "Geographical Mobility and Extended Family
    Cohesion." American Sociological Review 25 (June
    1960b):385-394.
_____. "Voluntary Associations and Neighborhood
    Cohesion." American Sociological Review 26 (April
    1961):358-371.
Litwak, Eugene and Figuera, Josephina. "Technological
    Innovation and Theoretical Functions of Primary Groups
    and Bureacuratic Structures." American Journal of
    Sociology 73 (January 1968):468-481.
Litwak, Eugene and Meyer, Henry. "A Balance Theory of
    Coordination Between Bureaucratic Organization and

Community Primary Groups." <u>Administrative Science</u>
<u>Quarterly</u> 2 (June 1966):33-58.

Litwak, Eugene and Szelenyi, Ivan. "Primary Group Structures
and Their Functions: Kin, Neighbors, and Friends."
<u>American Sociological Review</u> 34 (August 1969):465-481.

Litwak, Eugene; Shiroi, Earl; Zimmerman, Libby; and
Bernstein, Jessie. "Community Participation in
Bureaucratic Organizations: Principles and
Strategies." <u>Interchange</u> 1 (1970):44-60.

Liu, William and Duff, Robert. "The Strength in Weak Ties."
<u>Public Opinion Quarterly</u> 36 (Fall 1972):361-366.

Lopata, Helena Z. <u>Occupation Housewife</u>. New York: Oxford
University, 1971.

Lowenthal, Martin, "The Social Economy in Urban Working-Class
Communities." In G. Gappert and H. Rose (eds.) <u>The</u>
<u>Social Economy of Cities</u>. Volume 9, Urban Affairs
Annual Reviews. Beverly Hills: Sage.

Lurie, O. R. "Parents' Attitudes toward Children's Problems
and toward Use of Mental Health Services: Socio-
economic Differences." <u>American Journal of</u>
<u>Orthopsychiatry</u> 44 (1974):109-120.

Lynch, K. <u>The Image of the City</u>. Cambridge, Mass.: MIT
Press, 1960.

Maddox, J. G. "Persistence of Life Style among the elderly:
a Longitudinal Study of Patterns of Social Activity in
Relation to Life Satisfaction." <u>Proceedings, 7th</u>
<u>International Congress of Gerontology</u>: Vienna, 6,
(1966):309-311.

Mann, Peter. "The Concept of Neighborliness." <u>American</u>
<u>Journal of Sociology</u> 60 (September 1954):163-168.

Martinez, Thomas. "Alternative Mental Health Resources for
the Spanish-speaking: Latin Helping Networks." Paper
presented at the annual meeting of the American
Psychological Association, August 1977.

Mayo, Elton. <u>The Social Problems of an Industrial</u>
<u>Civilization</u>. New York: Macmillan, 1945.

McCall, G., and Simmons, J. <u>Identities and Interaction</u>.
New York: The Free Press, 1966.

McBride, Steward D. "Gallup Urban Poll--Residents View Their
Cities." <u>Nation's Cities</u> 16 (11):316-48.

McKinlay, John B. "Social Networks, Lay Consultation and
Help-Seeking Behavior." <u>Social Forces</u> 51 (March 1973):
275-292.

McKnight, James P. "A Service Economy Needs People in Need."
<u>Co-Evolution Quarterly</u> 15 (1977):36-38.

Mechanic, David. "Social Structure and Personal Adaptation:
Some Neglected Dimensions." <u>Politics, Medicine and</u>
<u>Social Science</u>. New York: Wiley, 1974.

Mechanic, David and Volkart, Edmund. "Stress Illness Behavior and the Sick Role." American Sociological Review 26 (February 1961):51-58.

Michelson, William. Man and His Urban Environment, A Sociological Approach. Reading, Mass.: Addison Wesley Publishing Company, 1970.

Milgram, Stanley. "The Experience of Living in Cities." Science 167 (March 1970):1461-1468.

Mills, C. Wright. The Power Elite. New York: Oxford University Press, 1956.

Mills, Robert and Kelly, James G. "Cultural and Social Adaptation to Change: A Case Example and Critique." In L. Steward and C. Disdorfer (eds.) Handbook of Community Mental Health, New York: Appleton-Century-Crofts, 1972:157-209.

Minar, David W. and Greer, Scott. The Concept of Community: Readings with Interpretations. Chicago: Aldine Publishing Company, 1969.

Mitchell, Clyde, ed. Social Networks in Urban Situations. Manchester, England: Mancester University Press, 1969.

Mitchell, J. Clyde. "Social Networks." Annual Review of Anthropology 3:279-499.

Moore, W., and Tumin, M. "Some Social Functions of Ignorance." American Sociological Review 14 (1949): 787-795.

Moss, G. Illness, Immunity, and Social Interaction: The Dynamics of Biosocial Resonation. New York: Wiley-Interscience, 1973.

Murch, G. Visual and Auditory Perception. Indiana: Bobbs-Merrill, 1973.

Musto, David F. The American Disease. New Haven: Yale University Press, 1973.

Myers, Jerome, and Robarts, Bertram. Family and Class Dynamics in Mental Illness. New York: John Wiley and Sons, 1959.

Myers, Jerome, and Bean, Lee. A Decade Later: A Follow Up of Social Class and Mental Illness. New York: John Wiley and Sons, 1968.

Myers, J. K.; Lindenthal, J. J.; and Pepper, M. P. "Life Events, Social Integration and Psychiatric Symptomology." Journal of Health and Social Behavior 16 (1975):421-427.

Nisbet, Robert A. "Moral Values and Community." International Review of Community Development 5 (February 1960):82.

Nuckalls, K.; Cassell, John; Kaplan, Bertram. "Psychosocial Assets, Life Crises, and the Prognosis of Pregnancy." American Journal of Epidemiology 95 (1972):431-441.

Packard, Vance. A Nation of Strangers. New York: Pocket
     Book, 1974.
Pancoast, Diane. A Nation of Strangers. New York: Pocket
     Book, 1970.
Parsons, Talcott. "An Outline of the Social System." In
     Theories of Society, Foundations of Modern Sociological
     Theory, pp. 30-79. Edited by Talcott Parsons, Edward
     Shils, Kasper Naegele, and Jesse Pitts. New York:
     The Free Press, 1961.
Parsons, Talcott and Bales, Fred. Social Interaction Process
     Analysis. Glencoe, Ill.: The Free Press, 1955.
Pasley, S. "The Social Readjustment Rating Scale: A Study
     of the Significance of Life Events in Age Groups
     Ranging from College Freshmen to Seventh Grade." Paper
     presented as part of a tutorial in psychology, Chatham
     College, Pittsburgh, 1969.
Patterson, Shirley L. "Older Natural Helpers: These
     Characteristics and Patterns of Helping," Public
     Welfare. Fall 1971:400-403.
_____. "Indigeous Helper Value Orientations: An
     Examination of Differences and Similarities Between
     Age Groups," Journal of Social Welfare, University of
     Kansas, Fall 1974:45-50.
_____. "Toward a Conceptualization of Natuarl
     Helping," Hrete, University of South Carolina (3)
     (Spring 1977):161-173.
Phillips, Derek. "The True Prevalence of Mental Illness in
     a New England State." Community Mental Health Journal
     2/2 (Spring 1966):108-117.
Phillips, Derek, and Segal, Bernard. "Sexual Status and
     Psychiatric Symptoms." American Sociological Review
     34(1) (February 1969):58-72.
Phillips, Derek. "Rejection: A Possible Consequence of
     Seeking Help for Mental Disorders." American
     Sociological Review 28(6) (December 1963):963-972.
Piven, Frances Fox, and Cloward, Richard. Regulating the
     Poor: The Functions of Public Welfare. New York:
     Pantheon Books, 1971.
Polsky, Ned. Hustlers, Beats, and Others. New York:
     Doubleday and Company, Inc., 1969.
Poplin, Dennis E. Communities: A Survey of Theories and
     Methods of Research. New York: Macmillan Company,
     1972.
Pouissant, Alvin F. "Black Roadblocks to Black Unity."
     Negro Digest 18 (November 1968):11-19.
Powell, James J. "The Use of Self-help Groups as Supportive
     Reference Communities." American Journal of
     Orthopsychiatry 45 (1975):756-764.

President's Commission on Mental Health. vol. I, U.S. Government Printing Office, Washington, D.C., 1978.

Rahe, Richard H. "Social Stress and Illness Onset," Journal of Psychosomatic Research 8 (February 1964):35-44.

Rahe, Richard H., and Holmes, Thomas H. "Social, Psychological, and Psychophysiological Aspects of Inguinal Hernia." Journal of Psychosomatic Research 8 (July 1965):487-491.

Rahe, Richard H. "Life-Change Measurement as a Predictor of Illness." Proceedings of the Royal Society of Medicine 61 (May 1968):1124-1126.

Reiss, Albert. "Rural-Urban Status Differences in Inter-Personal Contacts," American Journal of Sociology 65 (September 1959):182-195.

Richart, Robert and Miller, Lawrence. "Factors Influencing Admission to a Community Mental Health Center." Community Mental Health Journal 4(1) (February 1968): 27-35.

Roethlisberger, F. J. and Dickson, W. J. Management and the Worker: Social Versus Technical Organization in Industry. Cambridge: Harvard University Press, 1939.

Rosenberg, Morris. The Logic of Survey Analysis. New York: Basic Books, Inc., 1968.

Rosenblatt, Daniel and Suchman, Edward. "The Underutilization of Medical-care Services by Blue Collarites." In Arthur Shostak and William Gomberg (eds.) Blue Collar World: Studies of the American Worker. Engelwood-Cliffs, N. J.: Prentice Hall, 1964:341-349.

Rosengren, William and Lefton, Mark (eds). Organization and Clients. Columbus, Ohio: Charles E. Merril Publishing Co., 1970.

Rosengren, William. "The Careers of Clients and Organizations." In Rosengren and Lefton (eds.) Organization and Clients. Columbus, Ohio: Charles E. Merril Publishing Co., 1970.

Rosow, Irving. Social Integration of the Aged. New York: Free Press, 1967.

_____. Socialization to Old Age. Berkeley: University of California, 1974.

Ruch, Libby O., and Holmes, Thomas H. "Scaling of Life Change: Comparisons of Direct and Indirect Methods." Journal of Psychosomatic Research 15 (June 1971): 221-227.

Ryan, W. Distress in the City: Essays in the Design and Administration of Urban Mental Health Services. Cleveland: The Press of Case Western University, 1969.

Saarinen, T. "Image of the Chicago Loop." University of Chicago (unpublished paper), 1964.

Sanders, Irwin T. The Community: An Introduction to a
Social System. New York: Ronald Press, 1966.

Sarason, Seymour B. The Psychological Sense of Community:
Prospects for a Community Psychology. San Francisco:
Jossey-Bass, 1974.

_____. "Community Psychology, Network, and Mr. Everyman."
American Psychologist 31:317-328.

Schaefer, Leslie and Myers, Jerome. "Psychotherapy and
Social Stratifications." Psychiatry 17 (February
1954):83-93.

Scheurell, Robert P. and Scherden, Kathleen. "Social Network
Analysis: a Salient Approach for Social Work." The
Wisconsin Sociologist, 9(2 & 3) (1972):43-66.

Schon, Donald. "Network-Related Intervention." National
Institute of Education paper, 1977.

Schuval, Judith. "Class and Ethnic Correlates of Causal
Neighboring." American Sociological Review (August
1956):453-455.

Seashore, Stanley E. Group Cohesiveness in the Industrial
Work Group. Ann Arbor: Survey Research Center, 1954.

Sellin, Johan and Wolfgang, Marvin E. The Measurement of
Delinquency. New York: John Wiley and Sons, Inc.,
1964).

Senter, R. J. Analysis of Data. Glenview, Illinois: Scott,
Foresman, and Company, 1969.

Shanas, Ethel. Family Relationships of Older People. New
York: Health Information Foundation, Research Series
20, 1976.

Shapiro, Joan. "Dominant Leaders among Slum Hotel
Residents." American Journal of Orthopsychiatry 39
(1969):644-650.

Sharp, Harry and Axelrod, Morris. "Mutual Aid Among
Relatives in an Urban Population." In Ronald Freedman
(ed.) Principles of Sociology. Revised edition. New
York: Henry Holt & Co., 1956:433-439.

Shibutani, Tamotsu. Society and Personality. Englewood
Cliffs, New Jersey: Prentice-Hall, 1961.

Shils, Edward A. "The Study of the Primary Group." In
Daniel Lerner and Harold D. Lasswell (eds.) The
Policy Sciences. Stanford, Cal.: Stanford University
Press, 1951.

Shostak, Arthur. Blue-Collar Life. New York: Random House,
1969.

Silverman, Phyllis. "The Client Who Drops Out: A Study of
Spoiled Helping Relationships." Ph.D. dissertation,
Brandeis University, 1969.

Silverman, Phyllis. "The Widow as Caregiver in a Program of
Preventive Intervention with Other Widows." Mental
Hygiene 54 (4) (1970:540-545.

Silverman, Phyllis R., and Murrow, H. G. "Mutual Help during Critical Role Transitions." The Journal of Applied Behavioral Science 12 (1976):410-418.

Slater, Philip. The Pursuit of Loneliness, American Culture at the Breaking Point. Boston: Beacon Press, 1971.

Smith, Sarah. Natural Systems and the Elderly: An Unrecognized Resource. Oregon State Programs in Aging and School of Social Work, Portland State University, 1975.

Speck, Ross and Attreave, Carolyn. Family Networks: Retribalization and Healing. New York: Pantheon, 1973.

Stack, Carol. All our Kin: Strategies for Survival in a Black Community. New York: Harper and Row, 1974.

Stein, Maurice. The Eclipse of Community. Princeton, N. J.: Princeton University Press, 1960.

Stevens, S. S. and Galanter, E. H. "Ratio Scales and Category Scales for a Dozen Perceptual Continua." Journal of Psychosomatic Research 54 (December 1957): 377.

Srole, Leo, et al. Mental Health in the Metropolis: The Midtown Manhattan Study. New York: McGraw Hill, 1962.

Suchman, E. A. "Stage of Illness and Medical Care." Journal of Health and Behavior 6 (Fall 1965):114-128.

Sussman, Marvin. "The Help Pattern in the Middle Class Family," American Sociological Review 18 (February 1953):22-28.

Suttles, Gerald D. The Social Order of the Slum. Chicago: The University of Chicago Press, 1968.

_____. The Social Construction of Communities. Chicago: The University of Chicago Press, 1972.

Tannenbaum, Deborah. "People with Problems: Seeking Help in an Urban Community." Research Paper No. 64, Centre for Urban and Community Studies, University of Toronto, 1974.

Todd, David M. "Contrasting Adaptations to the Social Environment of a High School: Implications of a Case Study of Helping Behavior in Two Adolescent Subcultures." In: J. G. Kelly et al., (ed.) The High School: Students and Social Contexts in Two Midwestern Communities. Commuity Psychology Series no. 4, New York: Behavioral Publications, Inc., 1977.

Todd, David M. "Helping Behavior for Citizens and Tribe: A Case Study of Two Adolescent Subcultures of a High School." Ph.D. dissertation, University of Michigan, 1971.

Tolsdorff, Christopher. "Social Networks, Support and
        Coping: An Exploratory Study." Family Process 15 (4)
        (1976):407-417.

Tomeh, Aida. "Informal Group Participation and Residential
        Patterns." American Journal of Sociology 70 (July
        1964):28-35.

Tonnies, Ferdinand. Community and Association. Trans. by
        Charles P. Loomis. London. Routledge and Kegan Paul,
        1961.

Torrey, E. Fuller. "The Irrelevancy of Traditional Mental
        Health Services for Urban Americans," paper presented
        at the Annual Meeting of the American Orthopsychiatric
        Association.

Trickett, Edison; Kelly, James G.; and Todd, David. "The
        Social Environment of the High School: Guidelines for
        Individual Change and Organizational Redevelopment."
        In Handbook of Community Mental Health, edited by
        Steward Golann and Carl Eisdorfer. New York:
        Appleton-Century-Crofts, 1972:331-406.

Verbrugge, Lois M. "Sex Differences in Health: Testing the
        Hypotheses." Women and Health. Paper presented at the
        American Public Health Association meetings,
        Washington, D.C., November 1977.

Volkart, Edmund, ed. Social Behavior and Personality,
        Contributions of W. I. Thomas to Theory and Social
        Research. New York: Social Sciences Research Council,
        1951.

Warren, Donald I. "Neighborhood Structure and Riot Behavior
        in Detroit: Some Exploratory Findings." Social
        Problems 16(4) (Spring 1969):464-484.

_____. "Neighborhoods in Urban Areas." In The
        Encyclopedia of Social Work, New York: National
        Association of Social Work, 1971:772-782.

_____. Black Neighborhoods: An Assessment of Community
        Power. Ann Arbor: The University of Michigan Press,
        1975.

_____. Neighborhood and Community Contexts in Help
        Seeking, Problem Coping, and Mental Health: Data
        Analysis Monograph. Ann Arbor: Program in Community
        Effectiveness, 1976.

Warren, Donald I. The Radical Center: Middle Americans and
        the Politics of Alienation, Notre Dame, Ind.:
        University of Notre Dame Press, 1976.

_____. "Social Bonds in the Metropolitan Community,"
        paper read at the meeting of the Cross-Societal
        Comparative Research Project on the Residential Areal
        Bond in Vienna, Austria, April 4-6, 1977.

_____. "The Neighborhood Factor in Problem Coping, Help
        Seeking and Social Support: Research Findings and

Suggested Policy Implications," paper presented at the 55th Annual Meeting of the American Orthopsychiatric Association, San Francisco, California, March 1978.

_____. "The Multiplexity of Urban Social Ties," paper presented at the 9th World Congress of Sociology, Uppsala, Sweden, August 1978.

Warren, Donald and Clifford, David. "Invoked Expertise and Neighborhood Type: Two Critical Dimensions in the Coordination of Bureaucratic Service Organizations and Primary Groups." Paper presented at the 69th Annual Meeting of the American Sociological Association, Montreal, Canada, August 1974.

Warren, Donald I. and Rachelle B. "The Helping Roles of Neighbors: Some Empirical Patterns." Paper presented at the 71st Annual Meeting of the American Sociological Association, Chicago, Illinois, September 1977.

_____. "Six Types of Neighborhoods." Psychology Today 9(1) (June 1975):74–79.

Warren, Rachelle and Warren, Donald. The Neighborhood Organizer's Handbook. Notre Dame, Ind.: University of Notre Dame Press, 1977.

Warren, Roland L. The Community in America. Chicago: Rand McNally and Company, 1963.

Warren, Roland L. "The Good Community: What Would it Be?" Journal of the Community Development Society 1(1) (Spring 1970):14–23.

Weiss, Robert, and Berger, Bernard. "Social Supports and the Reduction of Psychiatric Disability." Psychiatry 31(2) (May 1968):107–115.

Weiss, Robert. "The Fund of Sociability." Transaction 6 (July 1969):36–43.

Wellman, Barry, et al. "The Uses of Community: Community Ties and Support Systems." Research Paper No. 47, Center for Urban and Community Studies, University of Toronto.

Wellman, Barry; Craven, P.; and Whitaker, M. "Community Ties and Support Systems: from Intimacy to Support." In L. S. Bourne, (ed.) The Form of Cities in Canada. University of Toronto Department of Geography, 1980.

Wellman, Barry. "The Community Question." Research Paper No. 90, Center for Urban and Community Studies, University of Toronto, 1978.

Wellman, Barry, and Craven, Paul. "Informal Interpersonal Relations and Social Networks," Sociological Inquiry 43 3/4 1973.

Wellman, Barry. "Urban Connections." Research Paper #84, Centre for Urban and Community Studies, University of Toronto, 1976.

_____. "The Community Question: The Intimate Networks of East Yorkers," Centre for Urban and Community Studies, University of Toronto, April 1978.

Wellman, Barry; Craven, Paul; Whitaker, Marilyn; Dutoit, Sheila; and Stevens, Harvey. "Community Ties and Support Systems." Center for Urban Research, paper no. 1, July 1971.

Whyte, William H., Jr. The Organization Man. New York: Simon & Schuster, 1956.

Wireman, Peggy. "Meanings of Community in Modern America." Unpublished Doctoral Dissertation: The American University, Department of Sociology, Washington, D.C., 1976.

Wirth, Louis. "Urbanism as a Way of Life." American Journal of Sociology 44 (July 1938):3-24.

Young, Michael, and Willmot, Peter. Family and Kinship in East London. 2nd edition. Harmondsworth, Middlesex, England: Penguin Books, 1959.

Zald, Mayer N. "Demographics, Politics, and the Future of the Welfare State," Social Service Review 50 (March 1977):120-122.

Zola, Irving. "Illness Behavior of the Working Class." In Arthur Shostak and William Gomber (eds.) Blue Collar World: Studies of the American Worker. Englewood Cliffs, N. J.: Prentice-Hall, 1964.

Zola, Irving. "Culture and Symptoms--An Analysis of Patients Presenting Complaints." American Sociological Review 31(5) (October 1966).